I0902391

IMAGES
of America

JOHNSON COUNTY
GEORGIA

IMAGES
of America

JOHNSON COUNTY
GEORGIA

The Johnson County Historical Society

ARCADIA
PUBLISHING

ISBN 978-0-7385-0641-8

Published by Arcadia Publishing
Charleston, South Carolina

Printed in the United States of America

Library of Congress Catalog Card Number: 00-106895

For all general information contact Arcadia Publishing at:
Telephone 843-853-2070
Fax 843-853-0044
E-mail sales@arcadiapublishing.com
For customer service and orders:
Toll-Free 1-888-313-2665

Visit us on the Internet at www.arcadiapublishing.com

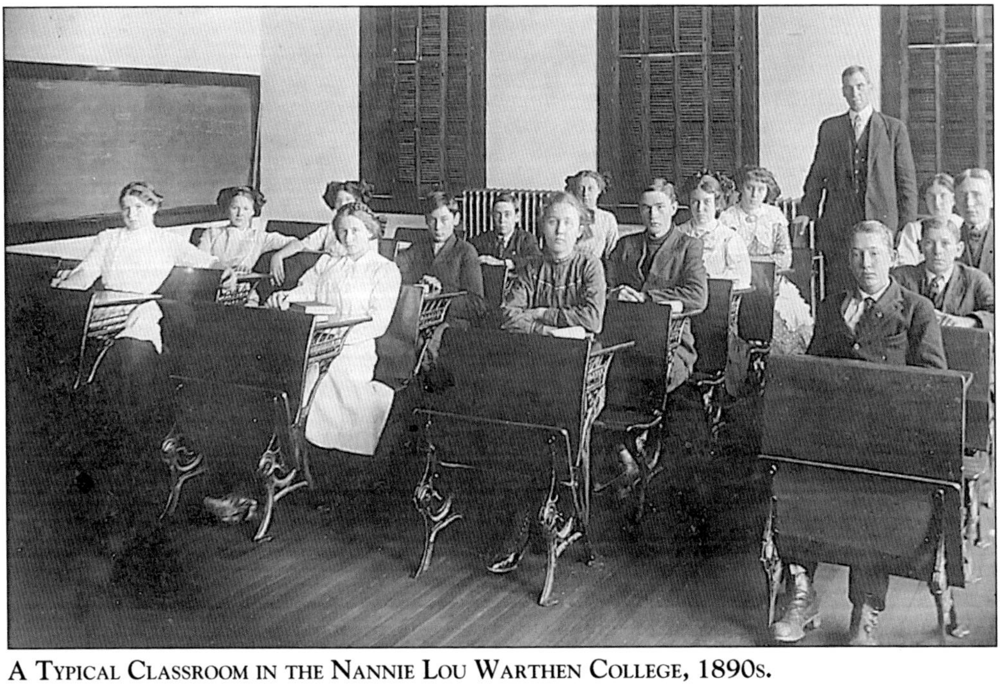

A TYPICAL CLASSROOM IN THE NANNIE LOU WARTHEN COLLEGE, 1890S.

Contents

Acknowledgments		6
Introduction		7
1.	Buildings and Streets	9
2.	Veterans	29
3.	Couples	51
4.	Styles and Fashions	81
5.	People of the Past and Present	93

ACKNOWLEDGMENTS

The members of the Johnson County Historical Society extend their sincere thanks and appreciation to everyone who helped make this book possible, including the *Wrightsville Headlight* and the *Johnson Journal* for printing feature articles and information about the book. To all those who contributed photographs and words of encouragement, we extend a special thank you. We hope that everyone enjoys this pictorial history of Johnson County.

THE JOHNSON COUNTY HISTORICAL SOCIETY OFFICERS

President: Virginia Josey
Co–Vice Presidents: Lois Holt and Donald Smith
Secretary: Susan Carey
Treasurer: Roger M. Webb

BOOK COMMITTEE

Roger M. Webb
Sue Webb
Virginia Josey
Claxton Josey
Lois Holt
Donald Smith

INTRODUCTION

The area now known as Johnson County was created on December 11, 1858 and was the 129th county to be organized in Georgia. It is located in East Central Georgia approximately 50 miles east of Macon, 60 miles southwest of August, 80 miles northwest of Savannah, and 135 miles from Atlanta. In the past, the county was considered a great site for a college because of its central location and convenience for train travelers.

The first inhabitants of this area were believed to be the Muscogean Indian, who became better known as the "Creeks" because they were found living along the creeks of the area. In the beginning when the land was being settled by the British, the Lower Creeks were friendly and, according to some, were even on the side of the British during the Revolutionary War. Chief Tecumseh of the Shawnees tried to influence the Creeks to turn against the British, but they continued to be loyal until they came under the leadership of Alexander McGillivary.

Under the influence of McGillivary, Creek warriors continued to pursue white settlers on the frontier east of the Oconee River. They continued to commit murder, take livestock, and burn the homes of these white settlers. They wanted their land back. To put an end to these raids, the legislature enlisted approximately 4,500 men to carry out a full-scale military operation against the Creek. The state did not have the funds to pay the soldiers and so promised them land in this area as payment. After much strife and many deaths, McGillivary decided to sign a treaty agreeing to return the Oconee lands, over which they had been fighting, to the State of Georgia. He signed the treaty on August 6, 1790. Even though a treaty had been signed, the settlements of the area were continuously hassled by the Creeks up until the death of their leader, Chief McGillivary.

Washington County was formed in 1784, Laurens County in 1807, and Emanuel County in 1812. Johnson County was created from its surrounding counties and is made up of Wrightsville, Kite, Adrian, and Scott. It was named for Hershel V. Johnson who served as the governor of Georgia from 1853 until 1857. He was also a candidate for vice president of the United States in 1860 when Stephen Douglas ran for president.

Many faces have passed through our towns and county. History has been made here and we continue to strive to preserve it. We are proud of our past and are looking forward to our future. The photographs that follow were gathered from the private collections of residents from all over the county. The majority of these pictures were taken for the benefit of family and friends, who have so graciously shared them with all of us. We greatly appreciate their generosity.

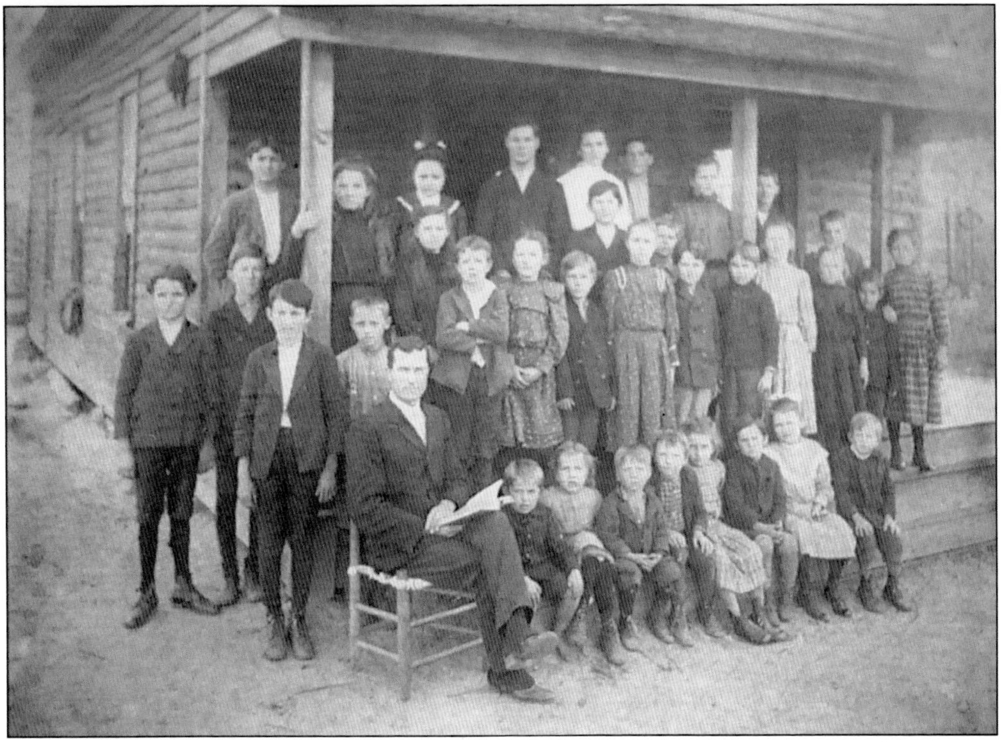

Davis School. The students of Davis School, along with their teacher, take a break from learning to pose for this photo.

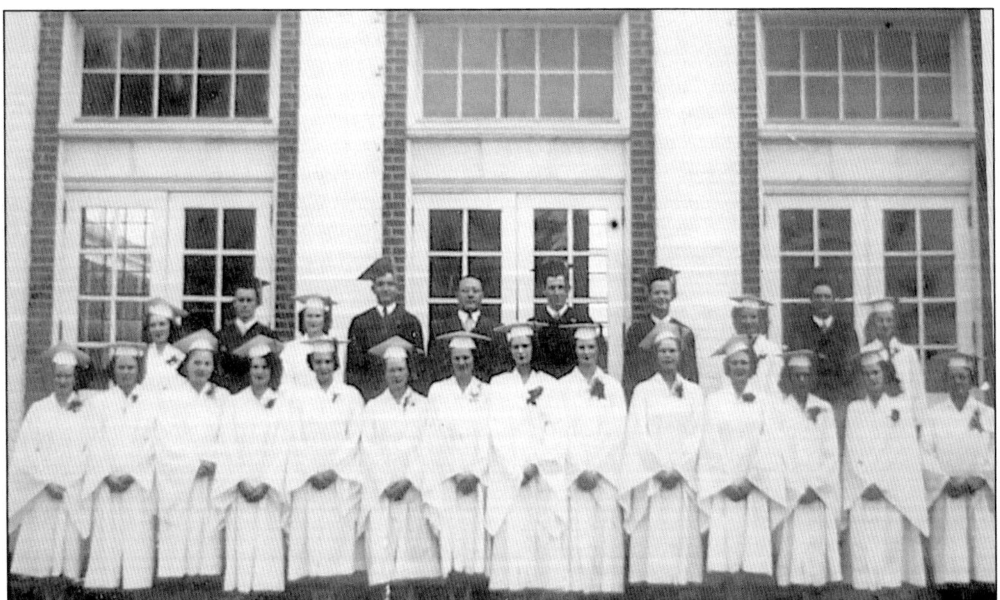

Kite High School Graduates of 1945. This building was destroyed by fire and replaced with a similar structure.

One

Buildings and Streets

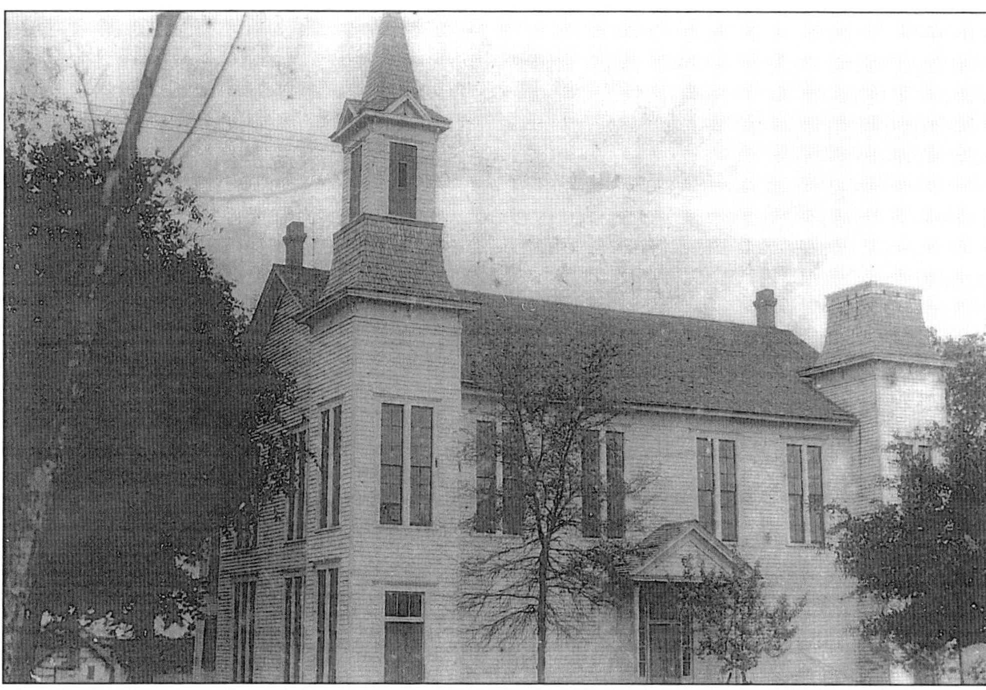

The First Nannie Lou Warthen Institute. Established by the Methodist Church, the institute was located at the corner of College and South Marcus Street in Wrightsville, Georgia. This picture was taken around 1900.

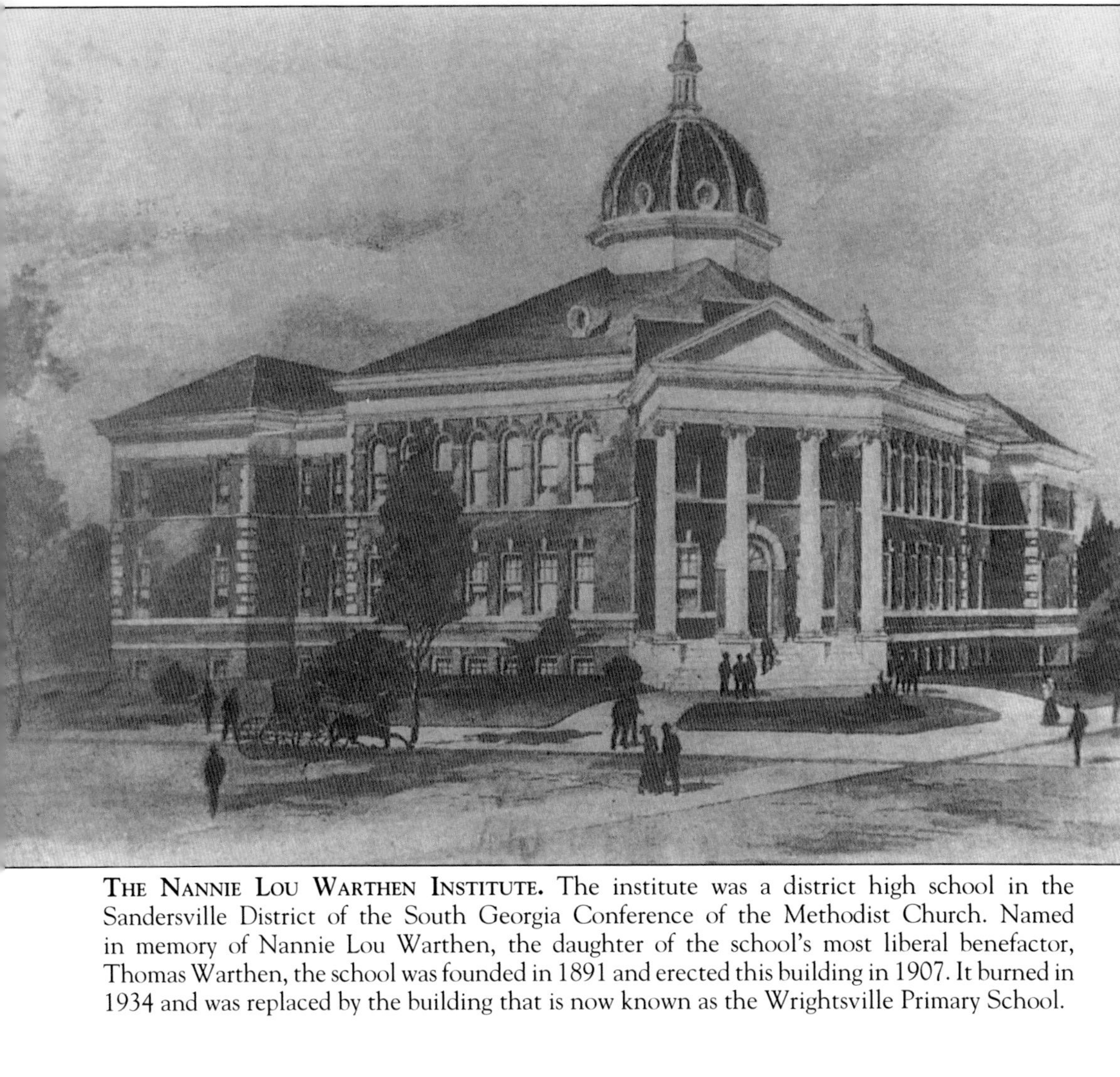

THE NANNIE LOU WARTHEN INSTITUTE. The institute was a district high school in the Sandersville District of the South Georgia Conference of the Methodist Church. Named in memory of Nannie Lou Warthen, the daughter of the school's most liberal benefactor, Thomas Warthen, the school was founded in 1891 and erected this building in 1907. It burned in 1934 and was replaced by the building that is now known as the Wrightsville Primary School.

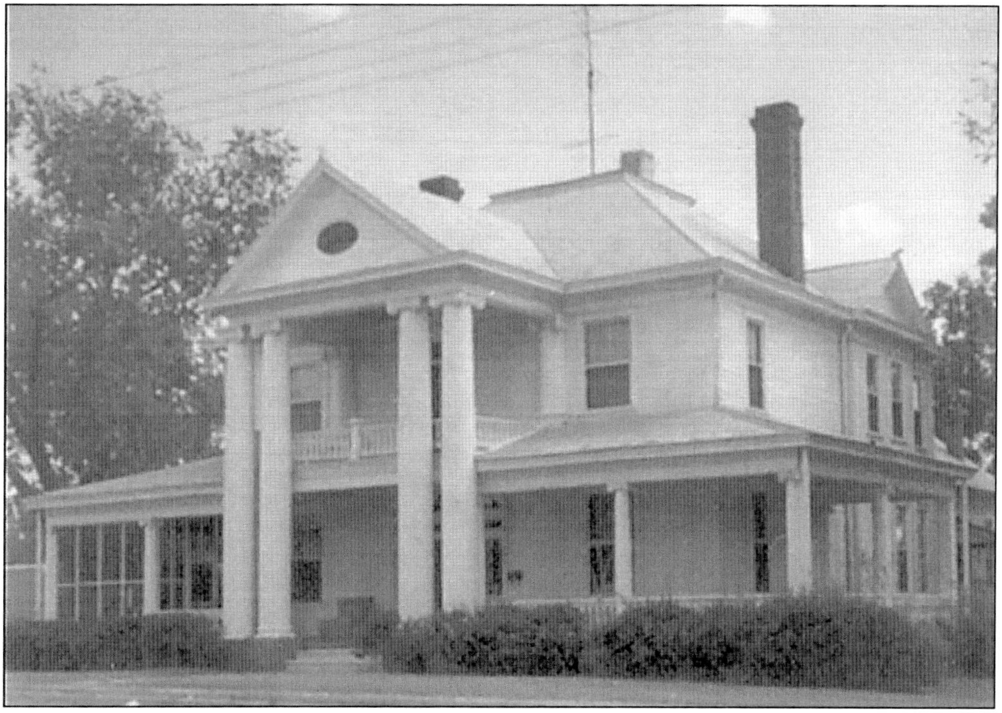

THE JOHNSON HOUSE. Located on West Elm Street in Wrightsville, this house was torn down and replaced by the Exchange Bank.

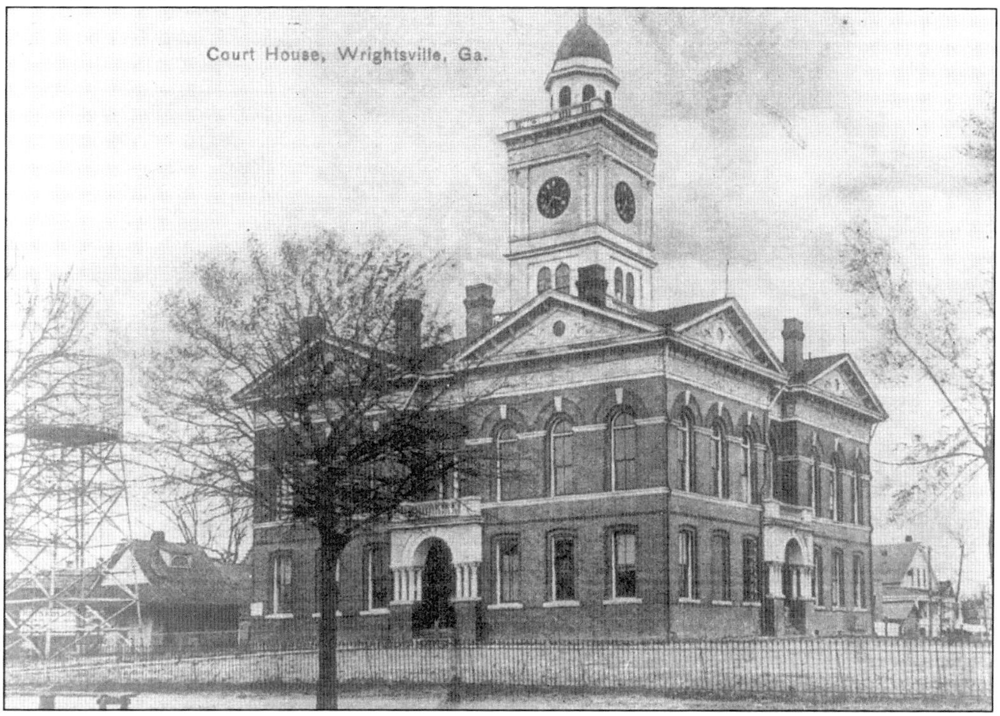

THE JOHNSON COUNTY COURTHOUSE. The statue of "Justice" was removed from the courthouse tower in 1938, but the building still maintained much of its original appearance.

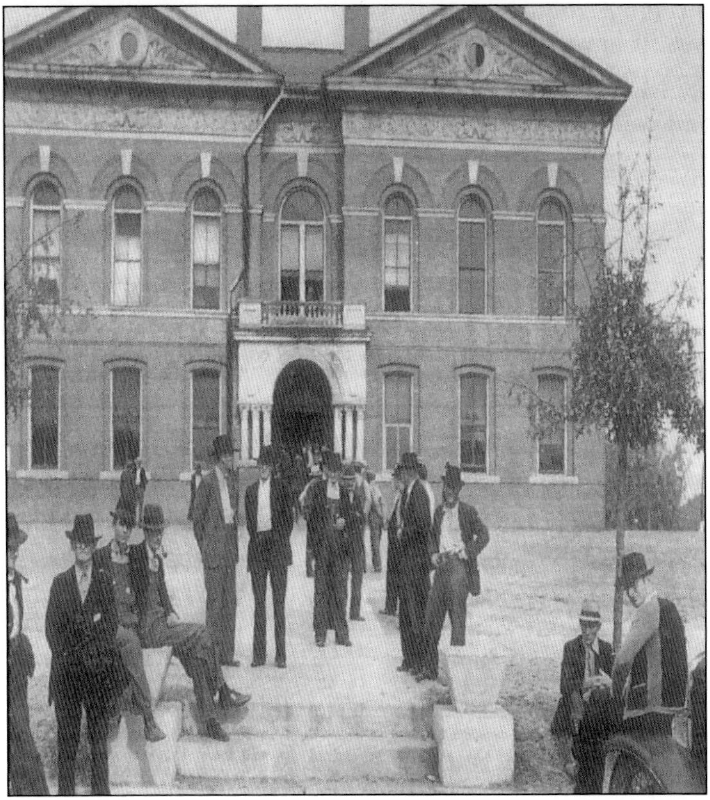

Johnson County Farmers. These farmers linger to talk with neighbors about organizing a conservation district following a hearing. A district was organized on February 17, 1940.

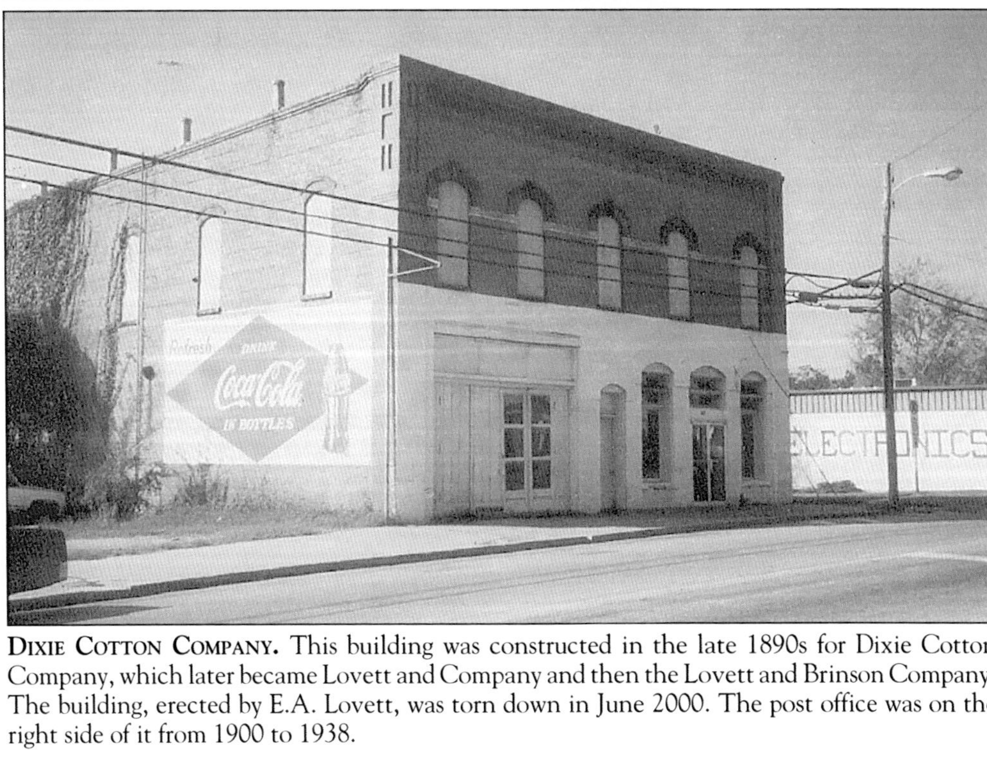

Dixie Cotton Company. This building was constructed in the late 1890s for Dixie Cotton Company, which later became Lovett and Company and then the Lovett and Brinson Company. The building, erected by E.A. Lovett, was torn down in June 2000. The post office was on the right side of it from 1900 to 1938.

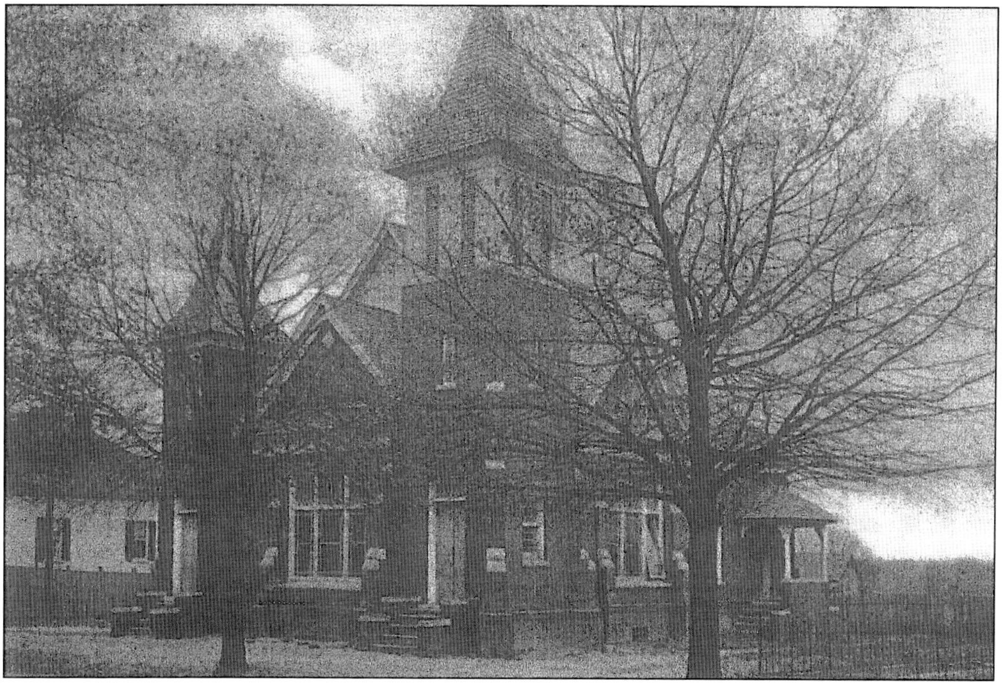

The Wrightsville Christian Church. The church was established by Elder T.M. Harris in 1897, and its charter members had some of the following names: Page, Waller, Dixon, Oliver, Hicks, Kent, Downs, Sammons, Walker, and Jenkins, among others.

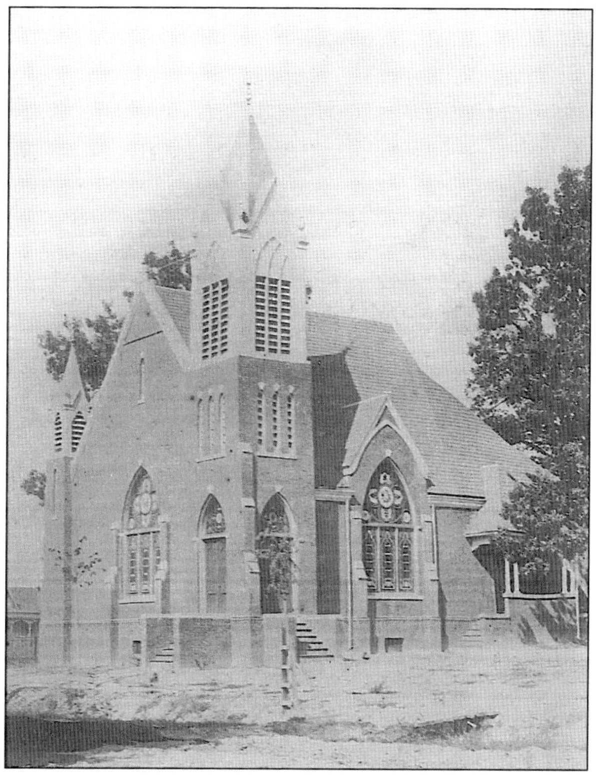

The Methodist Church. This building, home to the First United Methodist Church, was the first house of worship to be built in Wrightsville and dates back to 1882.

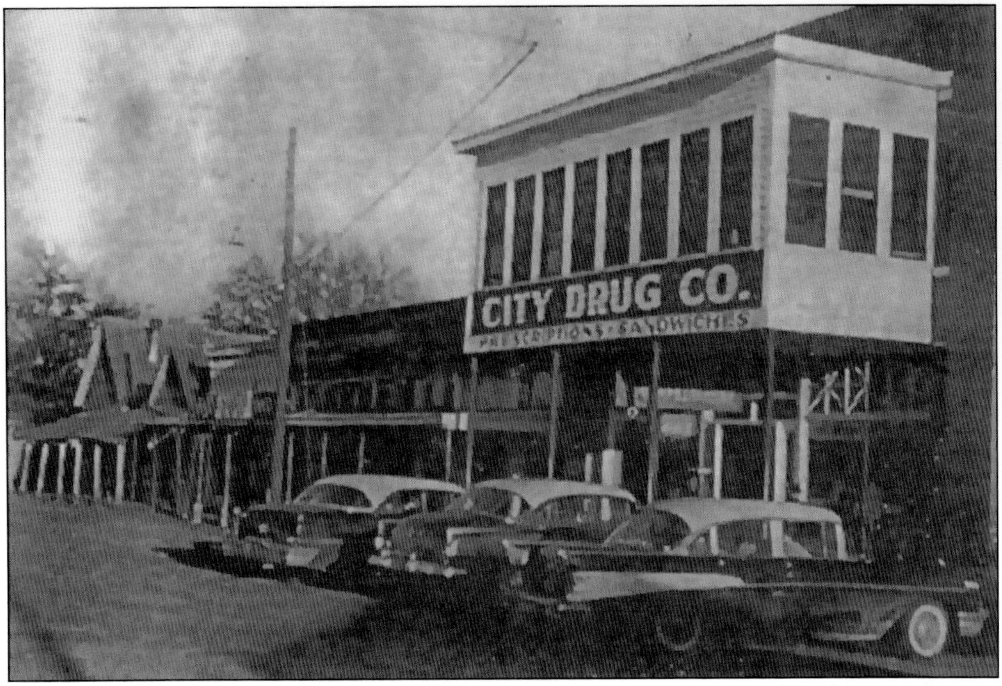

THE ELLIS CLAXTON DRUG STORE IN KITE, GEORGIA, C. 1956. This store later became the post office but is now a storage building for a private citizen.

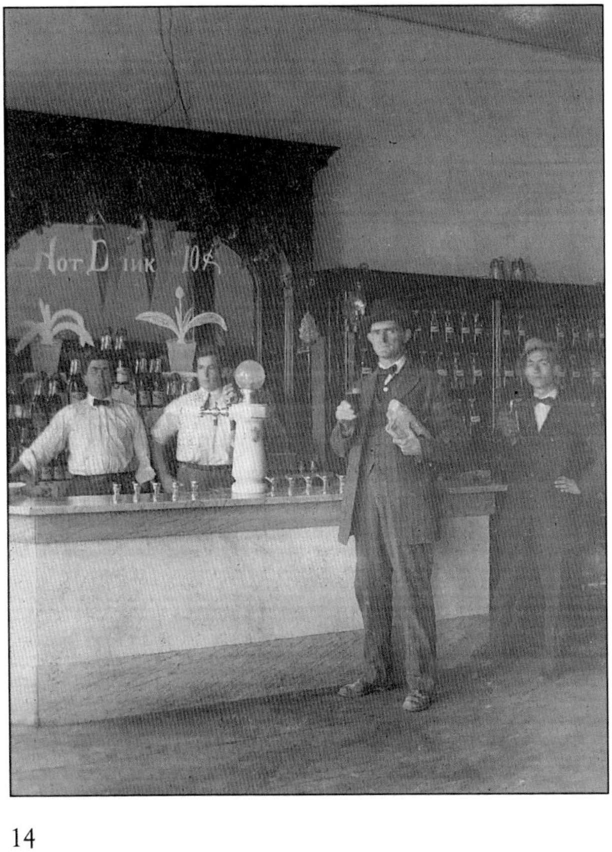

BRINSON'S DRUG STORE IN WRIGHTSVILLE, GEORGIA. This was the longest running drug store business in Wrightsville.

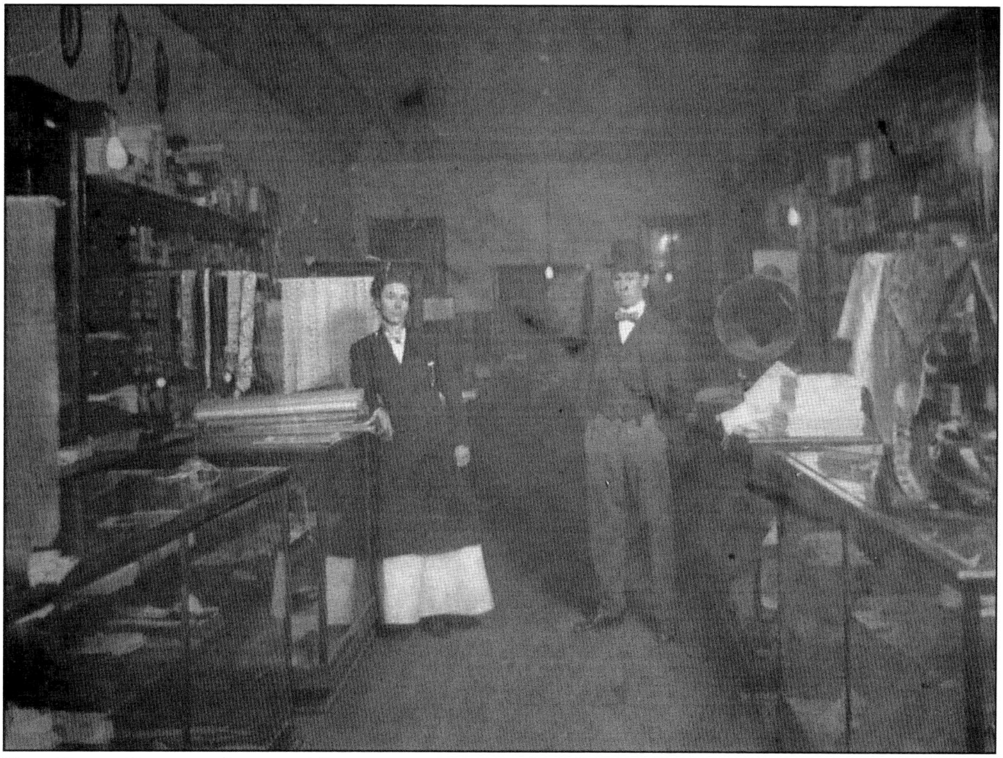

The Four Seasons Store. This store was owned and operated by Mr. and Mrs. Dunlap, the parents of Mrs. Nanelle Frost.

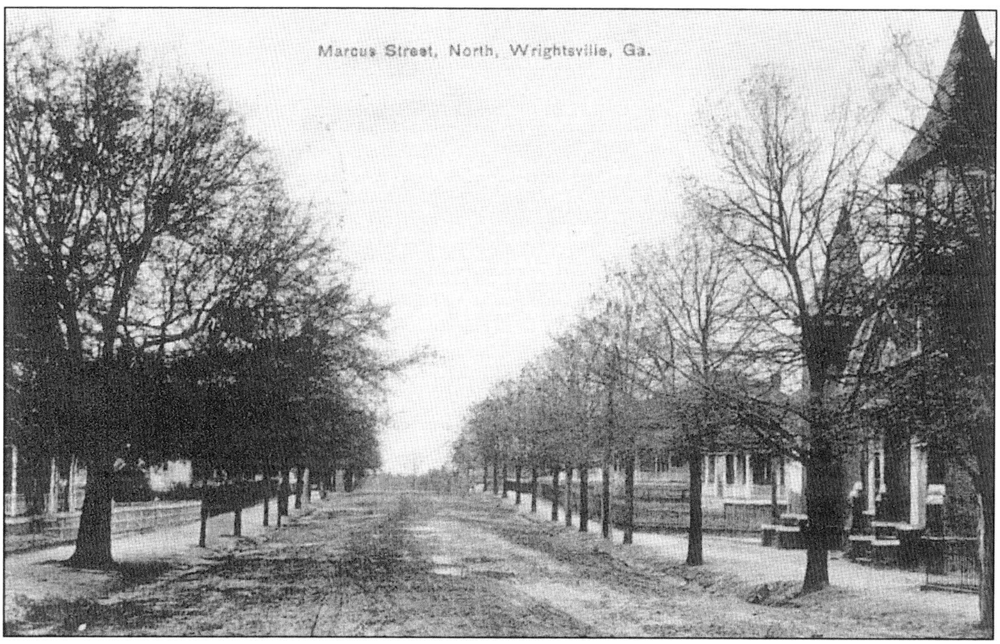

North Marcus Street in Wrightsville, Georgia. This picture was taken before any paving of our streets was ever done. The Wrightsville Christian Church is on now on the near right.

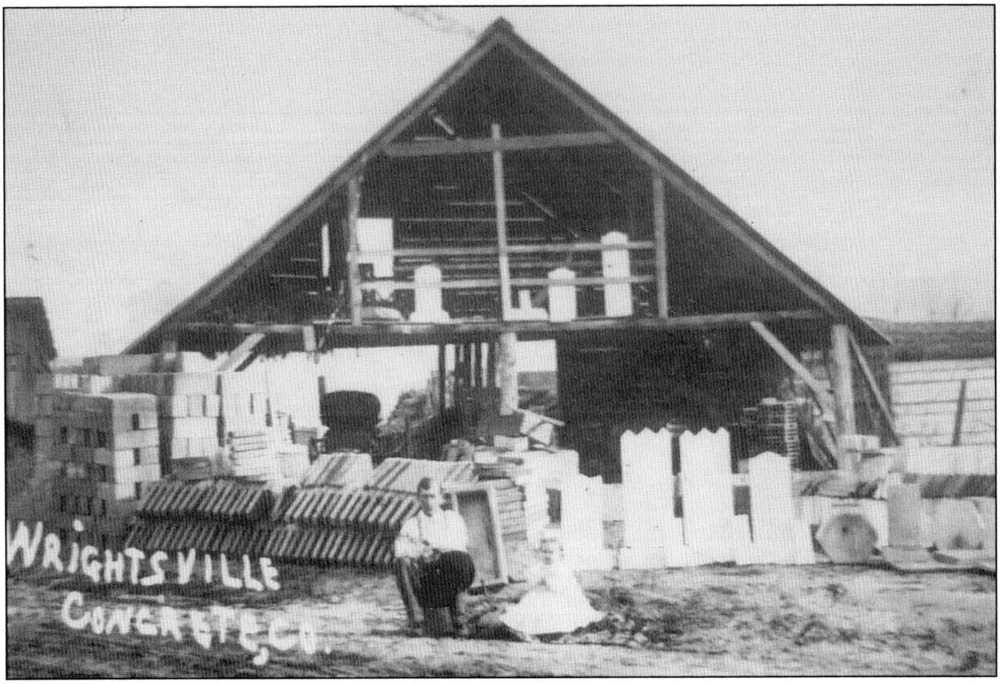

WRIGHTSVILLE CONCRETE COMPANY. This business, located on Highway 57 East, was owned by Frank F. Flanders, who made gravestones, water troughs, etc.

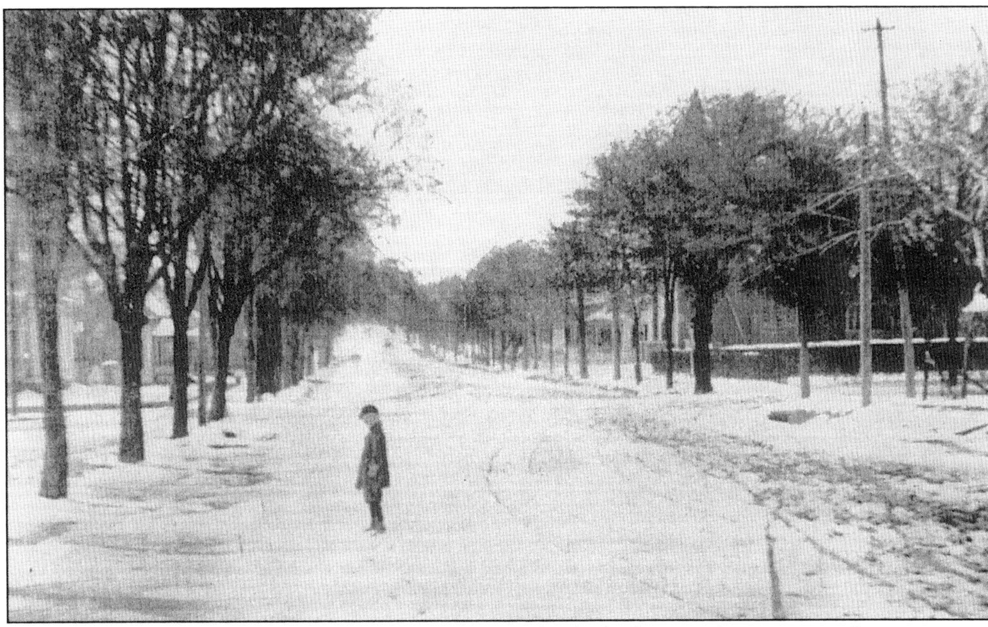

WEST ELM STREET IN WRIGHTSVILLE, GEORGIA. The little boy in this view is admiring a rare sight of snow in Wrightsville.

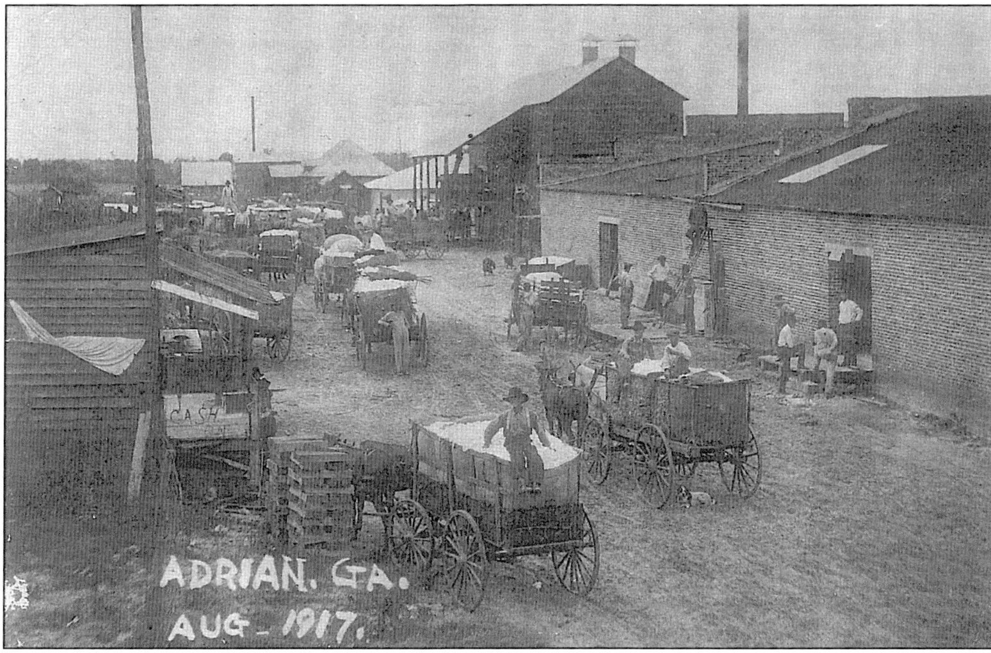

ADRIAN, GEORGIA DURING COTTON HARVEST TIME, 1917.

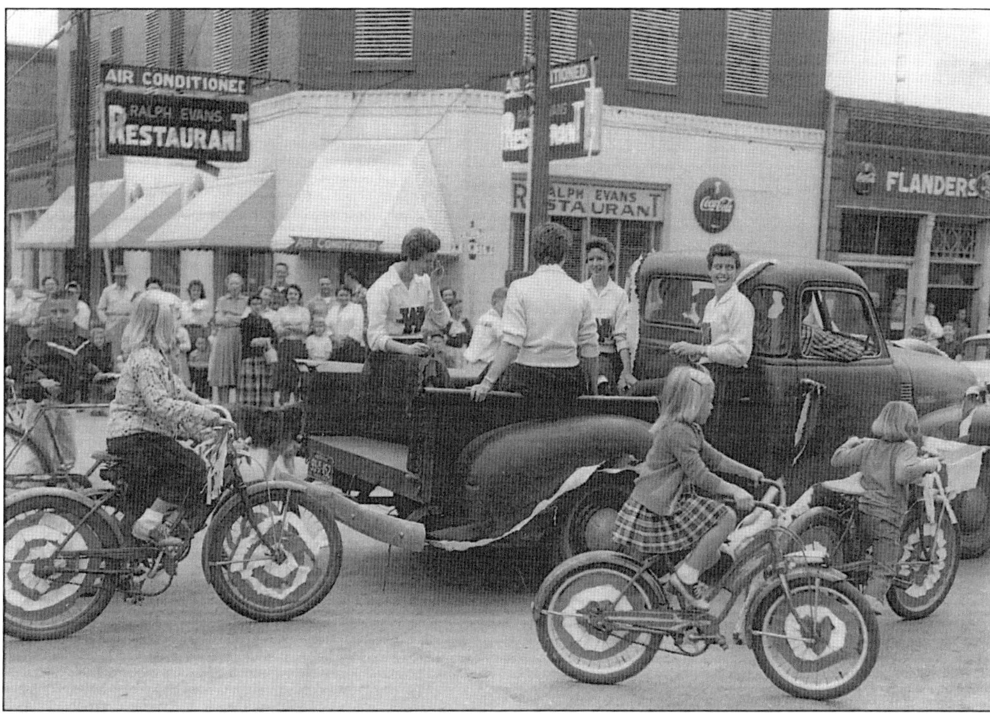

A HOMECOMING PARADE AT THE CORNER OF MARCUS AND ELM STREETS, 1956. Notice the sign at Ralph Evans Restaurant advertising air conditioning. The Flanders store, far right, now houses Hair Unlimited.

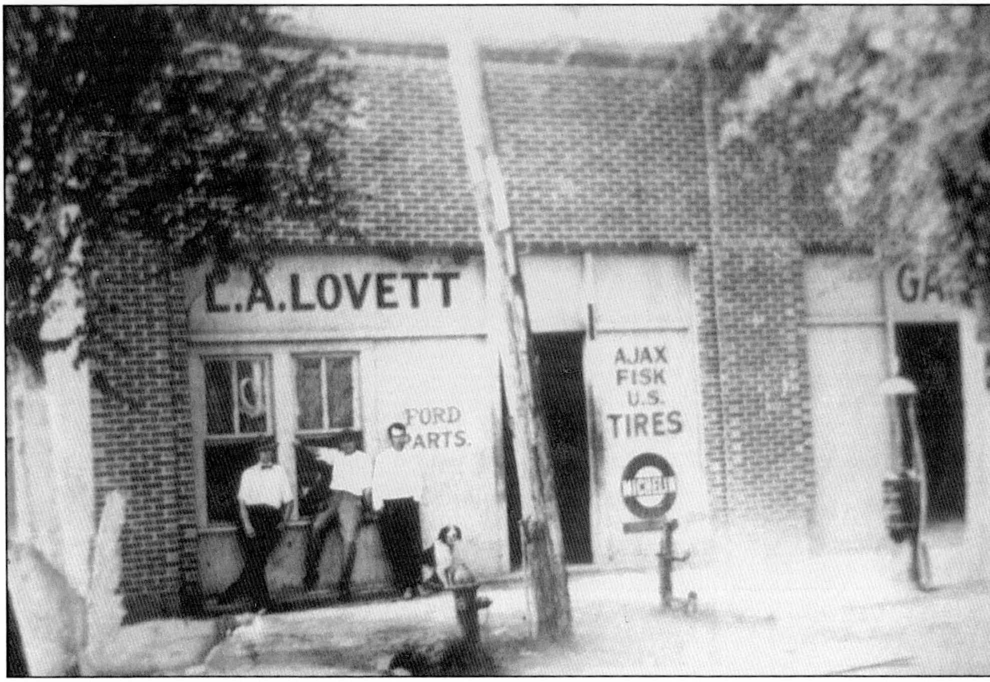

C.A. Lovett's Garage. This garage was located at the corner of South Bradford and College Streets.

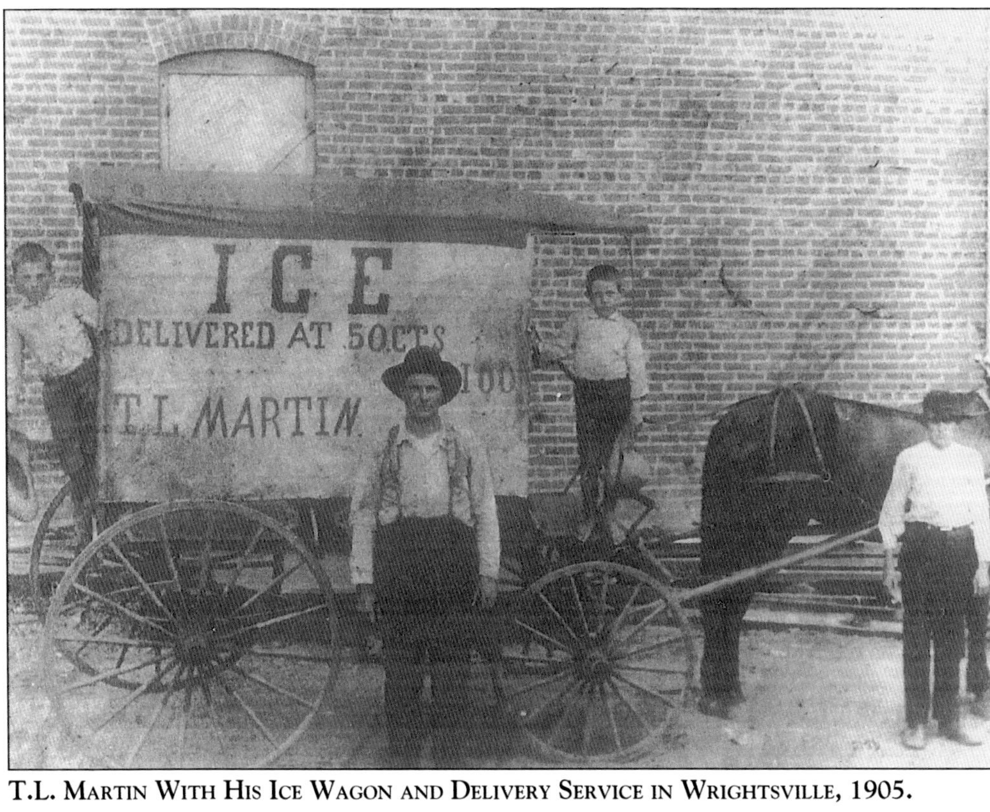

T.L. Martin With His Ice Wagon and Delivery Service in Wrightsville, 1905.

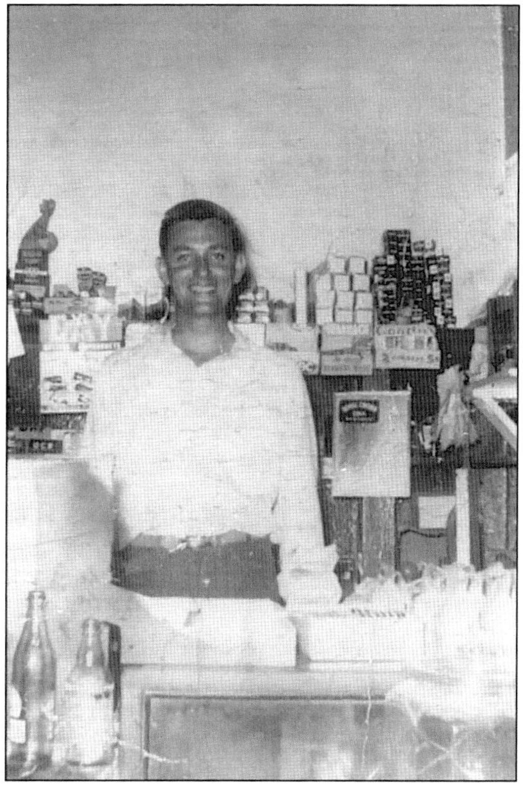

WEBB'S STORE. James Webb is pictured here in his father's store, which was located on the corner of Highway 319 and Union Hill Church Road.

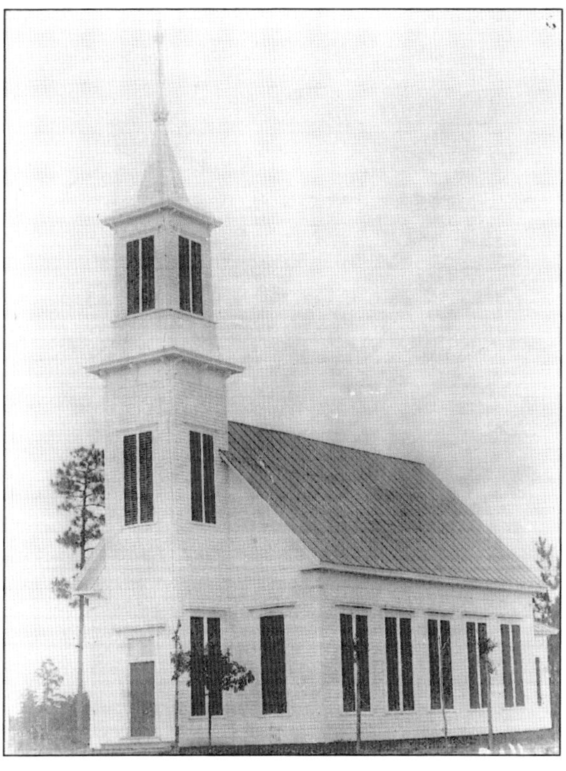

BEULAH BAPTIST CHURCH. Organized in 1890, this church was located near Donovan. The building shown here was once the Wrightsville Baptist Church (now known as Brown Memorial), which was dismantled, its boards numbered, hauled to its present location, and restored to its original appearance.

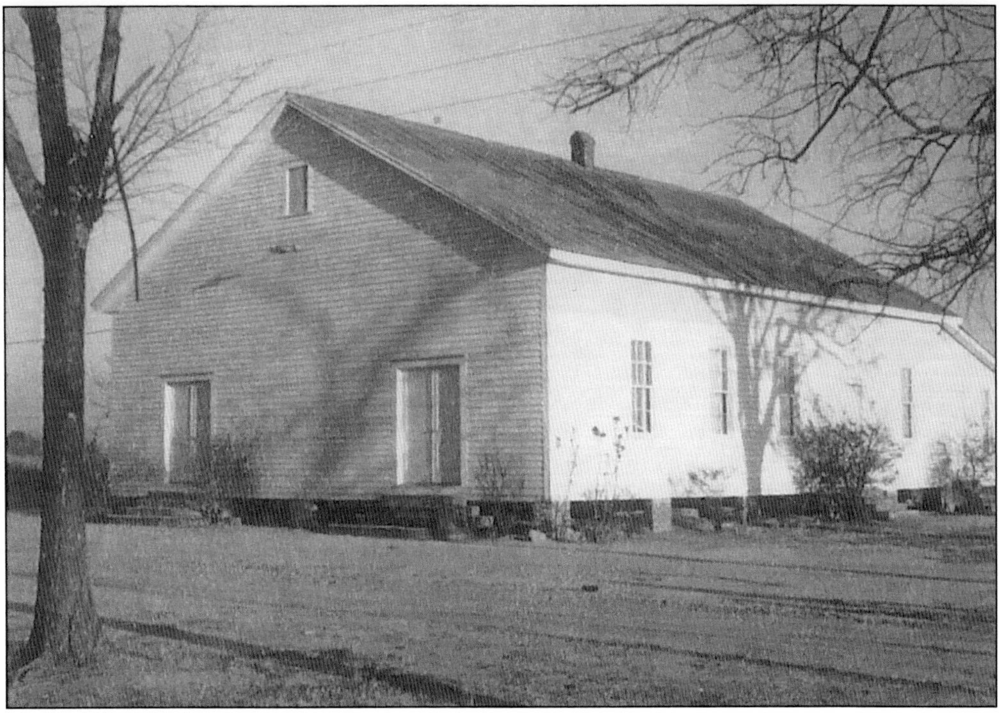

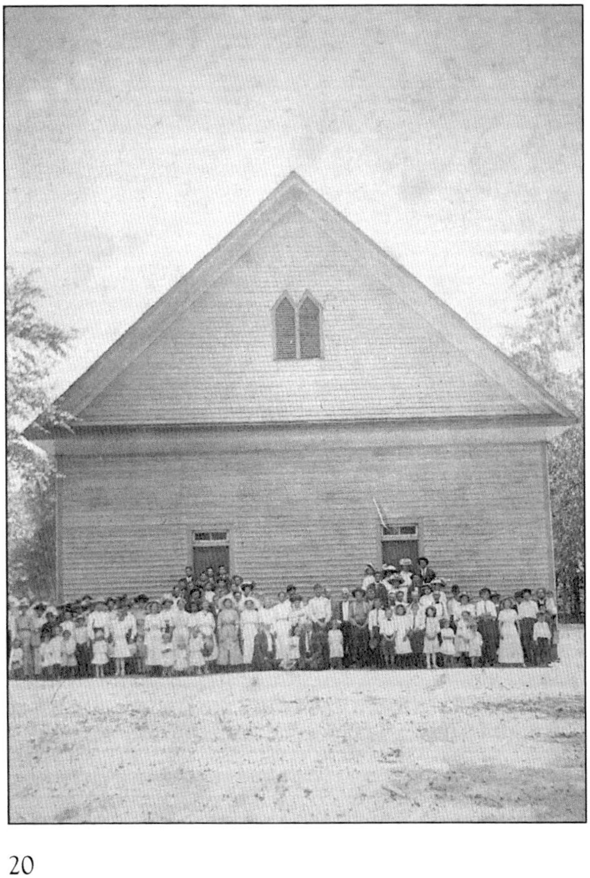

New Home Missionary Baptist Church. Formally known as Shiloh, this church was organized on September 19, 1886. The church was bricked in June of 1971.

Gumlog Primitive Baptist Church. Originally known as Mount Pleasant, this church was located on Highway 221, north of Kite and constituted in July 1880. The land was donated by Sheriff Lewis Davis.

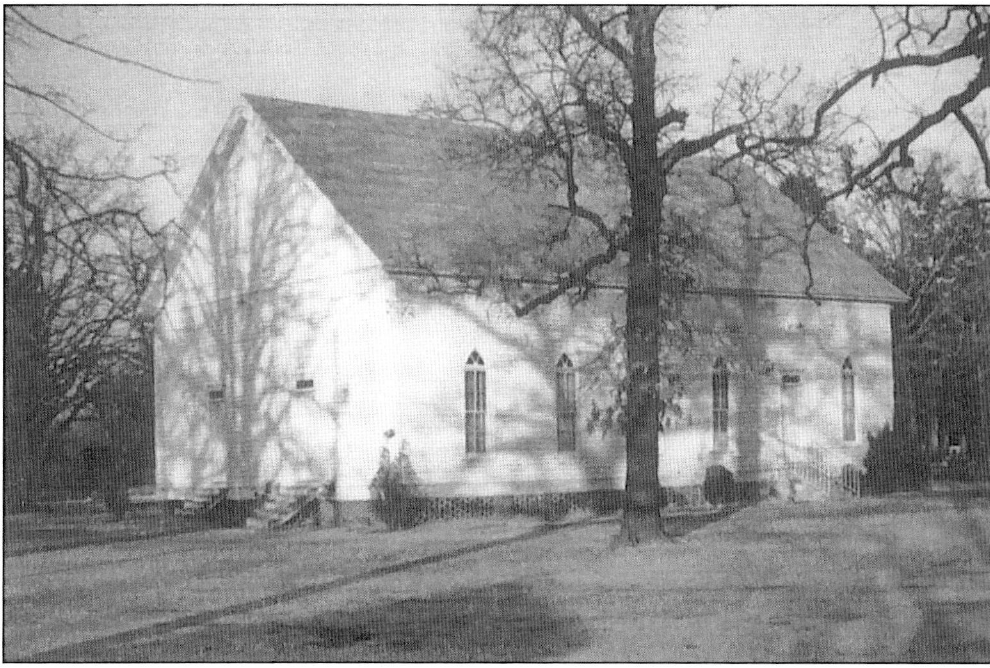

OAKY GROVE PRIMITIVE BAPTIST CHURCH. This church is located 10 miles from Wrightsville. It was organized August 5, 1818, and was originally called Gumlog until 1831, when the name was changed to Oaky Grove.

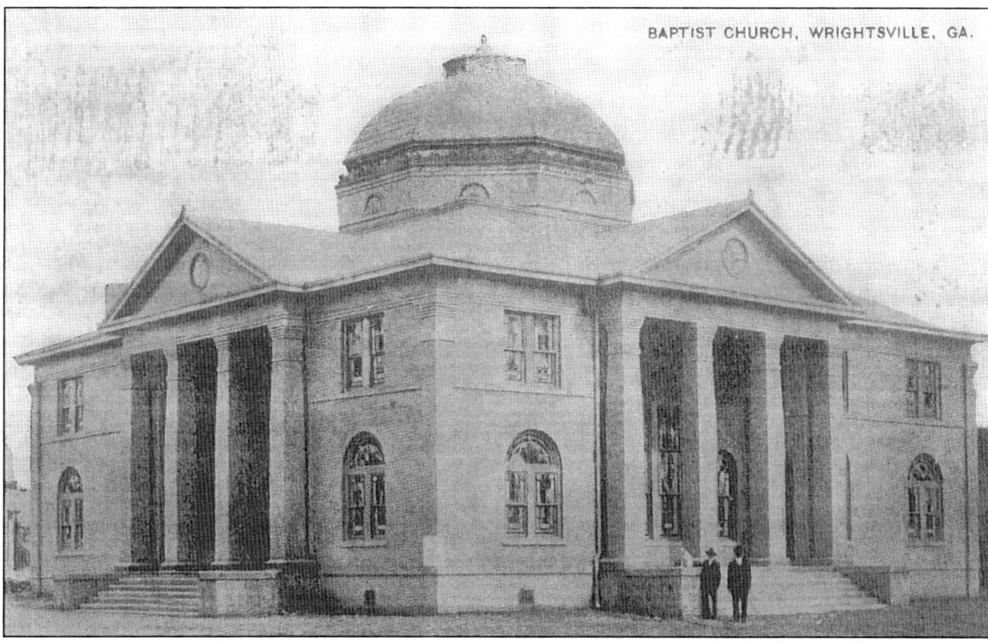

BROWN MEMORIAL BAPTIST CHURCH. In 1910, Mr. and Mrs. Ardis Brown willed their entire estate of $10,000 to Wrightsville Baptist Church for the purpose of constructing a new building. In 1914, the new church house was dedicated as Brown Memorial Baptist Church in memory of Mr. and Mrs. Ardis Brown. This building was used until November 1926, when it was destroyed by fire.

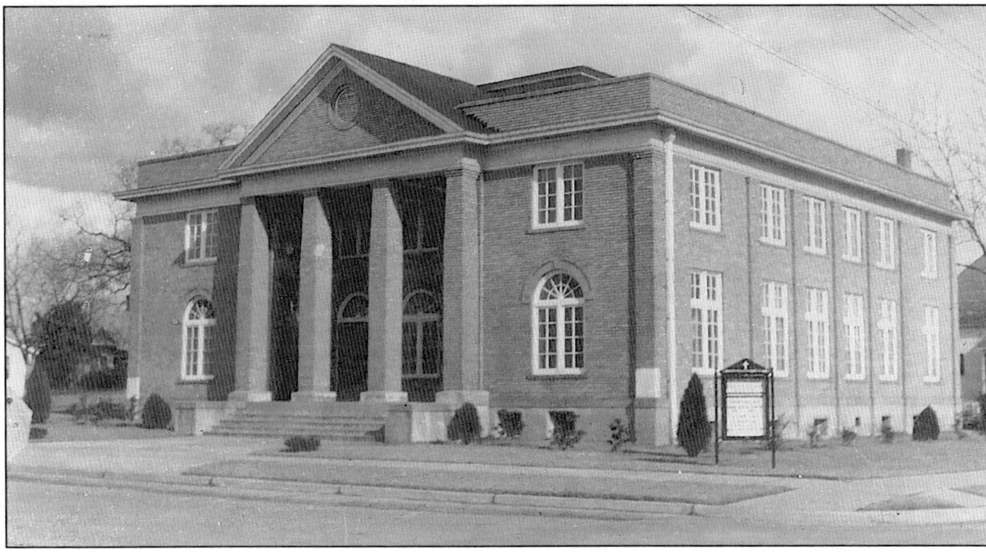

THE NEW BROWN MEMORIAL CHURCH. Pictured above is the building that replaced the burnt Brown Memorial Church. The new building, which cost $25,000, was erected under the leadership of Pastor Rufus Hodges and dedicated in 1927.

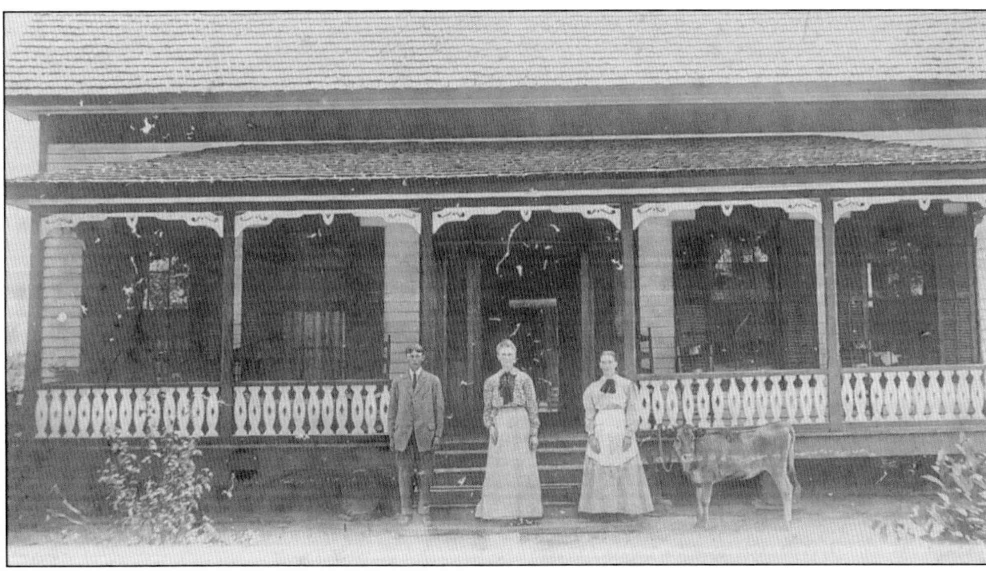

THE OLD NATHANIEL AND LUCINDA STOKES HOME, C. EARLY 1900S. Built before the Civil War on a part of the land given to Lucinda's grandfather Elisha Walker, this home still stands today. Mag and Martha Stokes, the twin daughters of Nathaniel and Lucinda, are pictured with farm overseer Bill Williams.

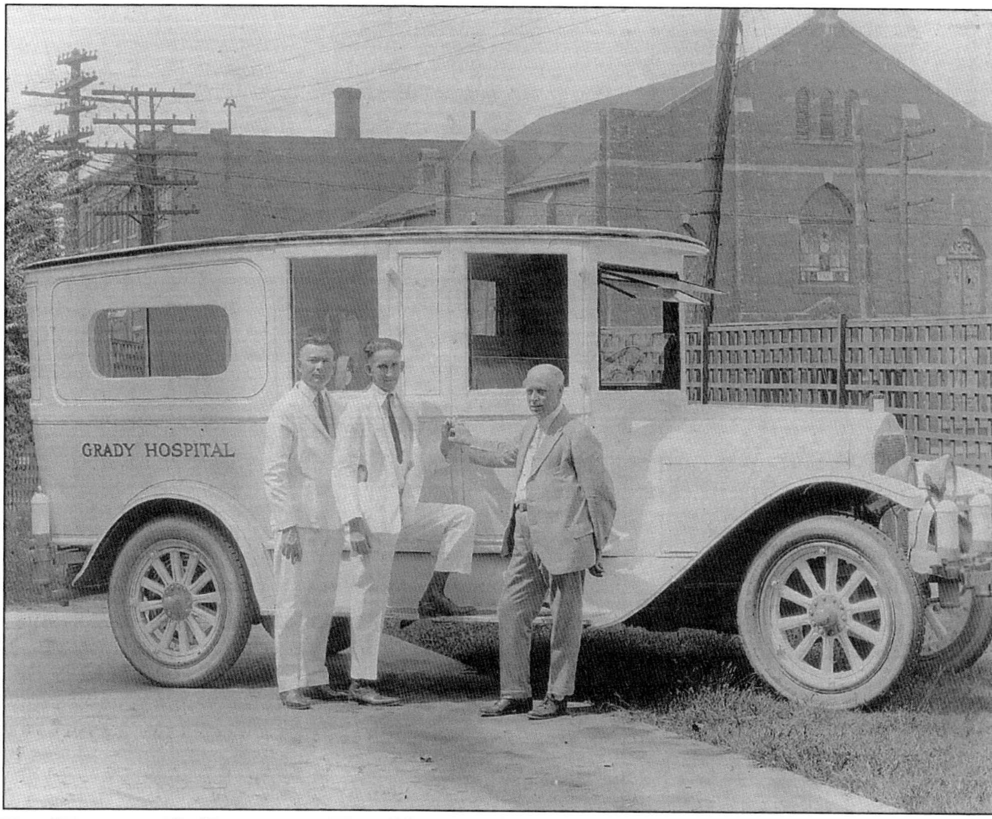

Dr. Herschel B. Bray with Two Medical Students, c. 1920s. Dr. Bray attended Emory University School of Medicine and interned at Grady Hospital in Atlanta. In 1935, he attended the Graduate School of Medicine and Surgery at Cook County Hospital in Chicago, Illinois. He served the citizens of Johnson County until his death in 1946.

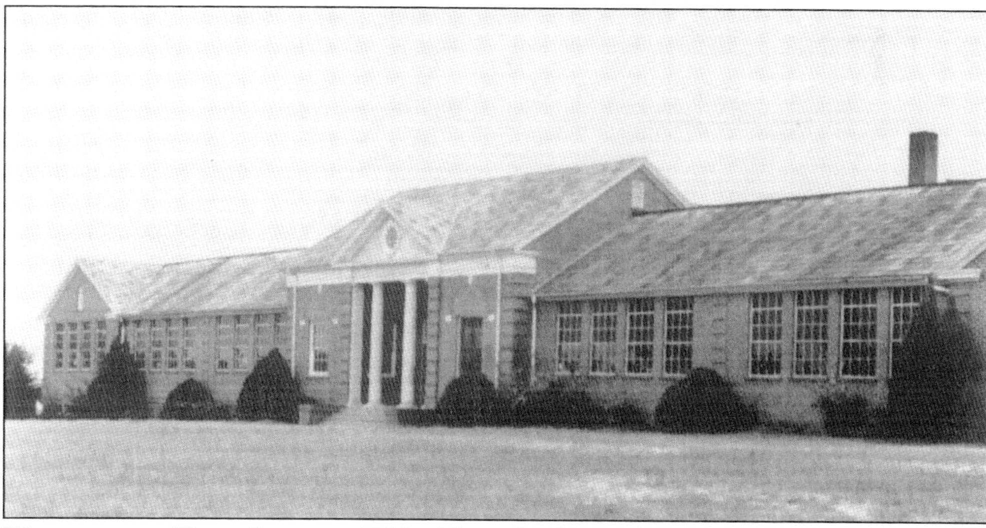

Wrightsville High School, 1920. The school was located on the site of the old Nannie Lou Warthen Institute. It later became the Wrightsville Primary School and is now used as a flea market.

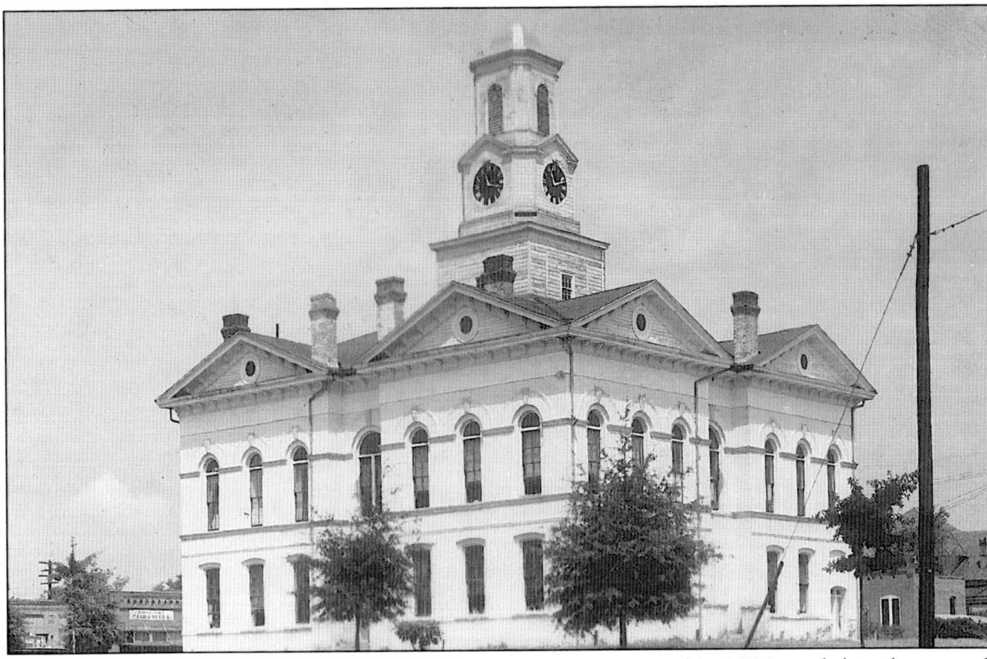

JOHNSON COUNTY COURTHOUSE. The courthouse was constructed in 1898, and this photograph was taken around 1923.

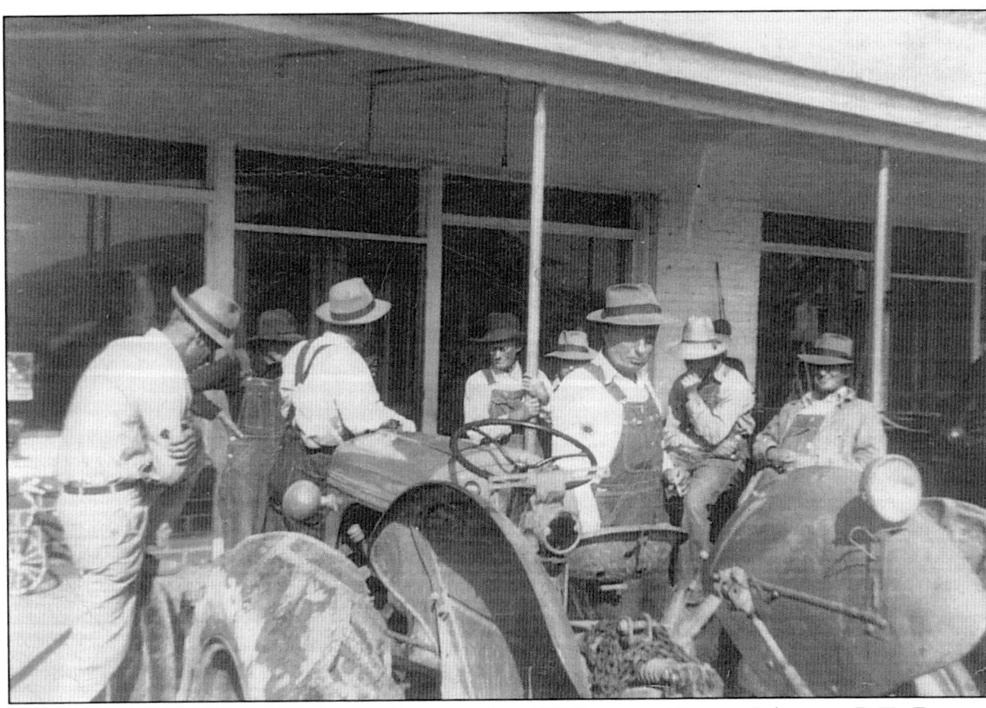

KITE, GEORGIA, C. 1948. Pictured here are Jim Wilkerson, George Johnson, R.T. Fortner, Talmadge Harrison, Ruel Martin, Kale Davis, and Manning Beasley.

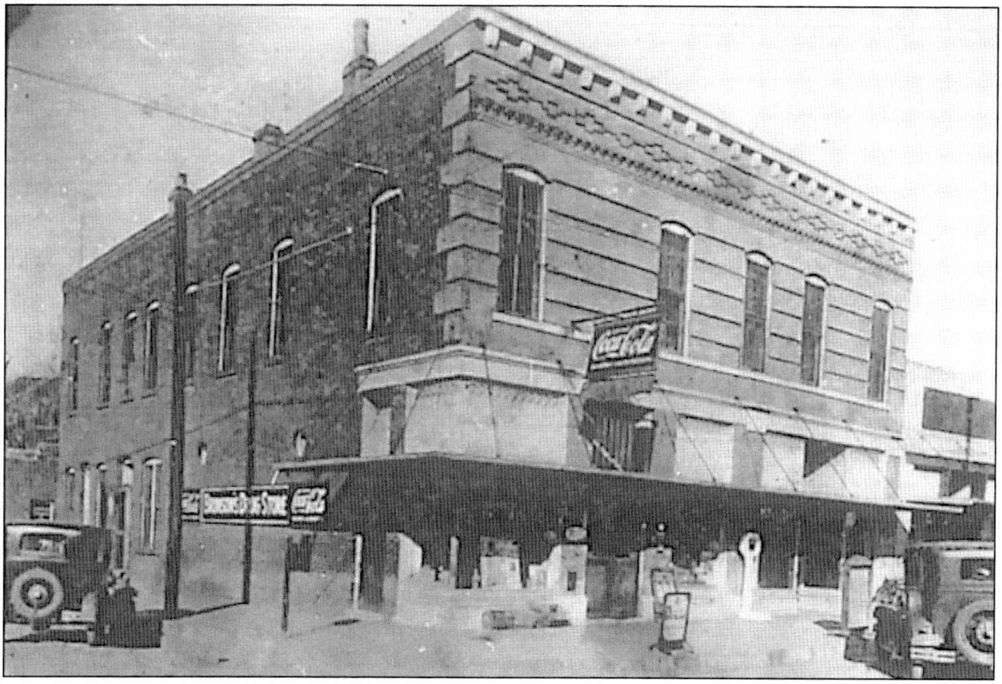

Brinson's Drug Store. The store was located on the corner of Elm and Marcus Streets and is currently the home of Superior Cleaners. Notice the penny scale on the street in front of the building.

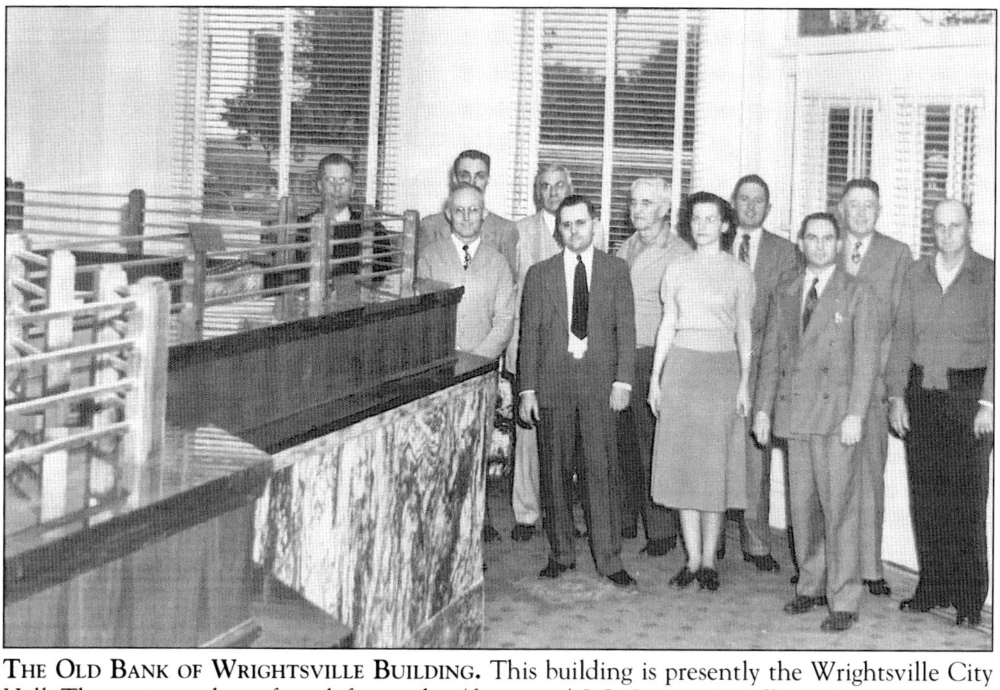

The Old Bank of Wrightsville Building. This building is presently the Wrightsville City Hall. Those pictured are, from left to right, (front row) L.L. Lovett, ? Collier, Mary Smith, and Joe Fulghum; (back row) R.A. Lovett, Perry Edge, Rozier Stephens, Flint Flanders, W.C. Lovett, W.H. Lovett, and T.L. Lovett.

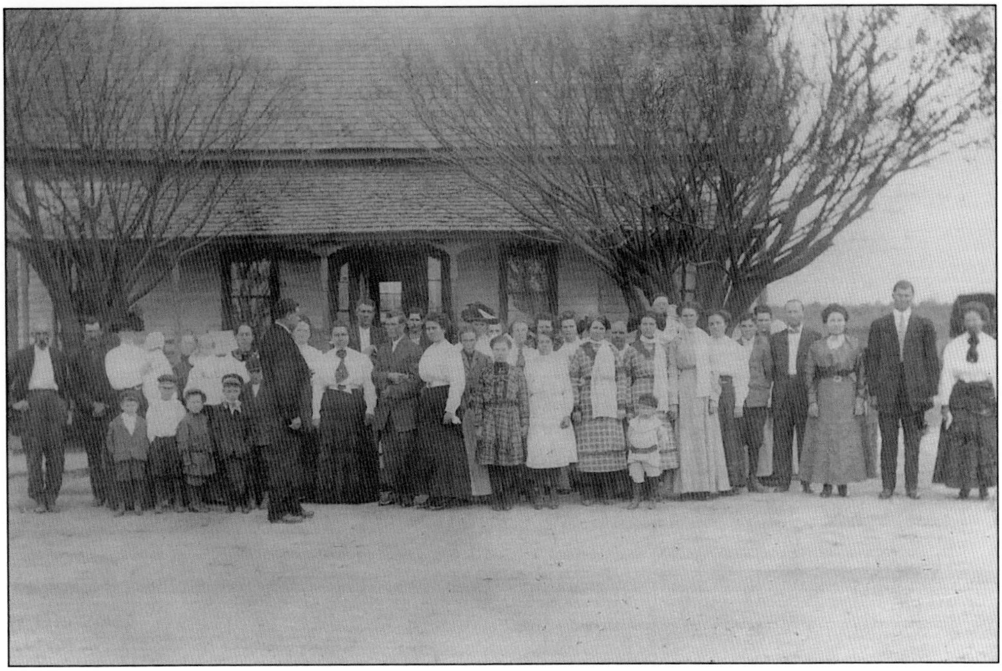

THE WEDDING OF CARRIE FROST AND HARVEY POOL, DECEMBER 1911. The group is pictured at the Donovan home of the bride's parents, William "Billy" Henry Frost and Nancy Norris Frost. Many descendants of Billy and Nancy Frost live in Johnson County today.

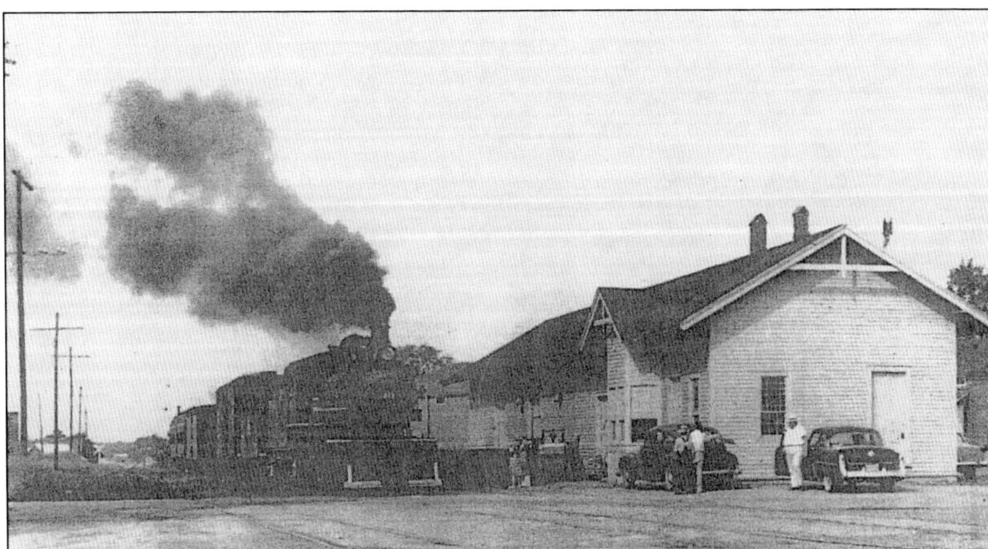

THE WRIGHTSVILLE AND TENNILLE RAILROAD MIXED TRAIN #4. The train is shown here northbound from Dublin to Tennille on July 5, 1954.

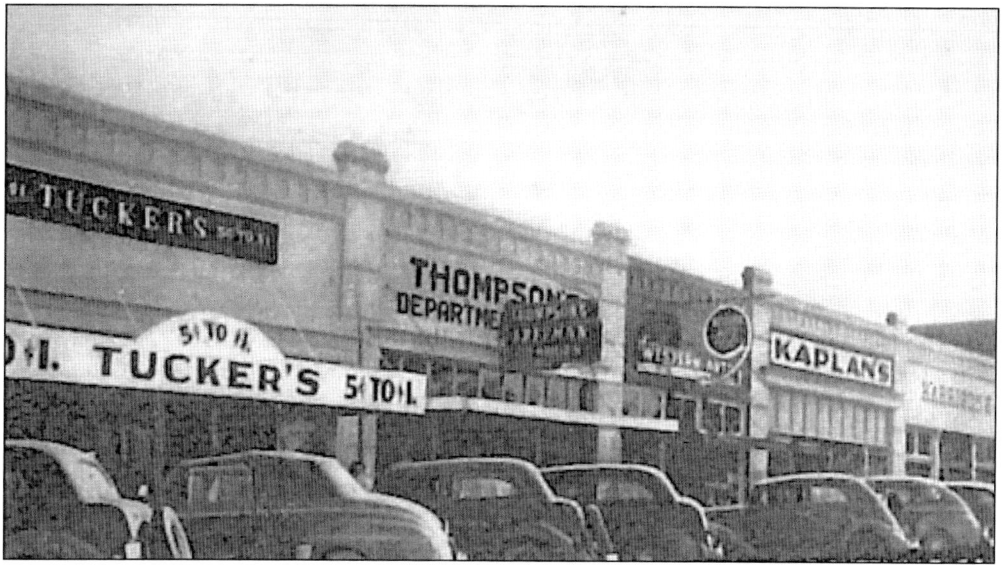

The Old Businesses of Wrightsville. Tucker's, Thompson's Department Store, Western Auto, Kaplan's (owned by the only Jewish merchant in town), and Harrison's are all seen in this photograph.

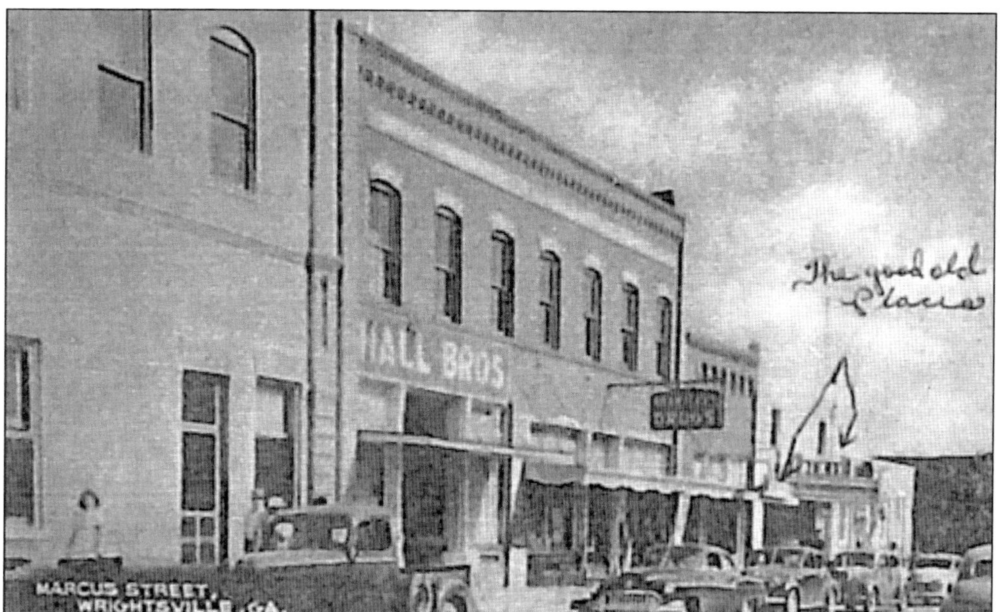

Marcus Street in 1939. Some residents called these the "good old places"—Brantley's Drug Store and Dixie Theatre.

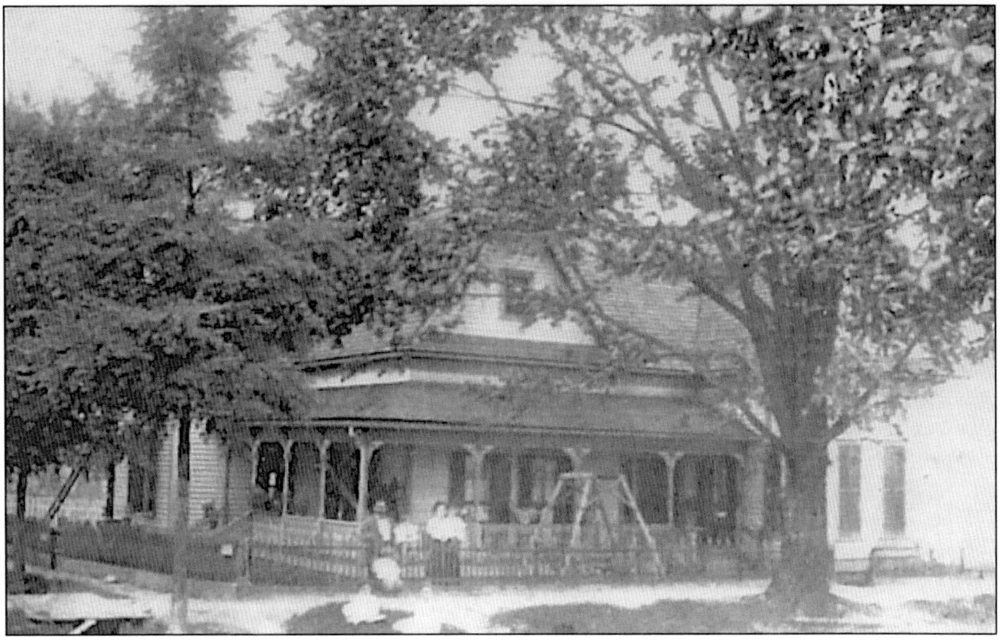

THE HOME OF MR. AND MRS. E.A.W. JOHNSON. This residence was located on South Myrtle Street around 1900.

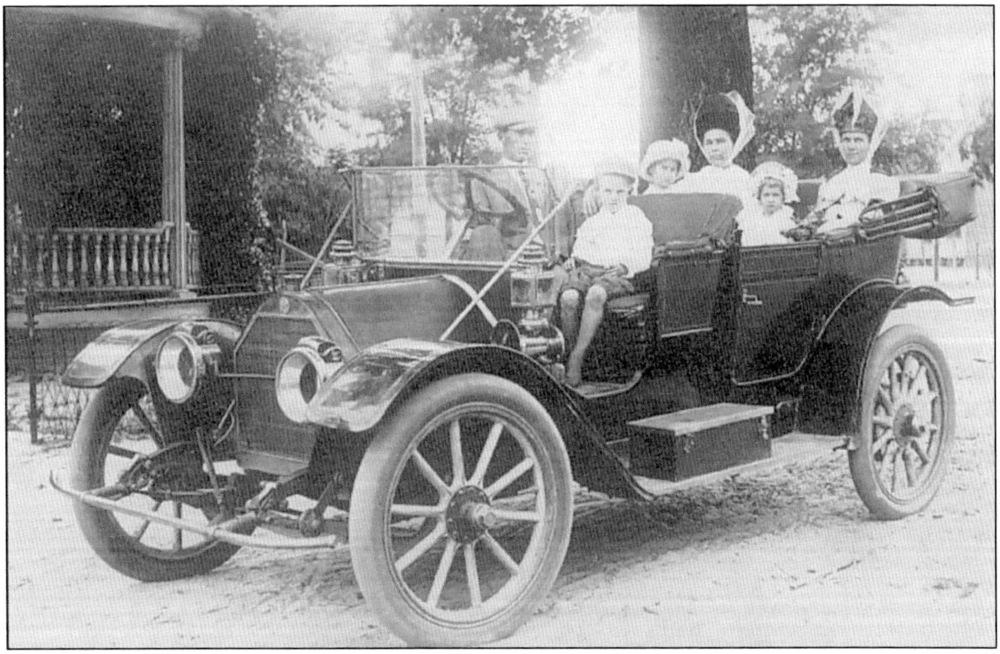

DRIVING ON MARCUS STREET. The Lovetts are seen sporting around in their new automobile. In the front seat are L.A. Lovett and T.L. Lovett. In the back seat are unidentified, Mrs. E.A. Lovett, unidentified, and Mrs. Maude Mixon.

Two

VETERANS

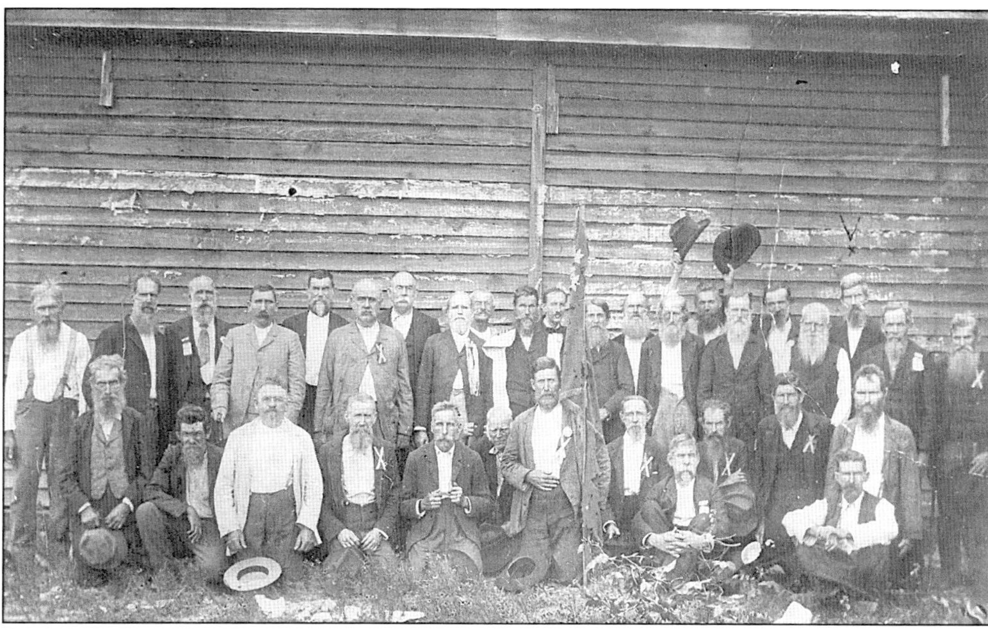

CONFEDERATE SOLDIERS REUNION IN KITE, GEORGIA, 1890. From left to right, are (seated) Jack Williams, Tom Sharp, George Schwalls, Will Mayo, Henry Hall, John Ellis, Elijah Beasley, Charles Wheeler, John Mixon, Andrew Sheley, Jimmy Anderson, Richard Mixon, and Andrew Atkinson; (standing) Harold Horton, Press Williams, Bennett Powell, Minter Burns, Math Bell, D.Z. Douglas, Arch Woods, Ben Fortner, H.G. Neal, B.Y. Wheeler, Captain John Martin, unidentified, C.T.J. Claxton, George Inman, John E. Meadows, Henry Wheeler, D.T. Johnson, Ramsey Powell, Jim Peebles, Jerd Norris, and Obie Fortner.

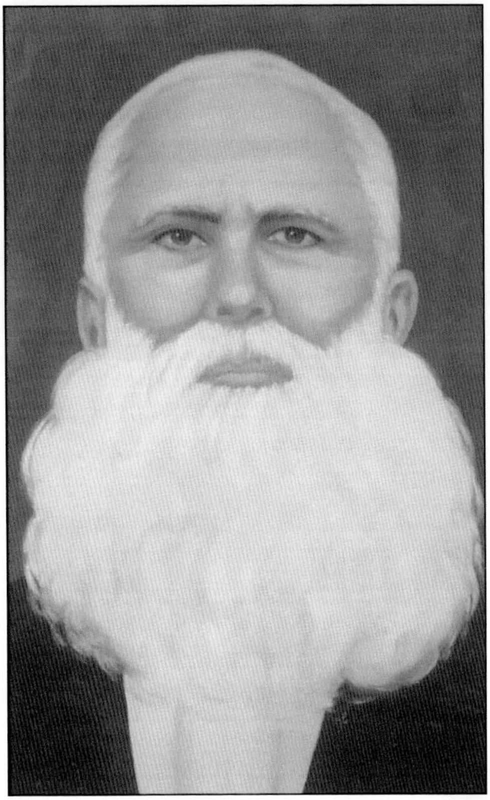

Charles Thomas Jefferson Claxton. Claxton enrolled as a private on February 15, 1863, in Co. D, 54th Regiment, Georgia Volunteer Infantry and was paroled at Augusta, Georgia on May 24, 1865. He was once the treasurer of Johnson County and the clerk of Gumlog Church.

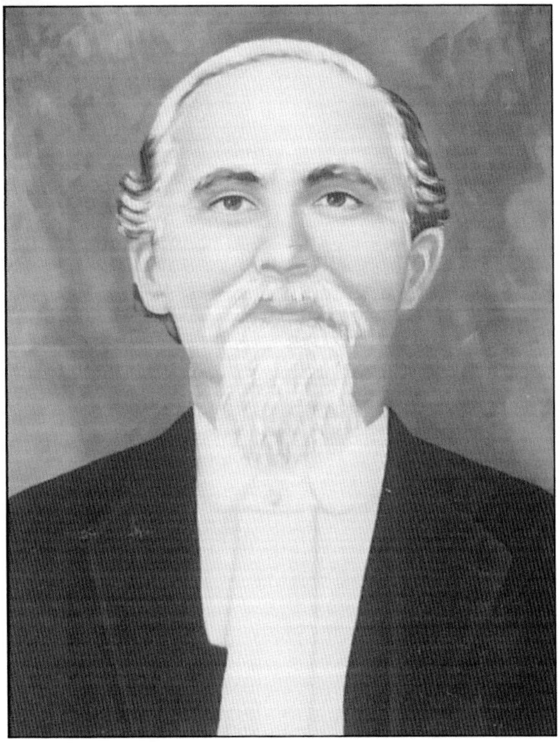

Elder Jordan Norris. Norris enrolled as a private on February 22, 1862, in Co. F, 14th Regiment, Georgia Volunteer Infantry. He was appointed first sergeant in 1864. He was also one of the ministers who officiated at the constitution of Gumlog Church.

JOHN L. MARTIN. Martin enrolled in Co. F., 62nd Regiment, Georgia Volunteer Infantry as a first lieutenant on July 1, 1862. He was transferred to Co. F, 8th Regiment, Georgia Cavalry on July 11, 1864. Pension records show that Martin was escorting President Jefferson Davis from Petersburg, Virginia in April of 1865.

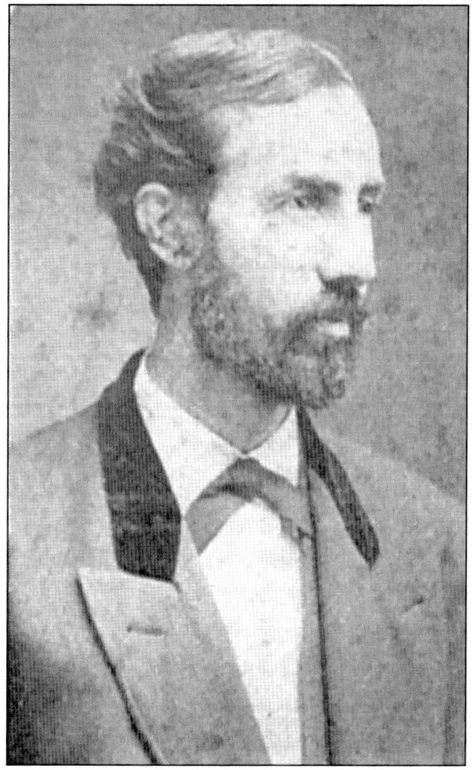

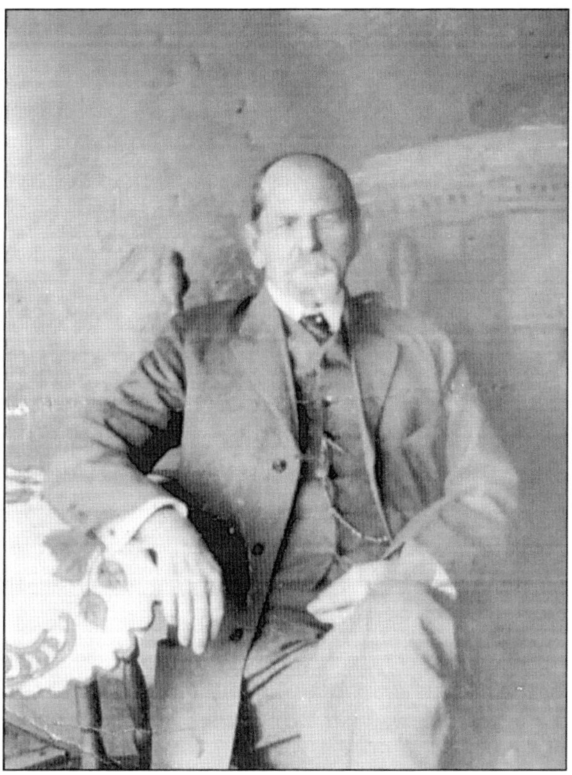

LEWIS BERRY LIGHTFOOT. Lightfoot became a private on April 26, 1861 in Co. A, 3rd Regiment Georgia Volunteer Infantry. He was wounded in Gettysburg, Pennsylvania on July 2, 1863, and in Spotsylvania, Virginia on May 14, 1864. After the war, Lightfoot became a lawyer.

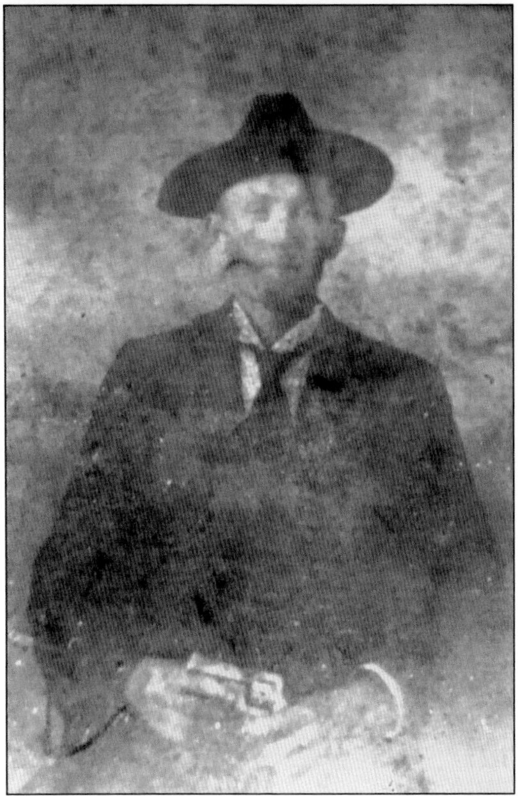

PHARO HUTCHENSON. Hutchenson enrolled as a private on May 7, 1862, in Co. G, 32nd Regiment, Georgia Volunteer Infantry. After fighting for almost three years, he surrendered in Greensboro, North Carolina on April 26, 1865.

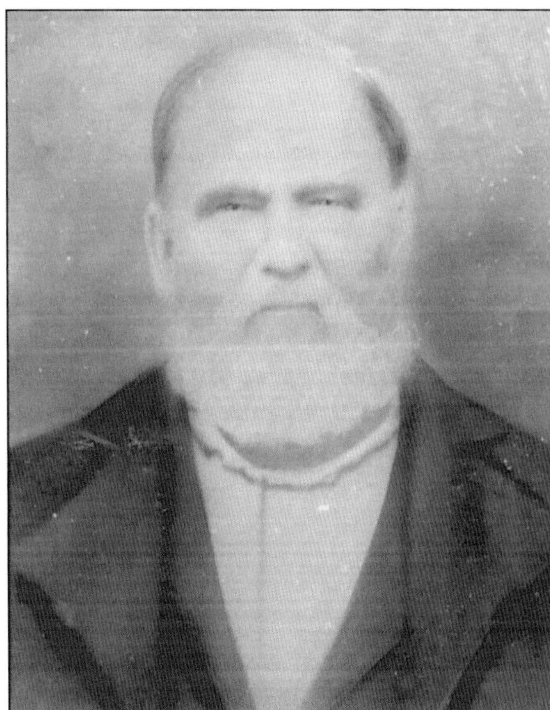

JOSEPH R.G. UNDERWOOD. Underwood enlisted as a private in Co. A, 2nd Regiment, 1st Brigade, Georgia State Troops on October 12, 1861. He was mustered out in April 1862 and then enlisted as a private in Co. G, 57th Regiment, Georgia infantry on May 6, 1862.

JOHN F. WILLIAMS. On August 10, 1862, Williams enrolled as a private in Co. D, 59th Regiment, Georgia Volunteer Infantry. He was wounded in the left temple, impairing his sight, in Tennessee on November 29, 1863, and he was wounded in his back near Petersburg, Virginia on June 3, 1864. John surrendered at Appomattox, Virginia on April 9, 1865.

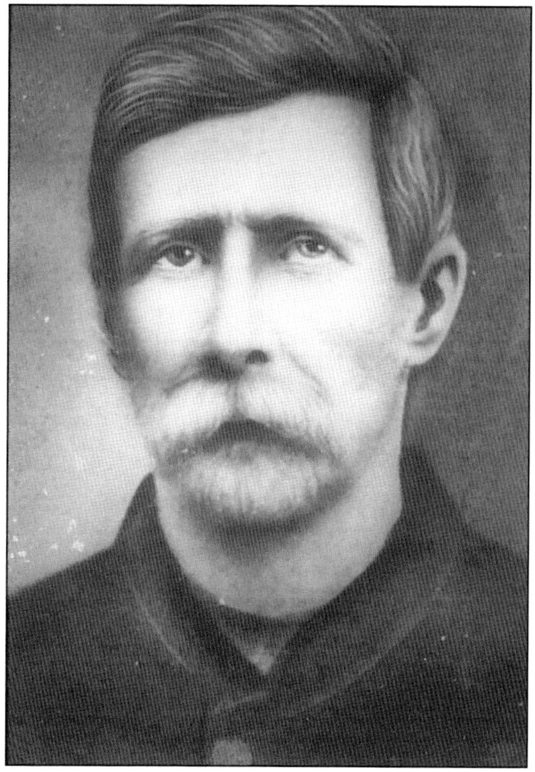

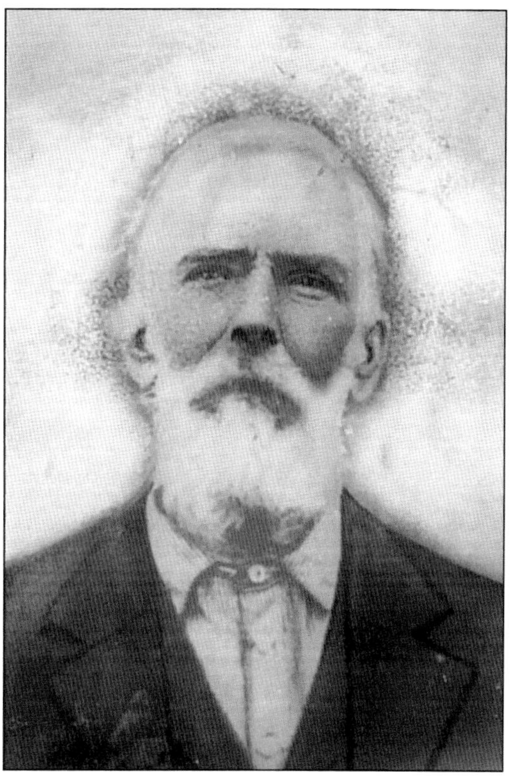

AMOS J. RINER. Riner enlisted as a private on March 4, 1862 in Co. F, 48th Regiment, Georgia Volunteer Infantry. He was wounded at Gettysburg, Pennsylvania on July 2, 1863 and was sent to Jackson Hospital in Richmond, Virginia on January 11, 1864. Pension records show that Riner was at home on sick furlough at the close of the war.

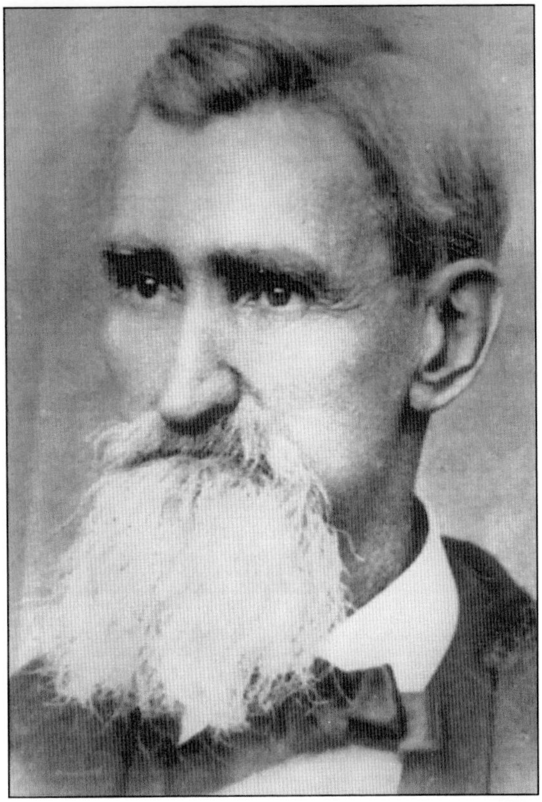

Dr. James Washington Flanders. Enlisted as a private in Co. C, 2nd Regiment on Nov. 18, 1861, Flanders was appointed a hospital steward on December 11, 1861 and was discharged for disability on January 23, 1862. He then enlisted as a private in Co. C, 57th Regiment Ga. Infantry on May 8, 1862 and was appointed a hospital steward on June 23, 1862. Flanders was captured at Vicksburg, Mississippi on July 4, 1863 and exchanged in August 1863.

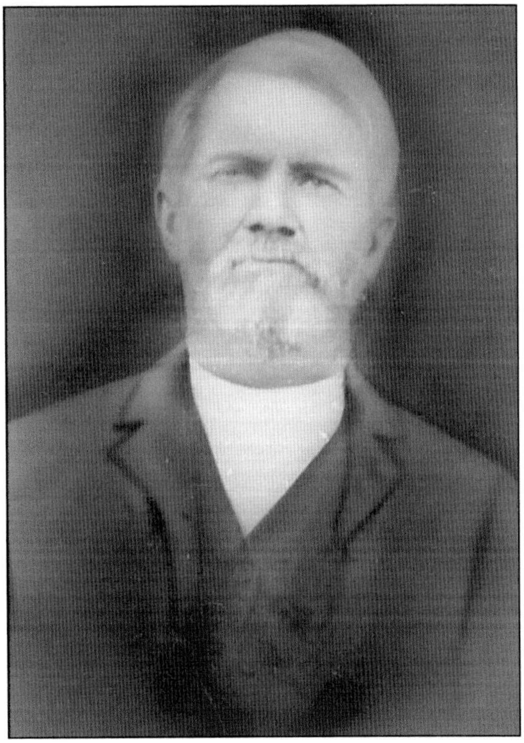

William Press Williams. This man enlisted as a private in Co. F, 3rd Regiment, Georgia Volunteer Infantry in 1861.

JACOB TAPLEY SNELL. He enlisted in the Georgia Militia at age 28 on March 10, 1864 and was assigned as first sergeant to Co. E, 2nd Regiment under the command of his brother James Christopher.

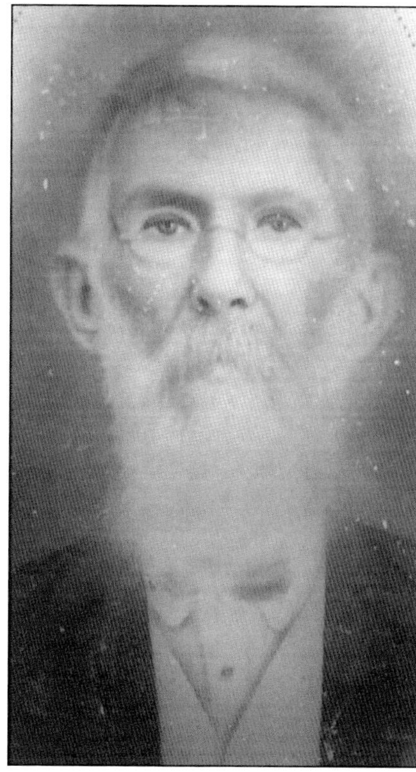

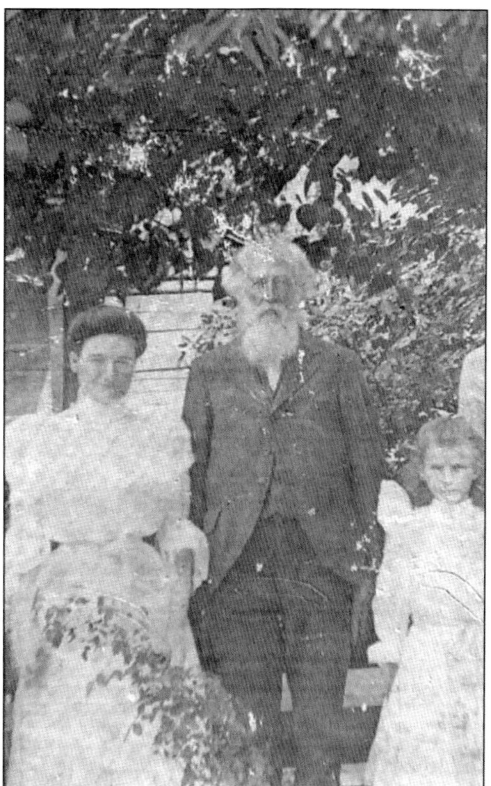

JOSEPH DRIVER WEBB. Webb enlisted as a private in Co. C, 2nd Regiment, 1st Brigade, Georgia State Troops on October 12, 1861. He was mustered out in April 1862. On May 8, 1862, he was appointed third sergeant of Co. C, 57th Regiment, Georgia Volunteer Infantry. On July 4, 1863, he was captured at Vicksburg, Mississippi and was exchanged in August 1863. He surrendered at Greensboro, North Carolina on April 26, 1865.

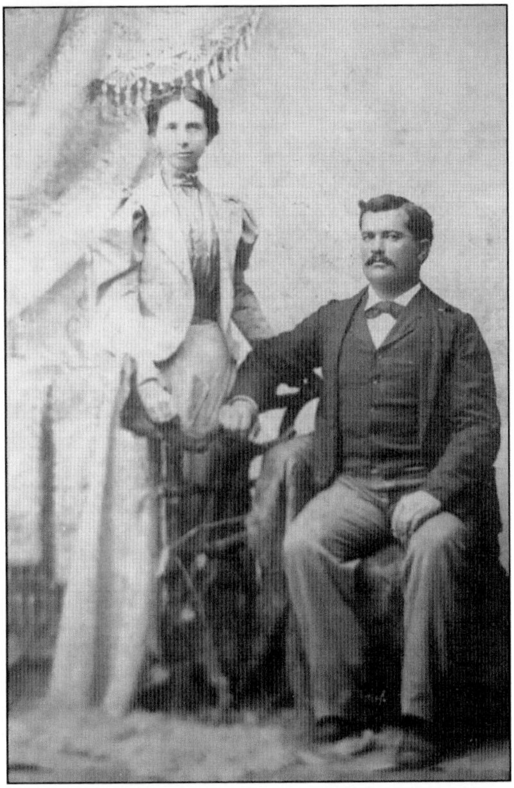

Joseph E. Page and His Wife, Elizear. Page enlisted in Co. D, 59th Regiment, Georgia Volunteer Infantry. He was wounded in the shoulder and knee.

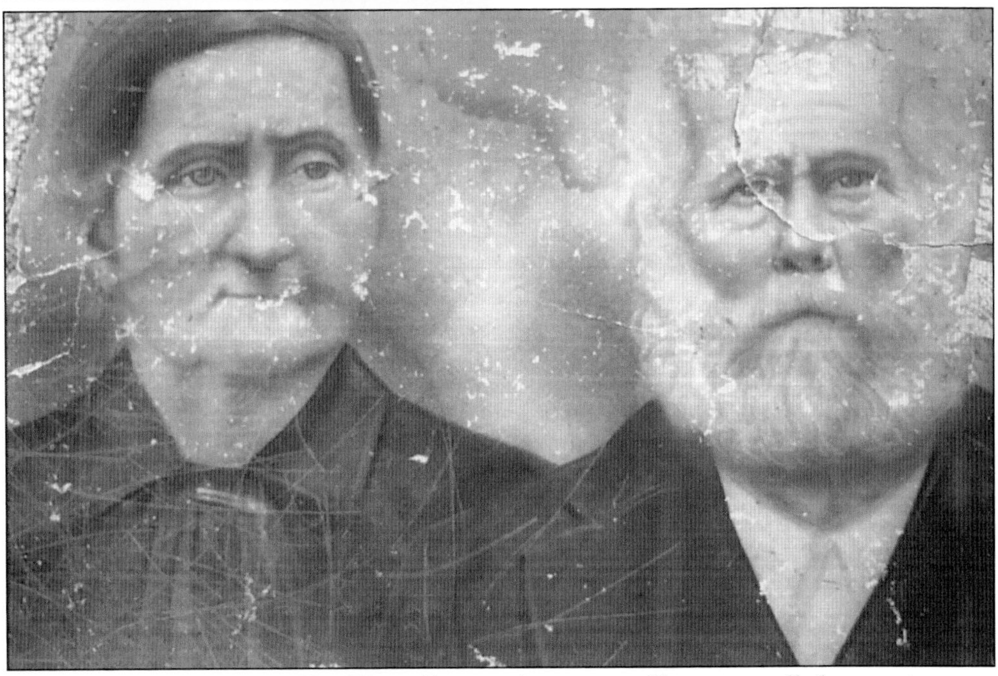

William I. Claxton and His Wife, Zilphia Anderson. Claxton enrolled as a private on July 25, 1862 in Co. D, 54th Regiment, Georgia Volunteer Infantry. He was paroled at Augusta, Georgia on May 30, 1865. Zilphia was the daughter of James and Eady Anderson.

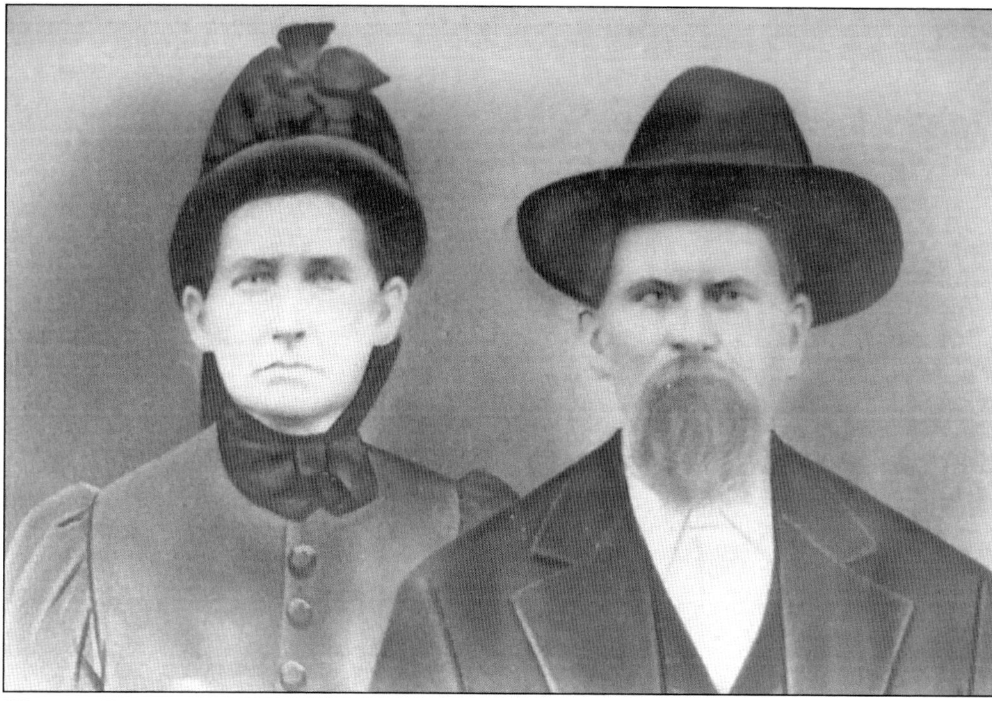

WILLIAM PAGE AND HIS WIFE, MARY WALKER. William enlisted as a private on May 8, 1862 in Co. D, 59th Regiment, Georgia Volunteer Infantry. He was appointed first sergeant in 1864. Mary is the daughter of Mr. and Mrs. Lott Walker.

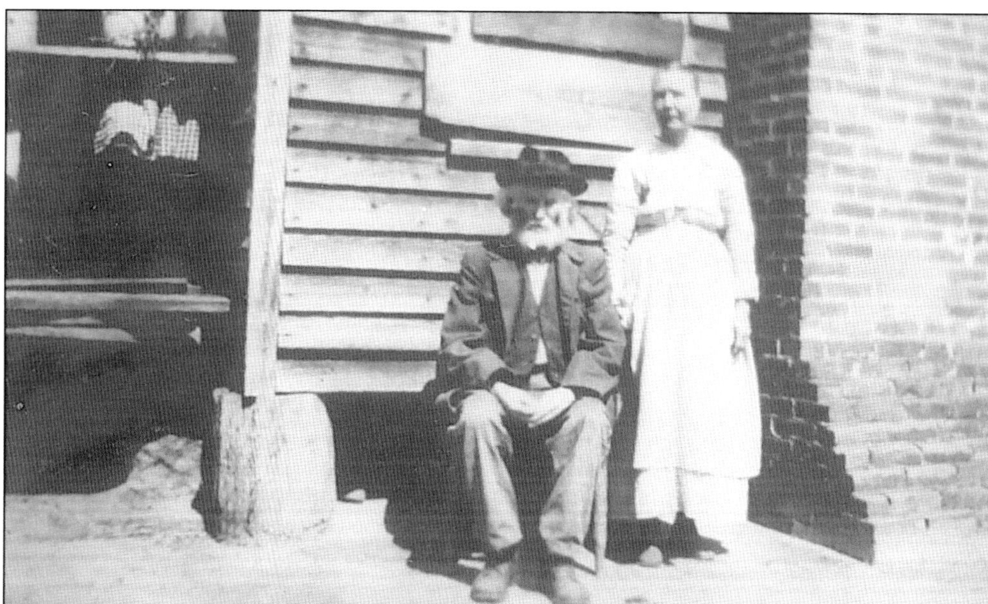

GEORGE ALBERT HALL AND HIS WIFE, NANCY FOSKEY HALL. Mr. Hall served as a soldier in the Civil War.

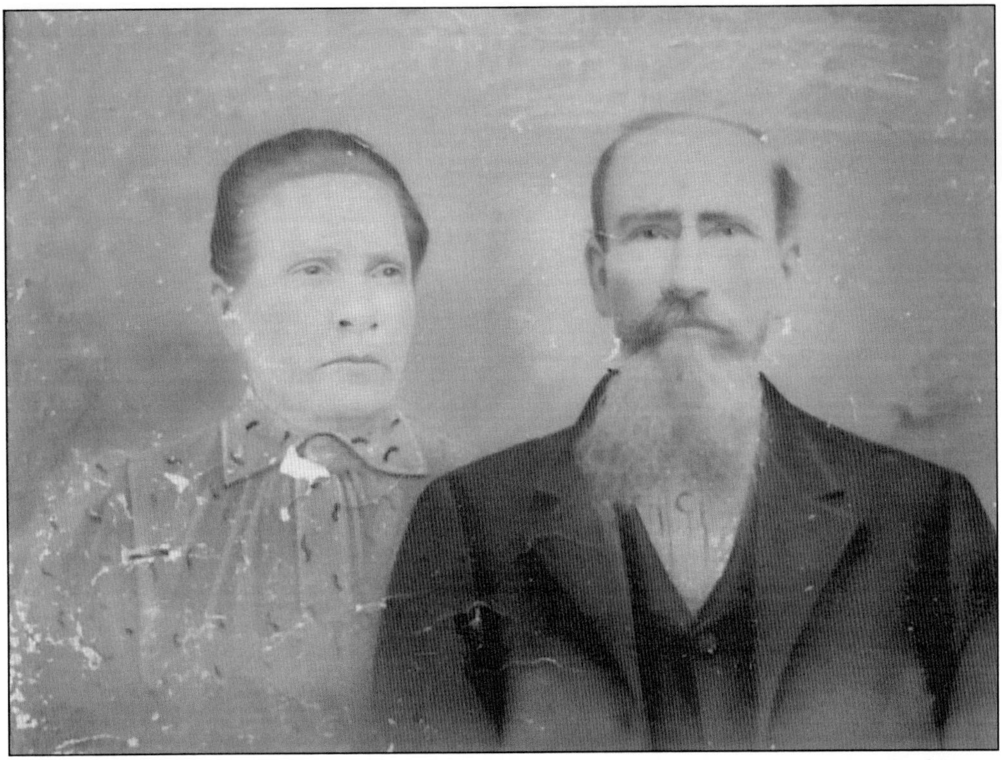

Jerry T. Dixon and His Wife, Dolly Kent Dixon. Mr. Dixon also served in the Civil War.

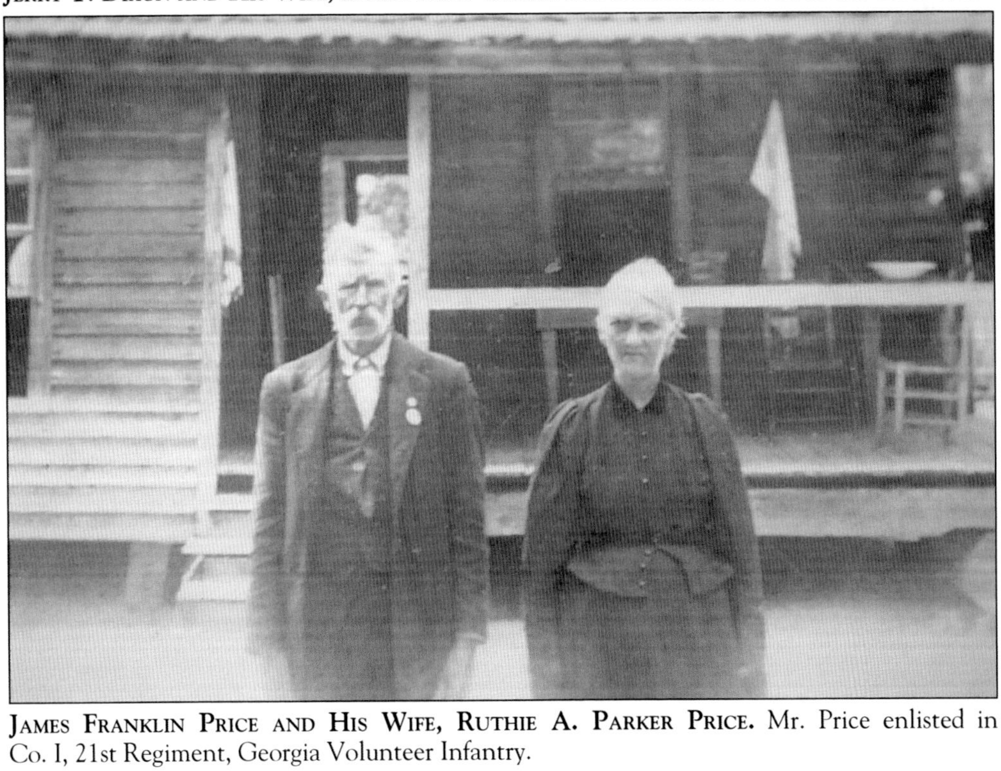

James Franklin Price and His Wife, Ruthie A. Parker Price. Mr. Price enlisted in Co. I, 21st Regiment, Georgia Volunteer Infantry.

Henry Brinson Caneega. Caneega fought for freedom during World War I.

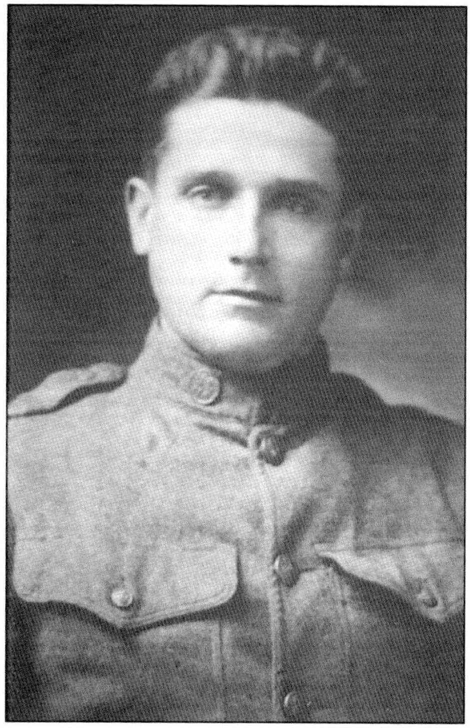

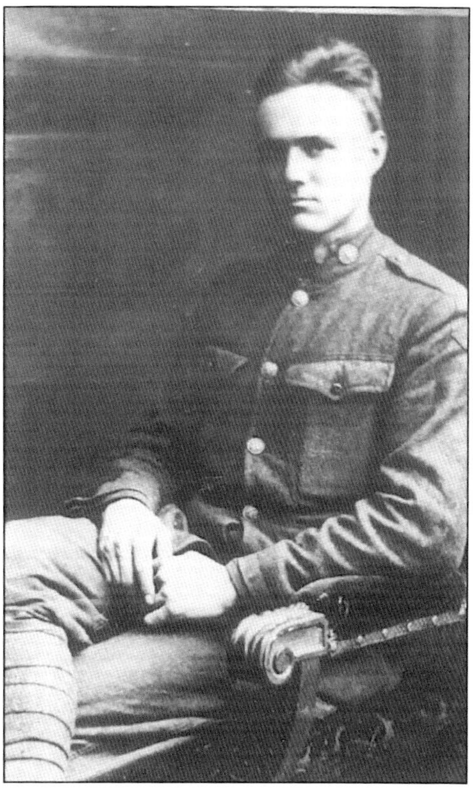

Brannan Snell. Snell was a private in the U.S. Army during World War I.

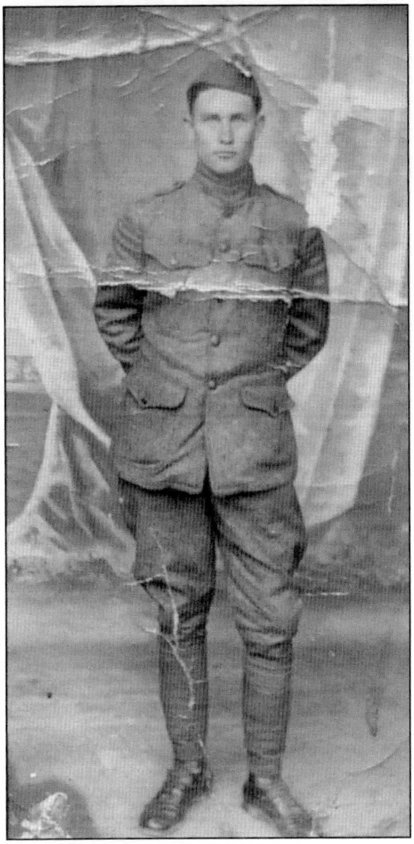

Clifford Smith in His World War I Uniform.

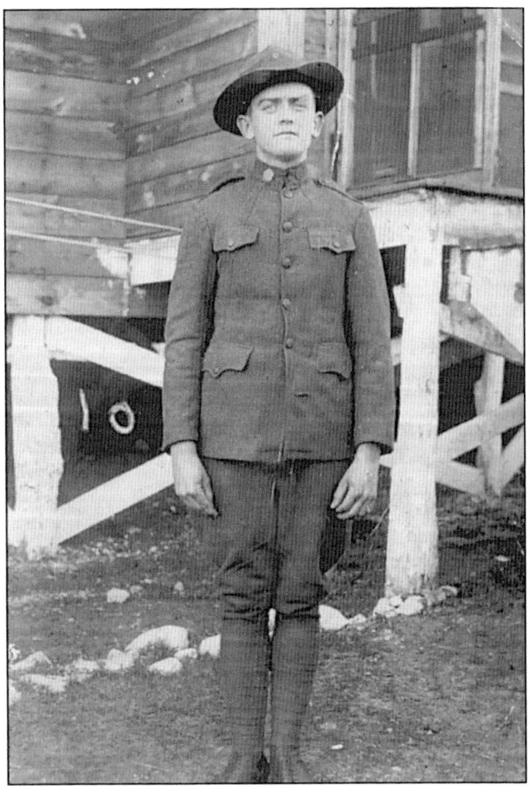

Henry Seals. Seals takes a moment from his duty during World War I to pose for the camera.

Tom Williams. Williams was in active duty during World War I.

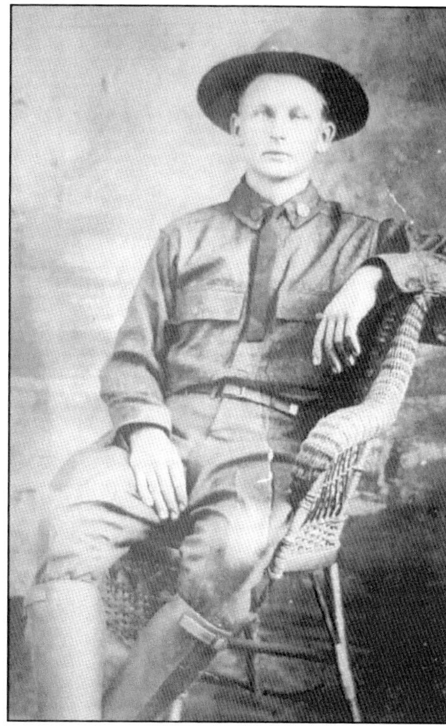

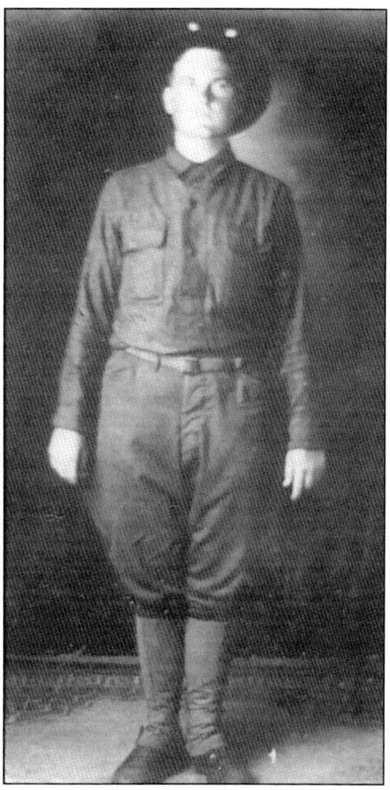

Will Bush. Bush was a private during World War I.

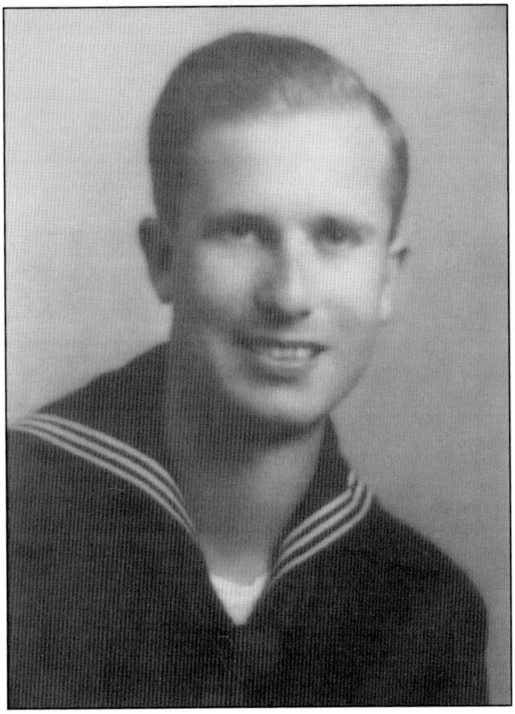

Ralph Lovett. Lovett was in active duty during World War II. He was engaged in three battle clusters in the Pacific Theatre.

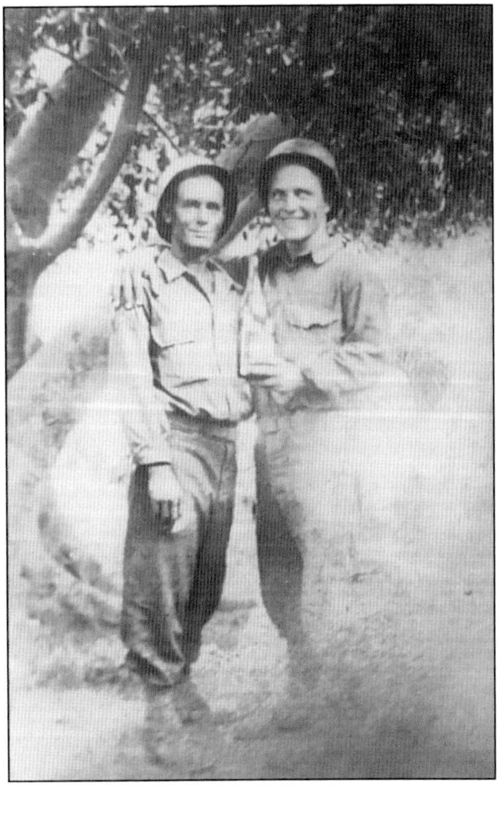

Corporal Elmer Cordry (Left) With Private First Class Steve Tribus. This picture was taken in Sicily in September 1943 during World War II.

PRIVATE PAUL PERKINS DURING WORLD WAR II.

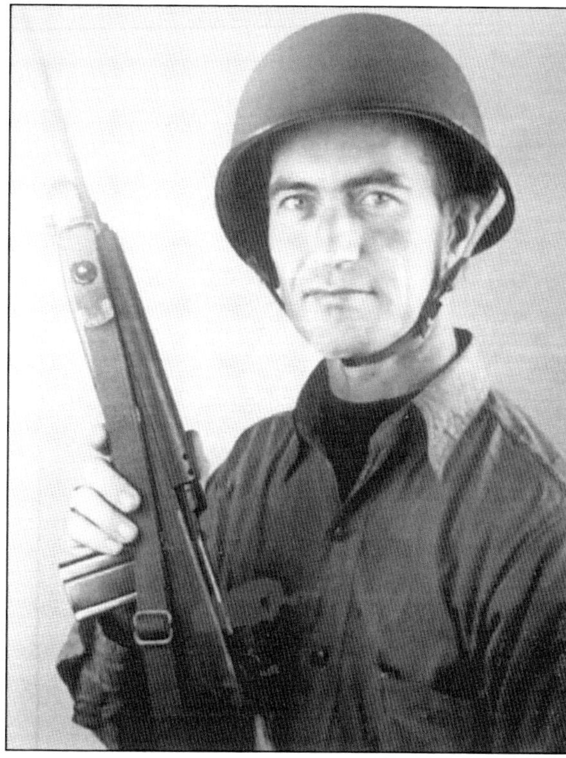

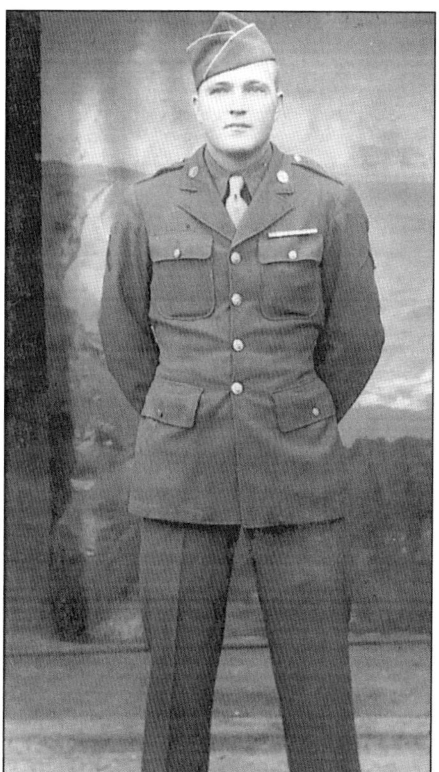

ROBERT EDWARD WEBB. Webb served his country during World War II. He was inducted on February 11, 1942 at Fort McPherson, Georgia, and his military occupational specialty was Rifleman #745. Webb was engaged in the Battle of the Bulge and the Germany Campaign and was wounded in the European Theatre. Awards and medals he received included a Purple Heart, E.A.M.E. Campaign Medal, a Bronze Star, and Expert Rifleman. He was discharged on April 24, 1945.

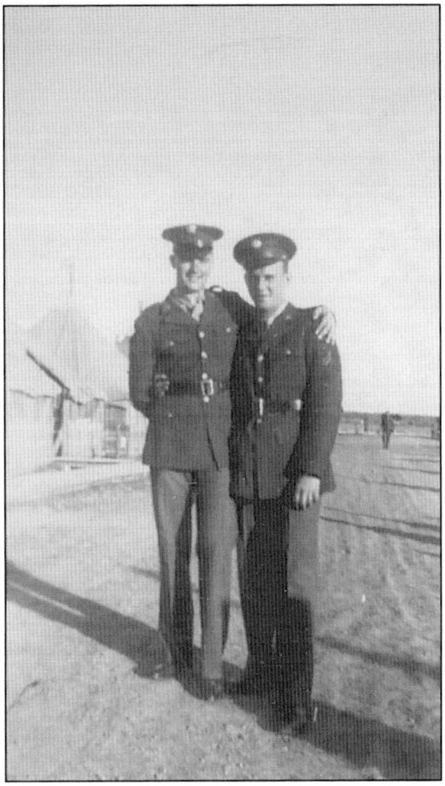

Hubert Brantley (Left) With George Harig From Germany. Brantley served in the Department of Patients during World War II. He was inducted into service on September 19, 1942 and received an honorable discharge on September 29, 1943.

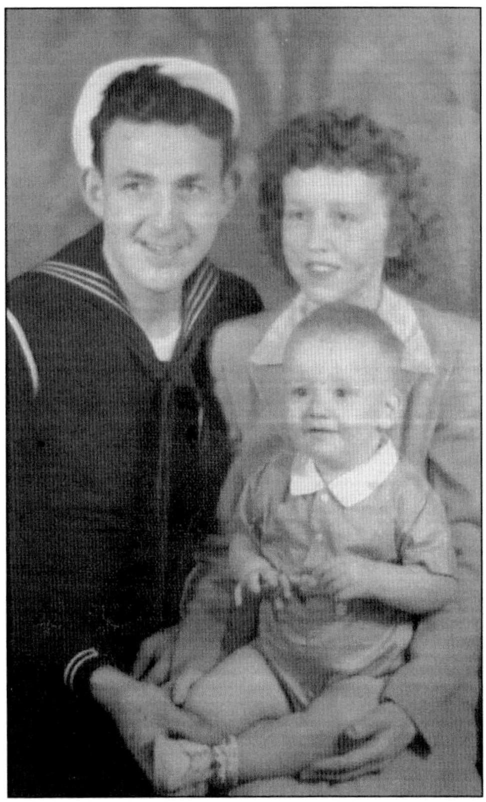

Harris Brantley With His Wife, Mildred, and Son James. Harris served in the Navy during World War II.

LOUIE E. ROWLAND. Rowland was inducted into the U.S. Army on November 14, 1942 and served in the battles of Normandy, Ardennes Rhineland, and Central Europe. Louie received a Purple Heart, a World War II Victory Medal, an E.A.M.E.T. Service Medal, a Meritorious Unit Award, an American Theater Ribbon, a Bronze Star, a Good Conduct Medal, and a Lapel Button.

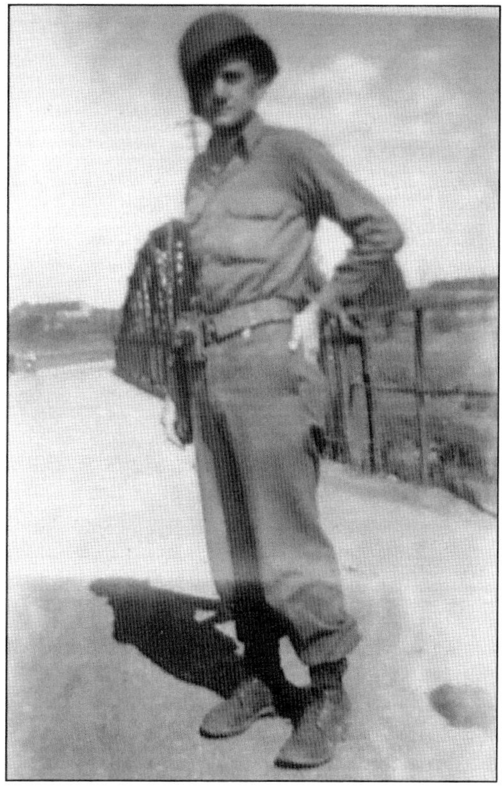

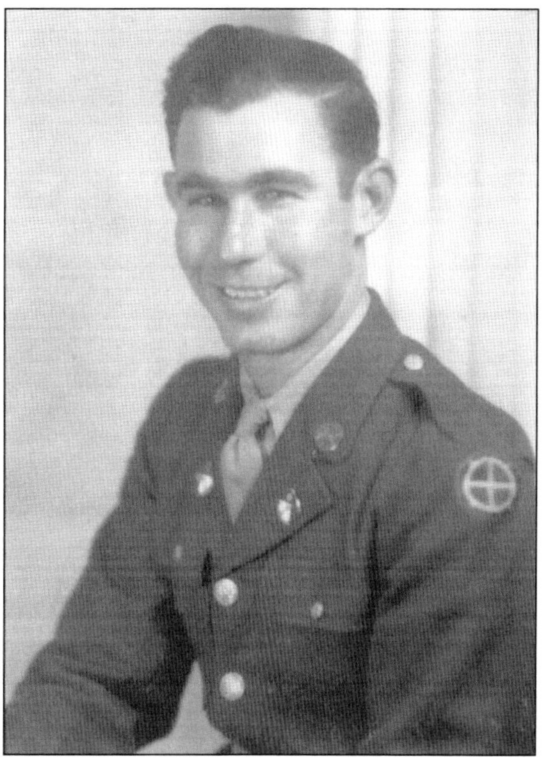

SERGEANT RANDOLPH SHEPARD. Shepard was inducted into the U.S. Army on September 5, 1942 and had a military occupational specialty of Squad Leader. He was in the battles of Normandy, Northern France, and Rhineland, and he received a Combat Infantryman Badge on July 23, 1944. Other medals and awards Shepard received included an E.A.M.E Campaign Medal with three Bronze Stars, a Good Conduct Medal, a Purple Heart with one Oak Leaf Cluster, a Distinguished Unit Badge, and a Lapel Button.

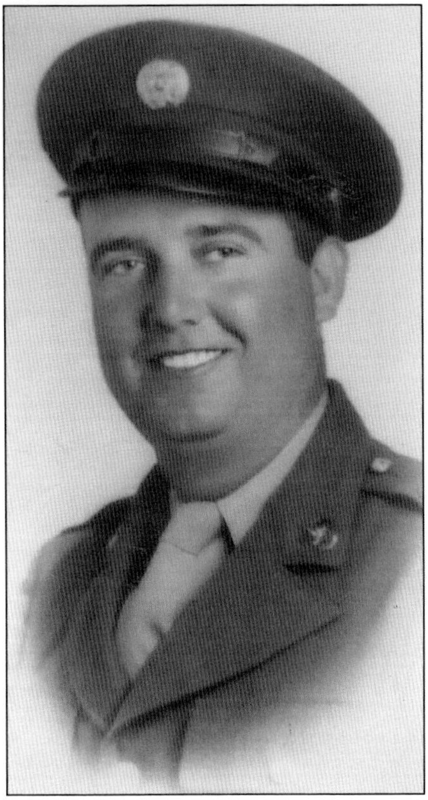

HUBERT OUTLAW. Outlaw was in active duty during World War II.

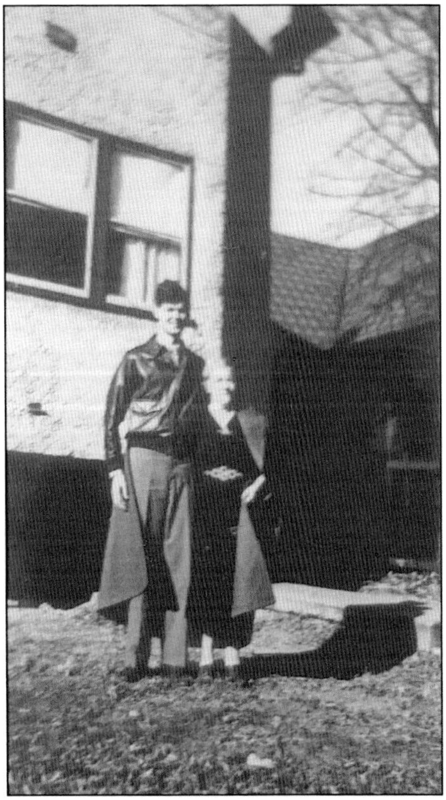

LAUDICE BRANTLEY WITH HIS LANDLADY MRS. ALLARDICE. Laudice served his country during World War II in the United States Air Force.

PRIVATE WILMER C. WILKERSON DURING WORLD WAR II.

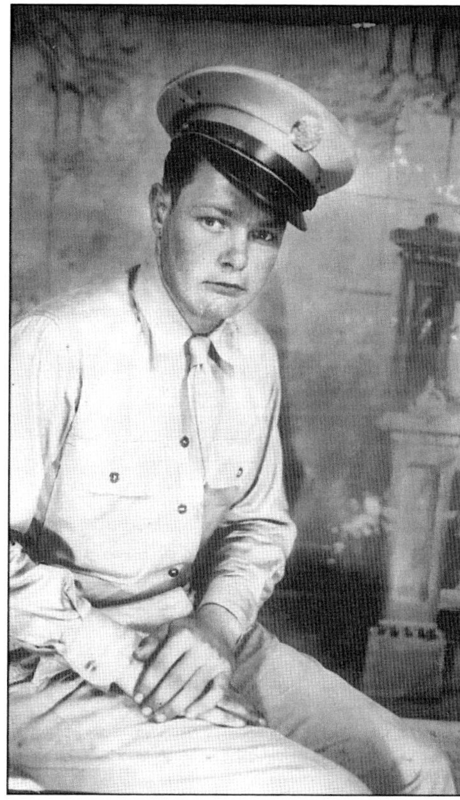

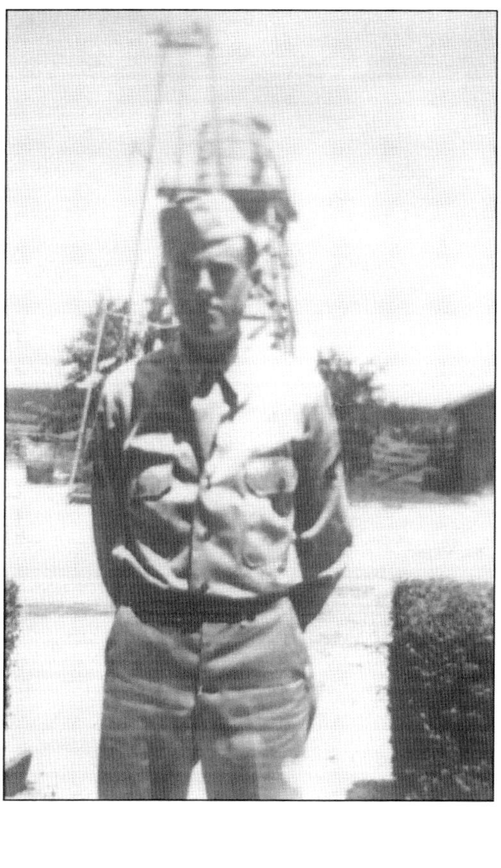

J.Q. IVEY DURING WORLD WAR II, 1943.

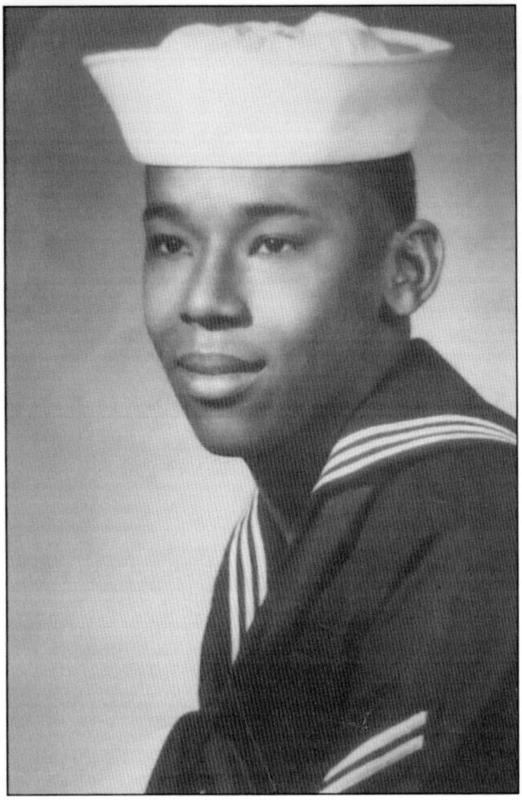

WILLIE C. CORDY. He proudly served his country during World War II.

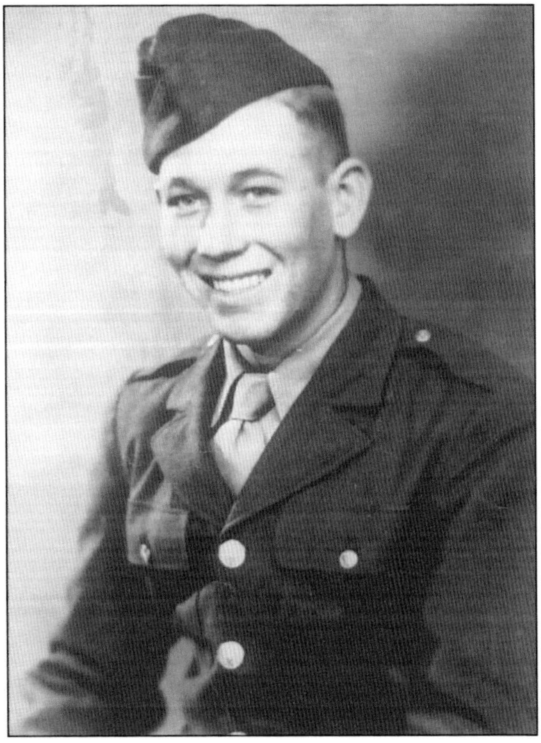

HUBERT JOSEY. The son of Milo Josey and Missouri Powell Josey, Hubert served during World War II.

Henry Lee Josey and His Wife, Pauline Claxton Josey. Henry Lee served in the U.S. Navy Seabees during World War II.

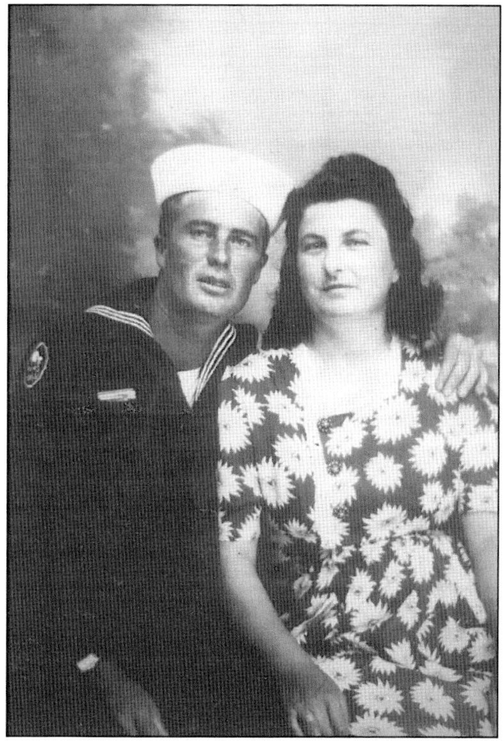

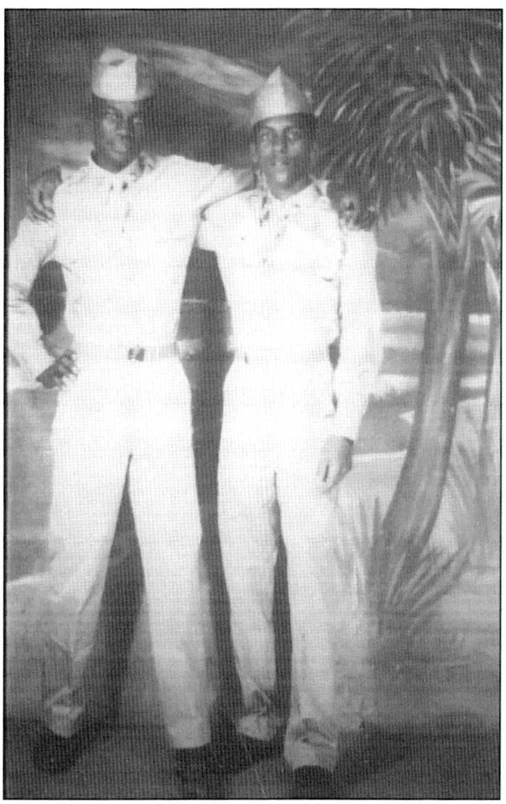

Douglas Wesley (Left) and Friend Willie H. Wright. Both young men were very proud to be serving their country during World War II.

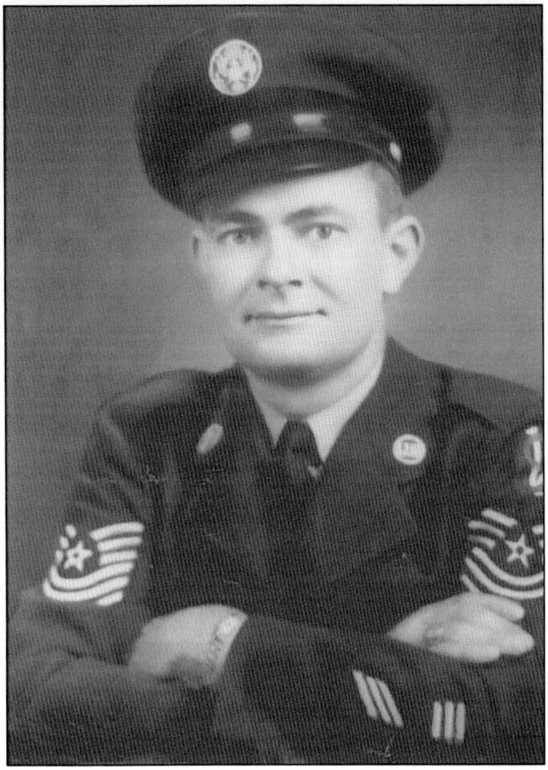

Fred Kight of Kite, Georgia. Kight is pictured here in his dress blues during World War II.

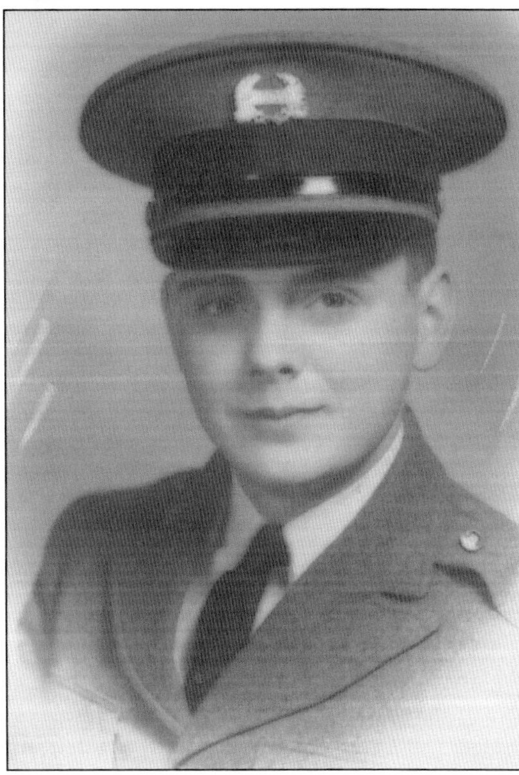

Marion Brantley in his World War II Uniform.

Three

Couples

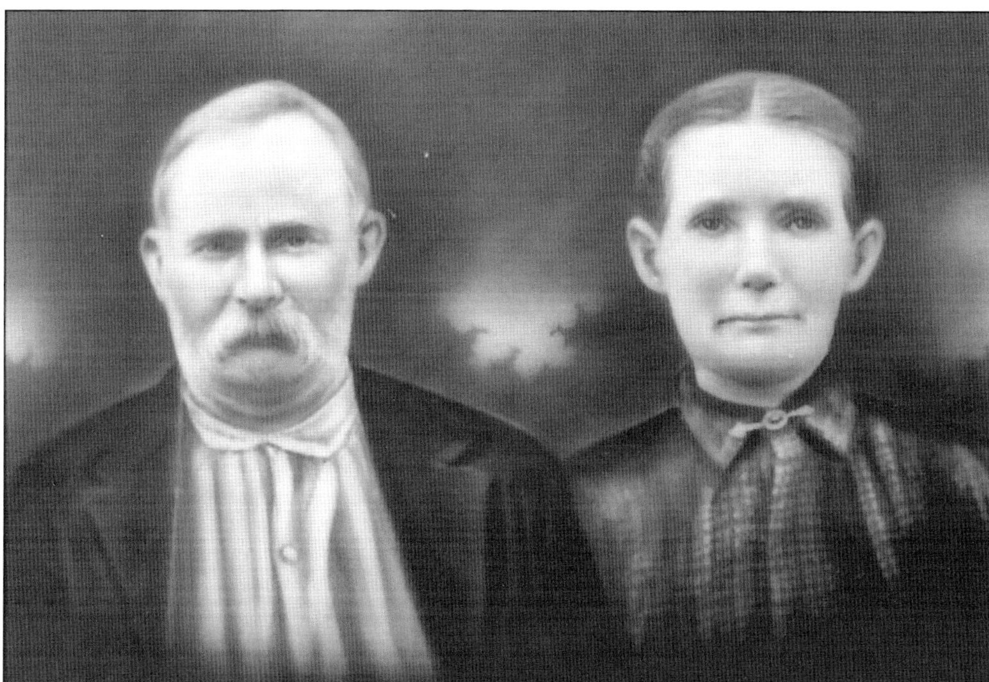

William Amos Heath and Louisanian "Lula" Lord.

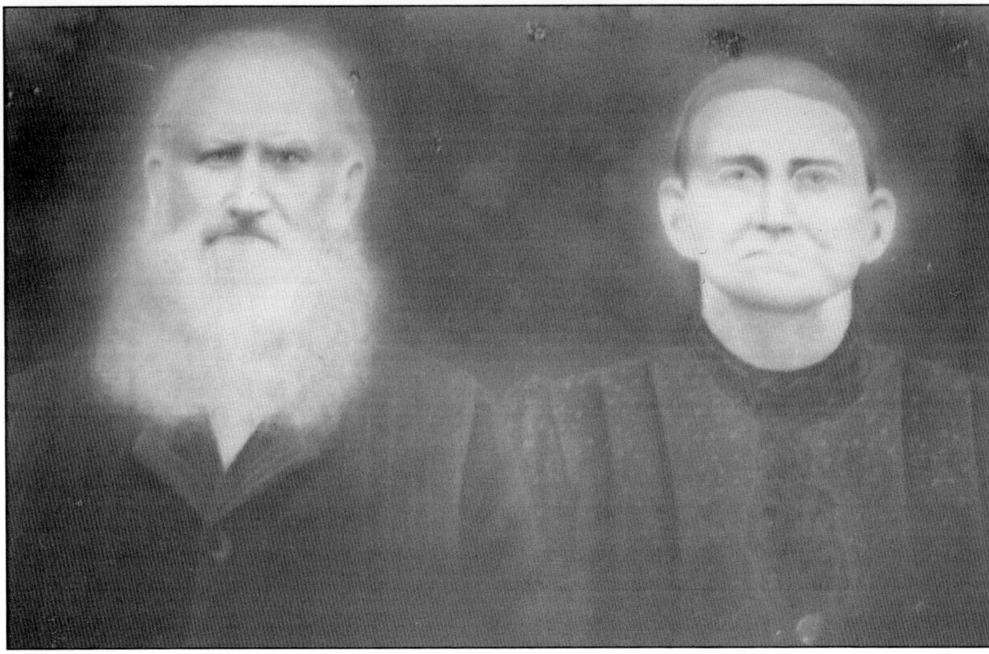

David Z. Lindsey and Eliza S. Tanner Lindsey.

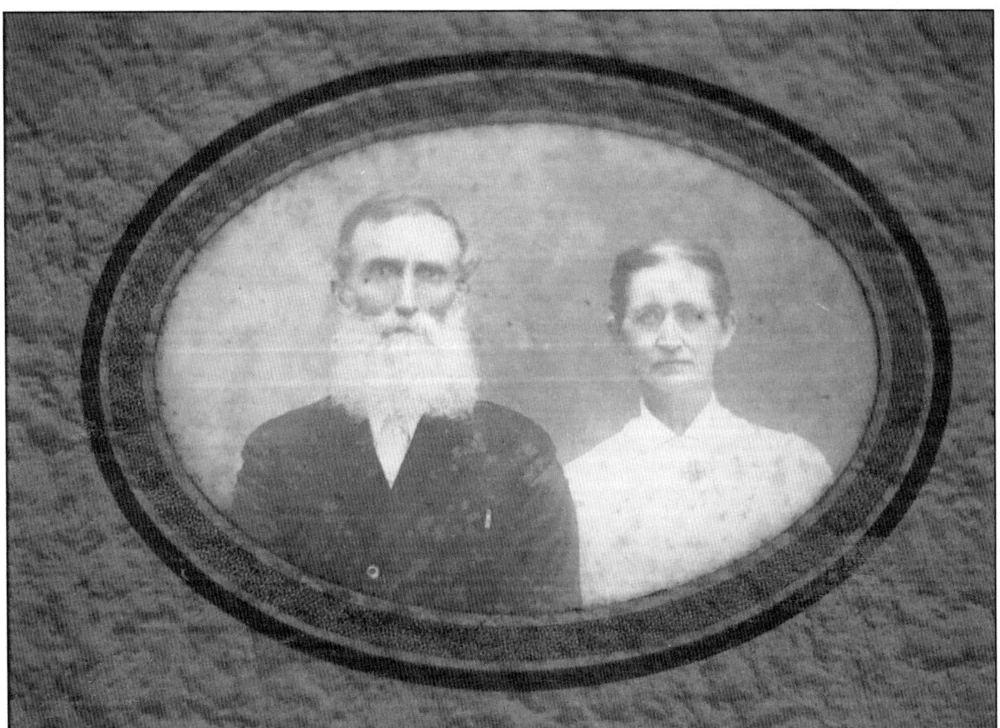

Alexander "Alex" Steven Mayo and Meddie Lindsey Mayo.

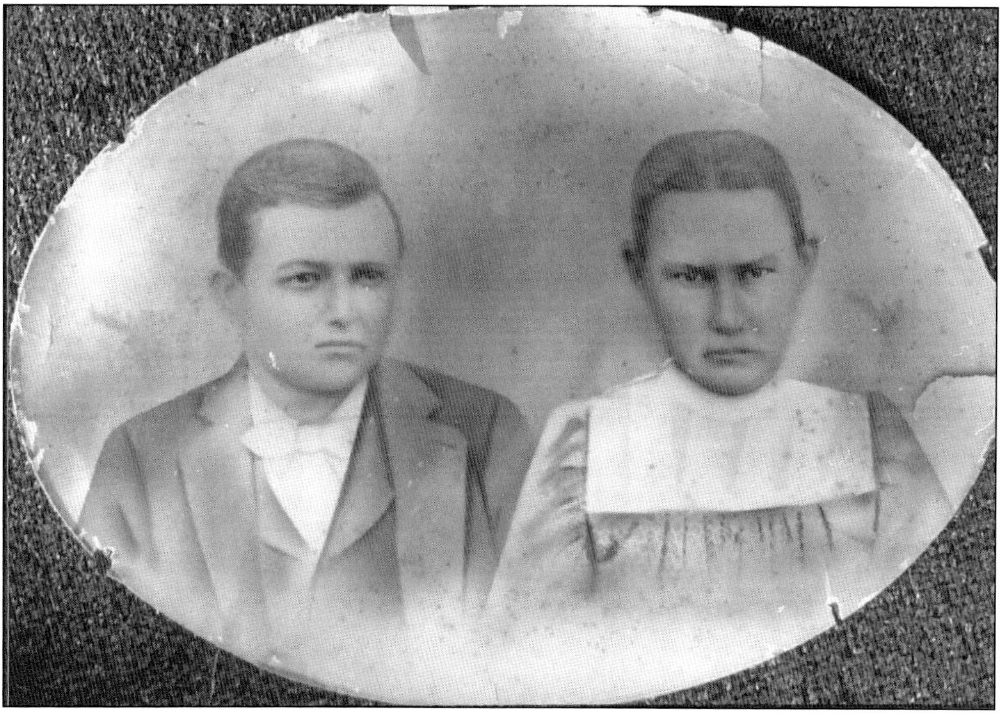

Corneleus "Pat" Johnson and Viola Holton Johnson.

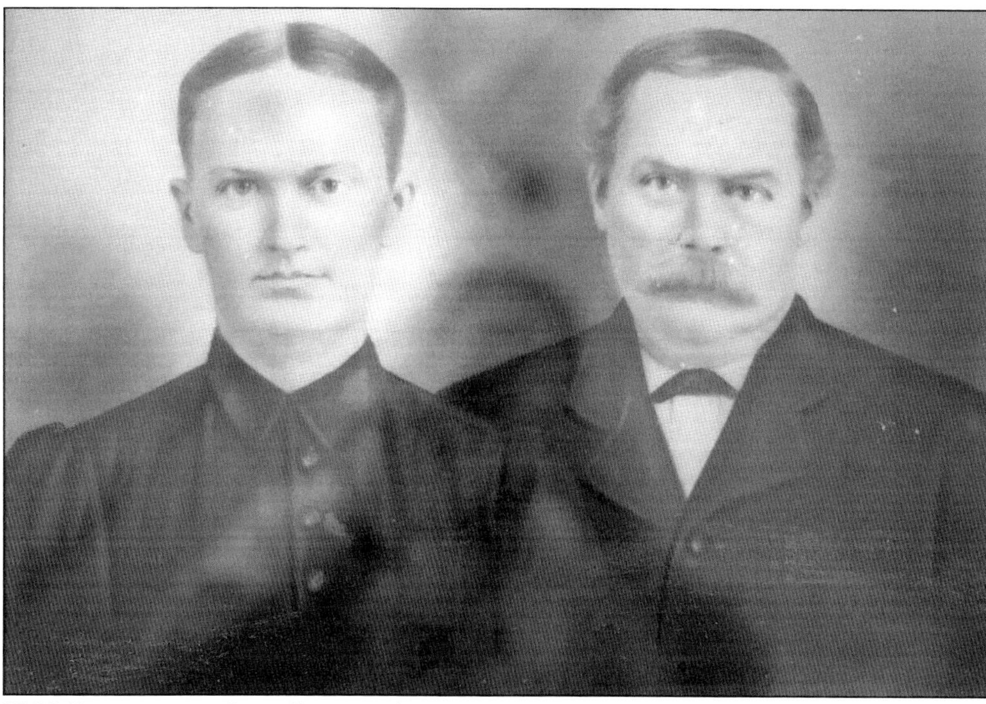

W.H. Blizzard and Lula Frances Coleman Blizzard.

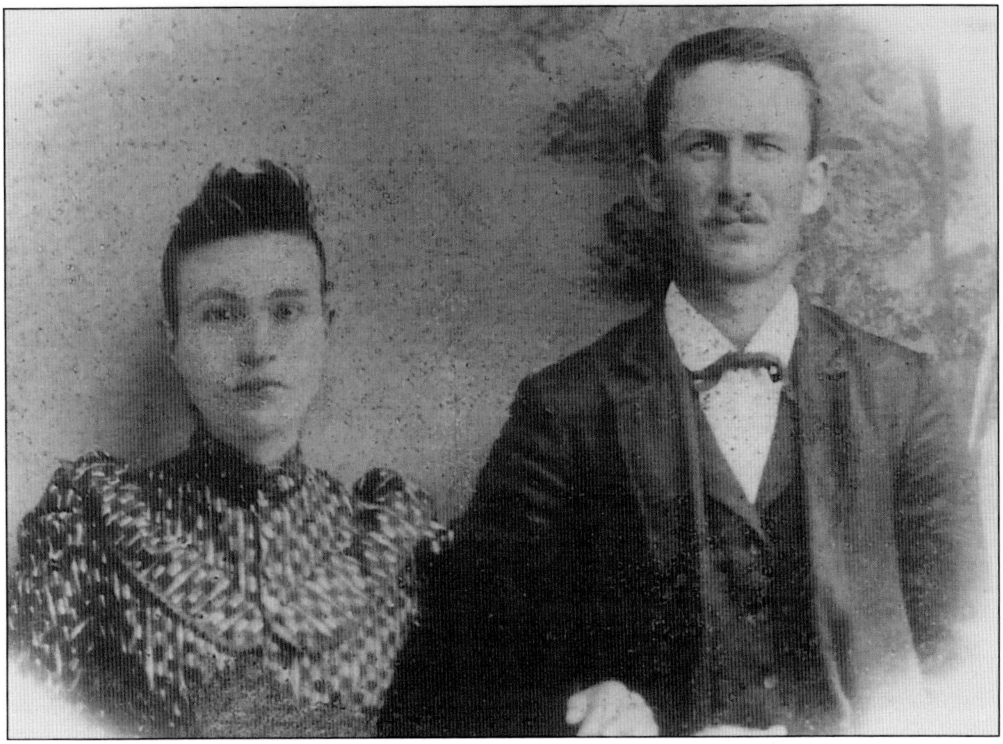

Julious Daniel Underwood and Jencie Ellen Underwood.

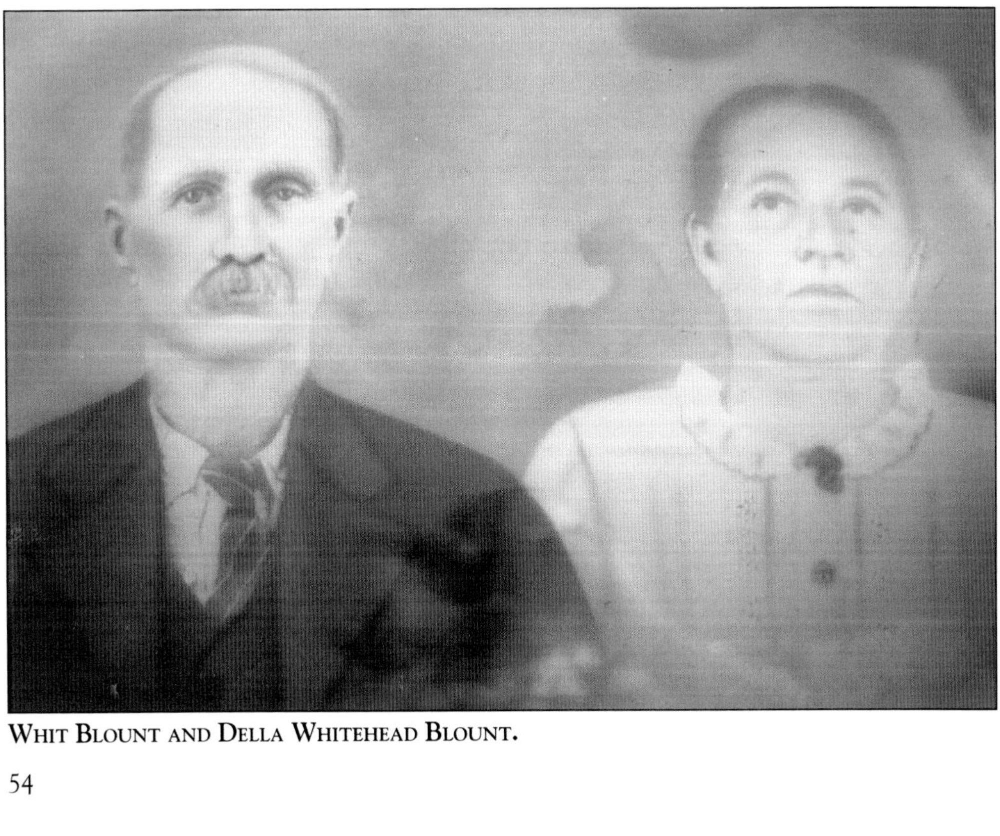

Whit Blount and Della Whitehead Blount.

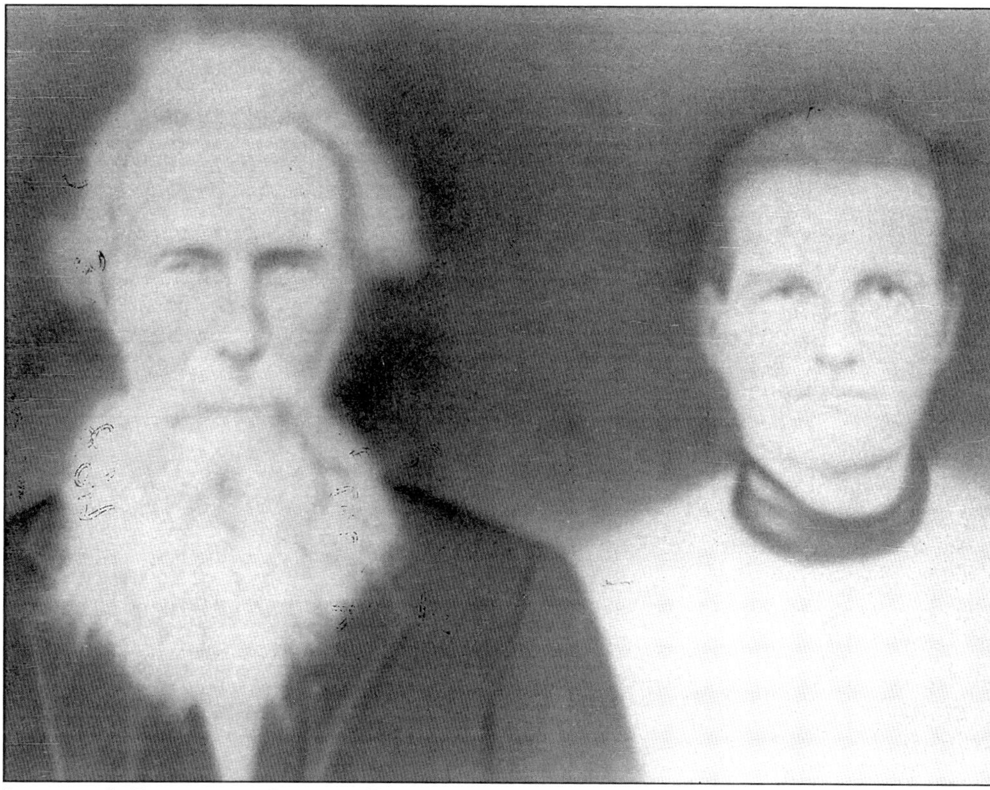

Leaston S. Powell and Latisha Powell.

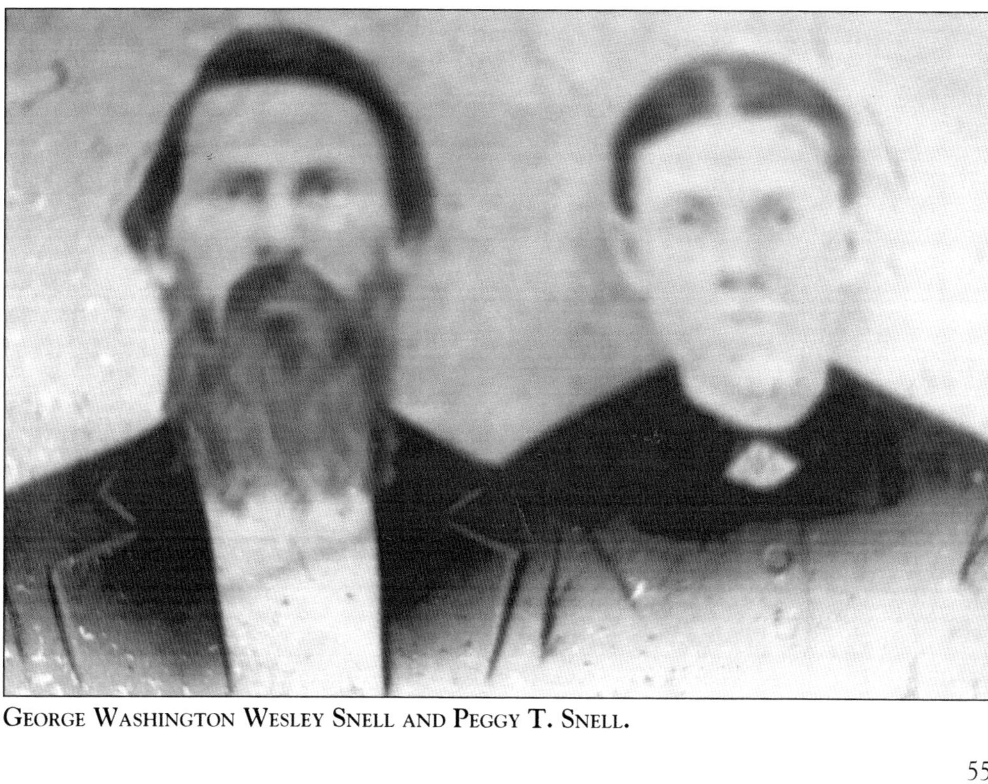

George Washington Wesley Snell and Peggy T. Snell.

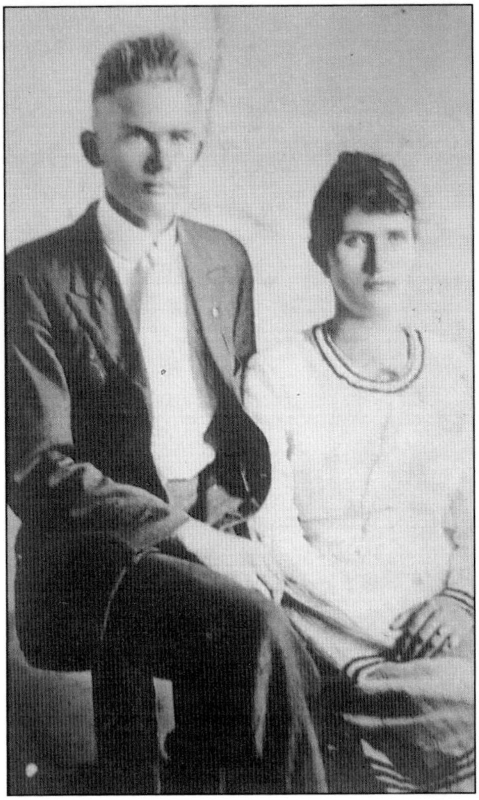

Willie Flarea Mayo and Harrell Mayo.

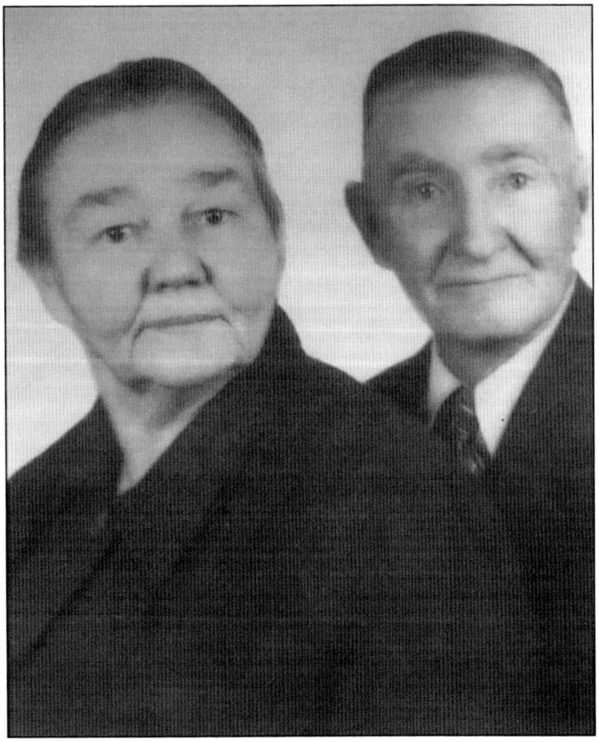

Eli Smith and
Sarah Ann Hammock Smith.

JACK STAPLETON AND NONA AKRIDGE STAPLETON.

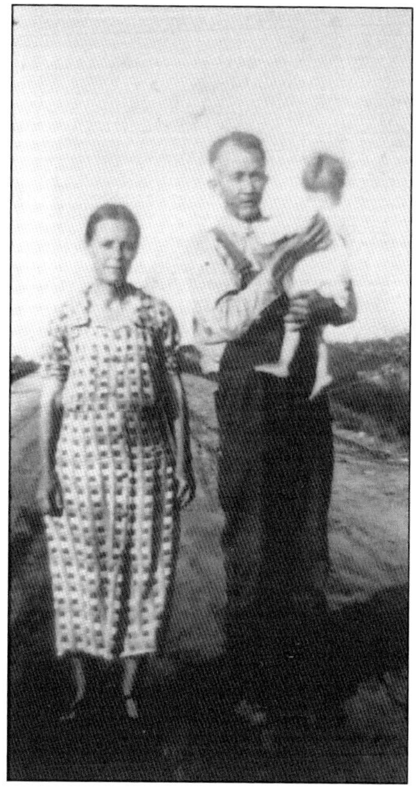

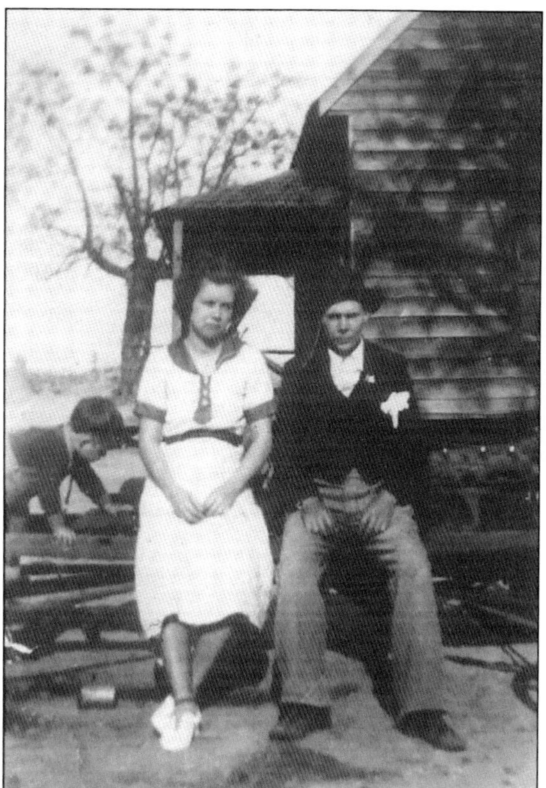

JIM TIMOTHY STAPLETON AND ETHEL PERNELL STAPLETON.

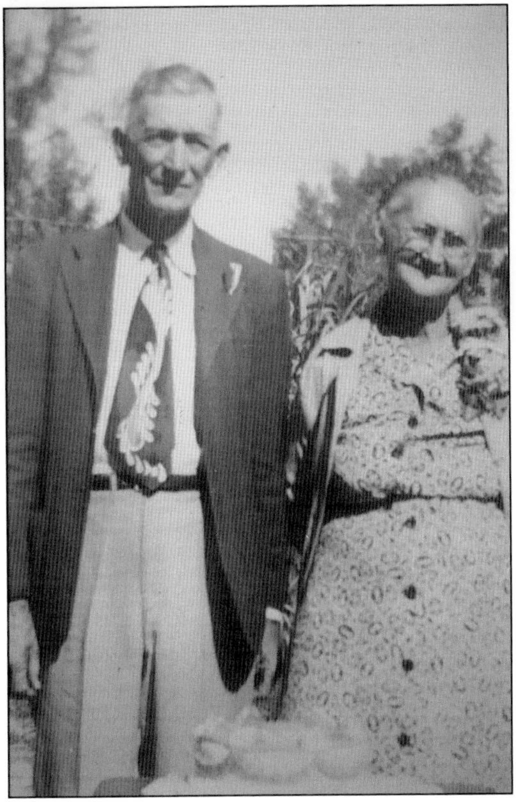

CORSBY FOREST BLOUNT AND SUSIE WARE BLOUNT.

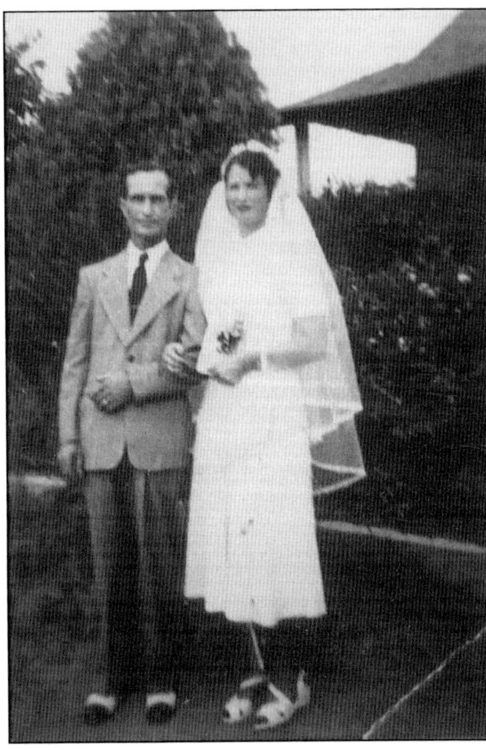

PAUL PERKINS AND VELMA WEBB PERKINS.

TOM AND MAUDE WILLIAMS.

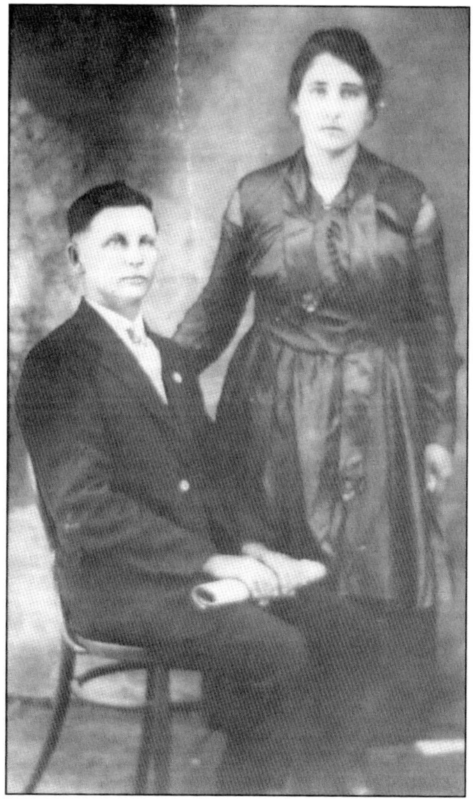

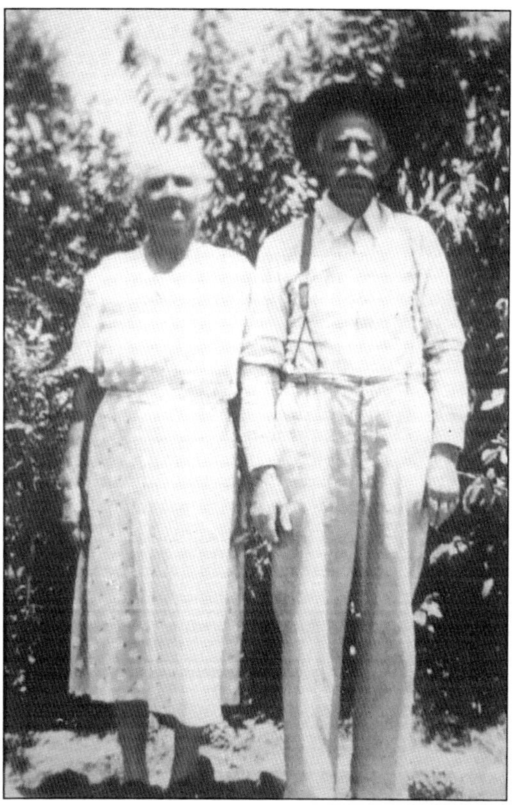

LONNIE KEEN PRICE AND JOHNNY PRICE.

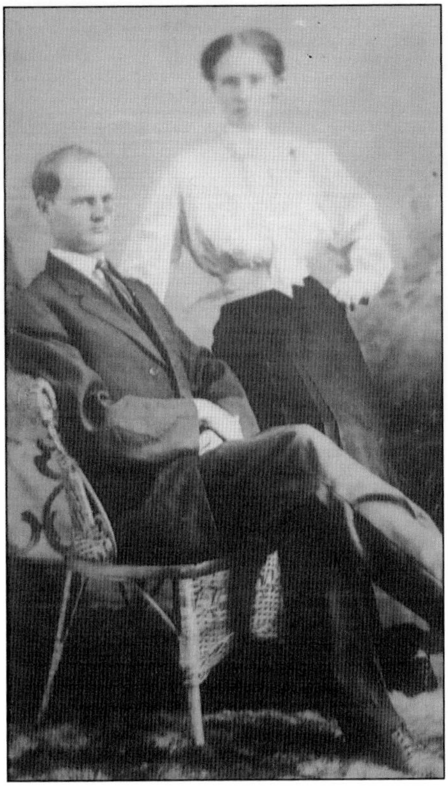

MACK BLIZZARD AND SALLY THARPE BLIZZARD.

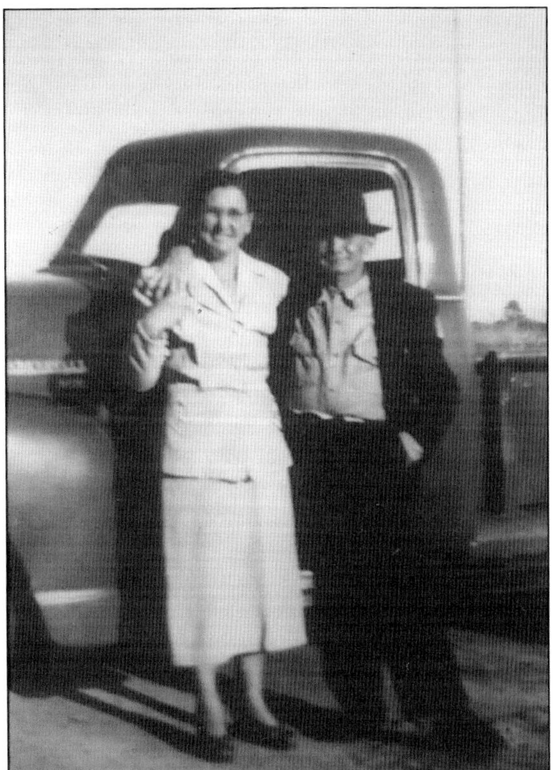

MELINDA AND ARLIE LINDSEY.

EHEN AND ALICE DIXON.

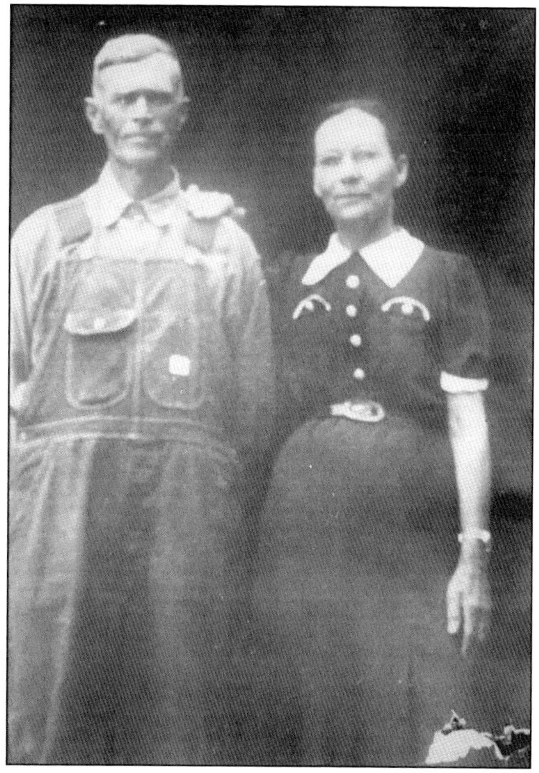

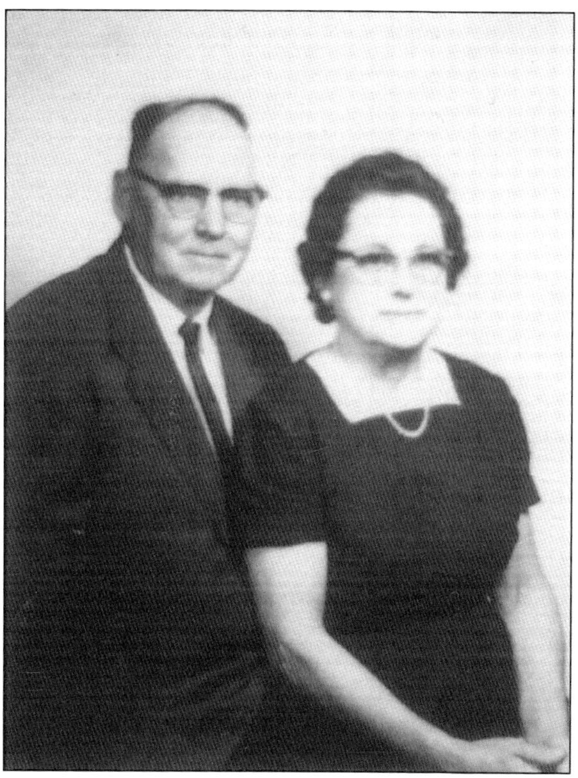

ROBERT POWELL AND
NELLIE SAMMONS POWELL.

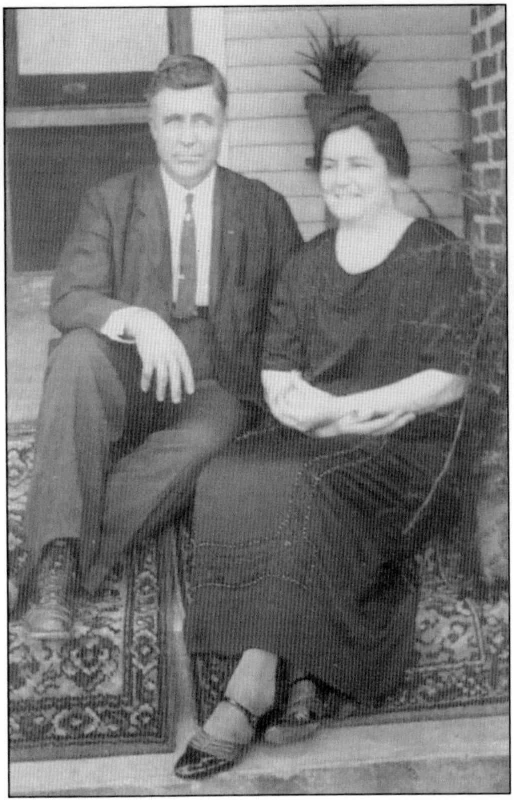

Joseph Benjamin Williams and Nancy Drake Williams.

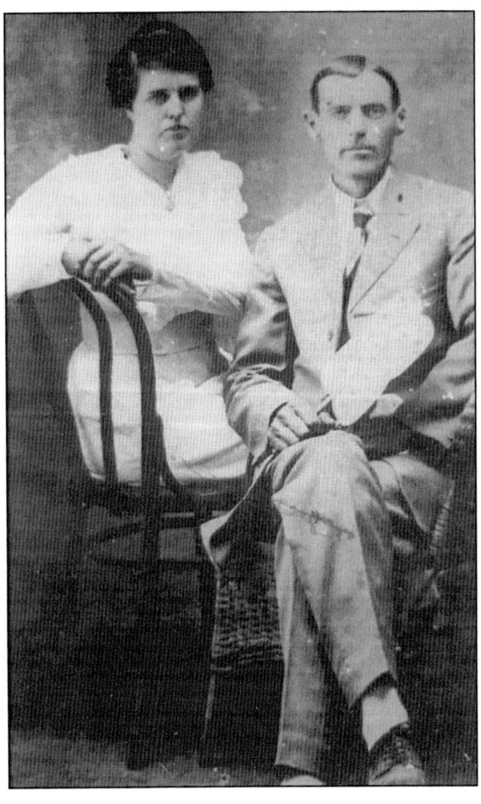

John Q. Ivey and Ethel Reese Ivey.

Mary Ann Elizabeth Hightower and John Ashley McAfee.

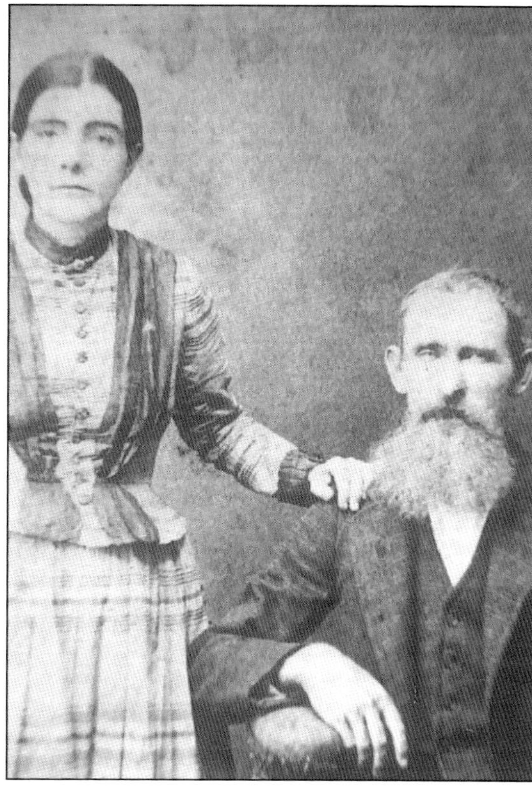

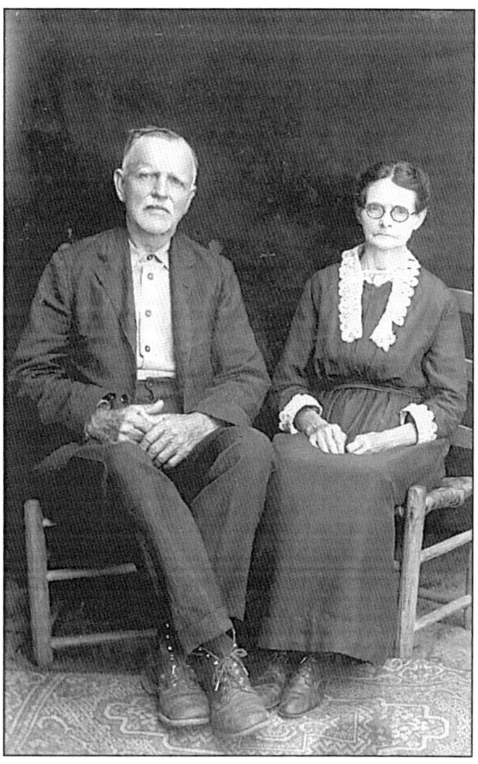

Joseph Brantley and Virginia Brantley.

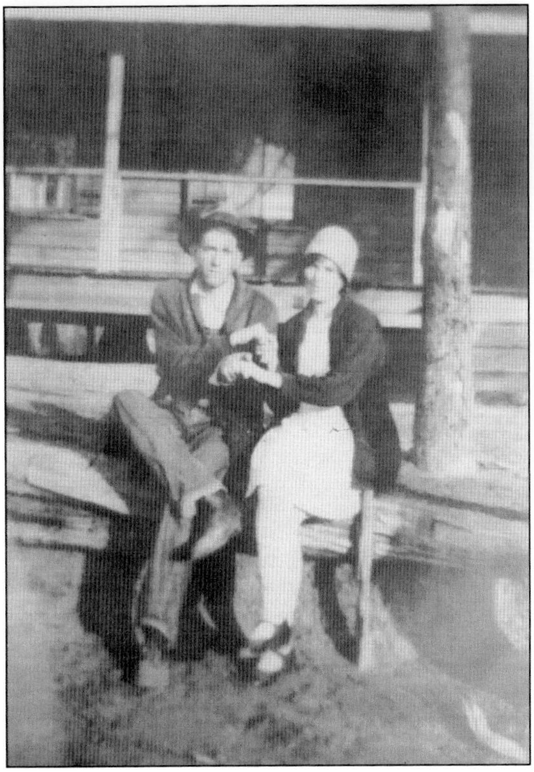

Ernest Lee Holt Sr. and Stella Mae Price Holt.

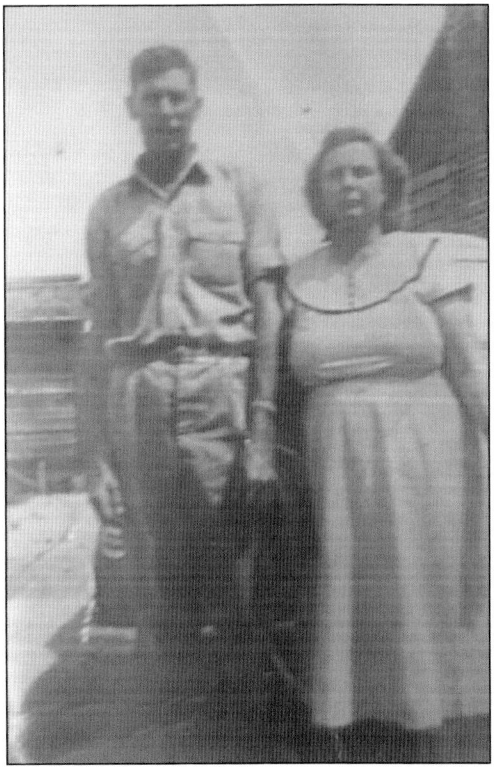

Roy Hall Sr. and Ruth Price Hall.

ELIJAH "B" JOHNSON AND FLORIA FORD JOHNSON.

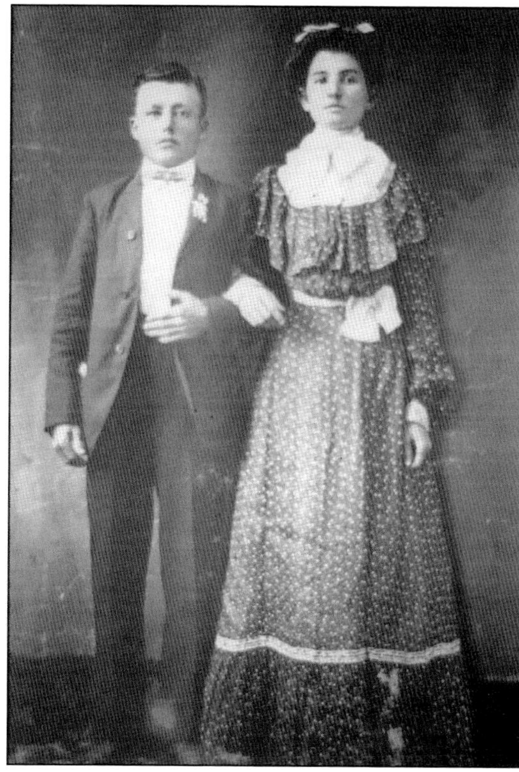

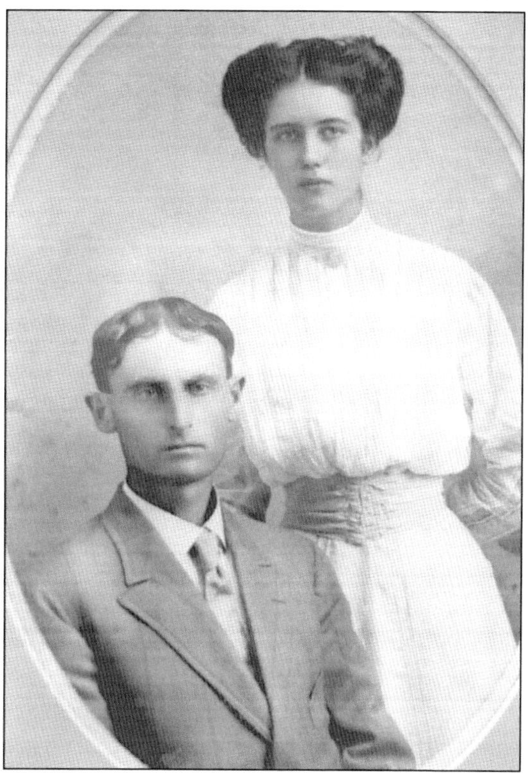

WILLIAM HARVEY BLIZZARD AND EVELLE MAYO BLIZZARD.

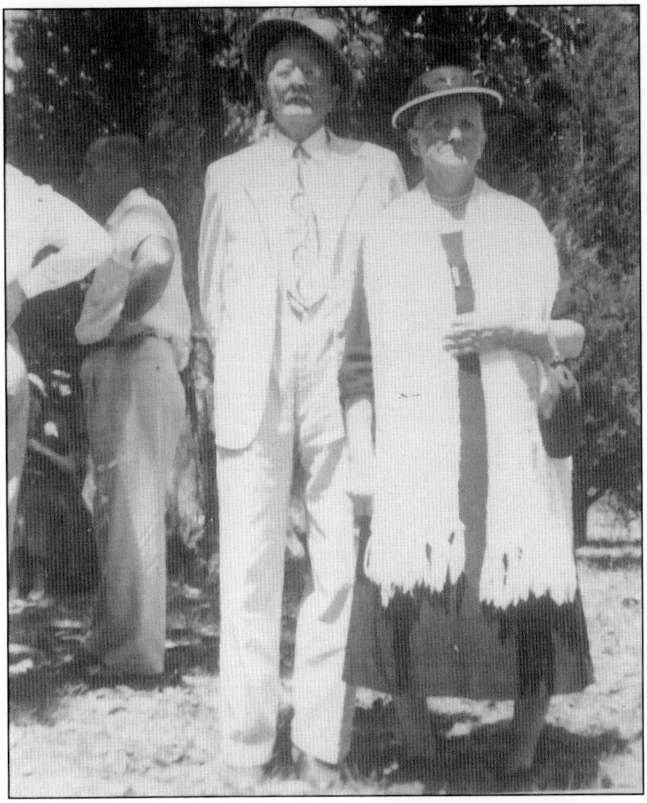

ROBERT "BOB" WEBB AND MINTA RAINES WEBB.

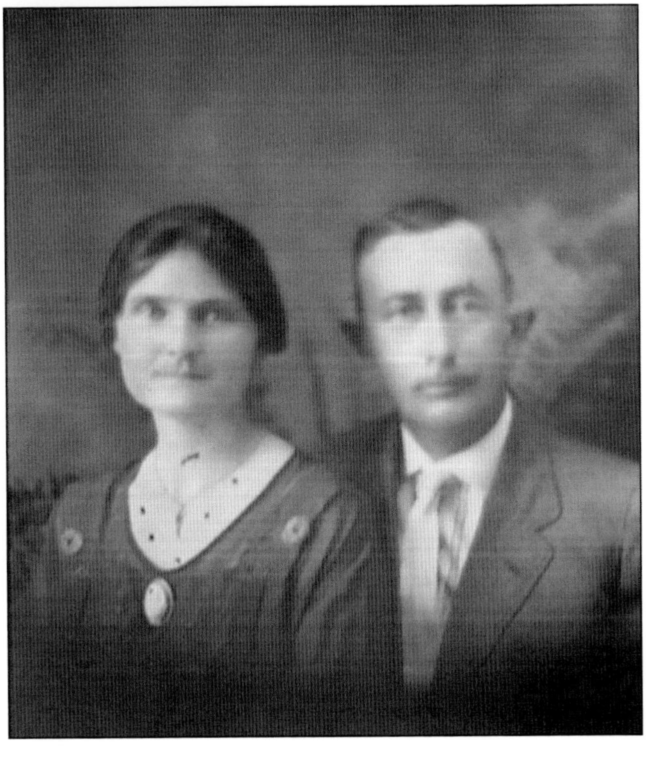

HENRY AND CLYDE CLAXTON.

ALONZO L. BRANTLEY AND MATTIE DEE PERNELL BRANTLEY.

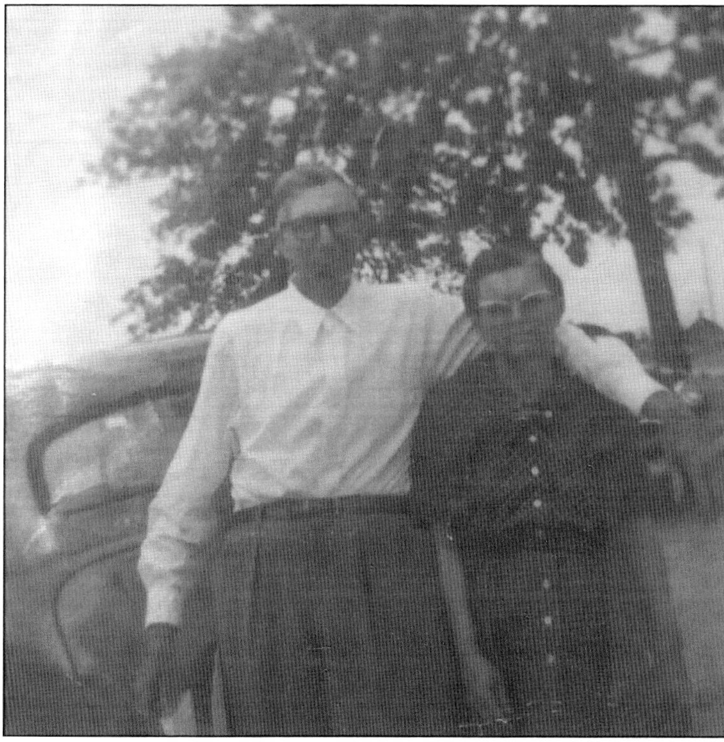

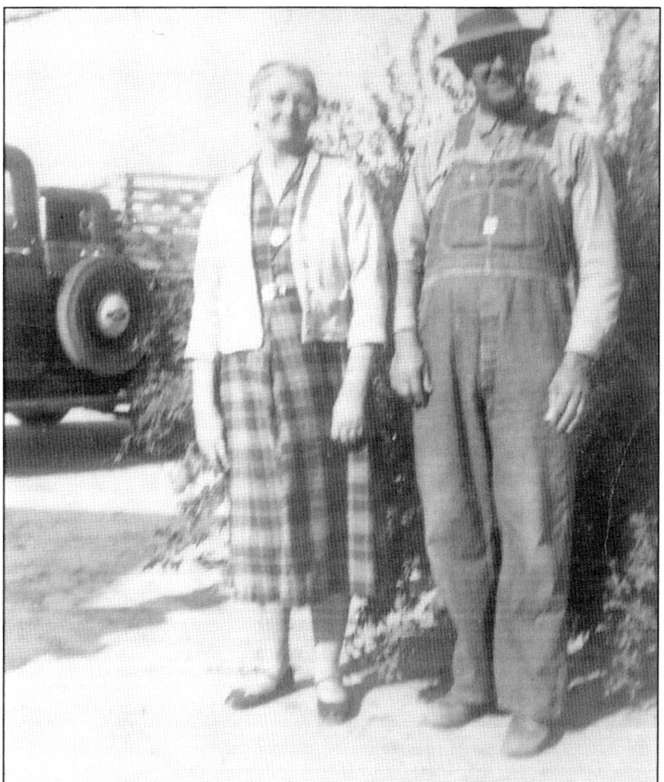

CLEO BRANTLEY AND VERA MAE WEBB BRANTLEY.

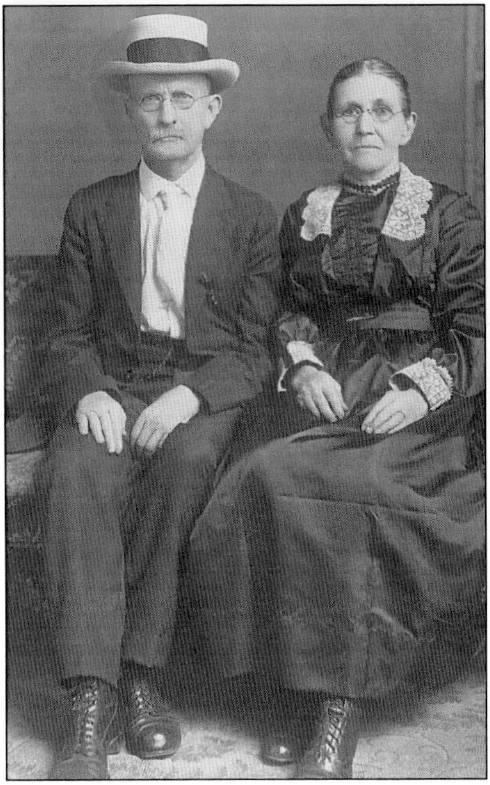

WILLIAM DAVID JORDAN SUMNER AND ELIZABETH BINA THOMPSON SUMNER.

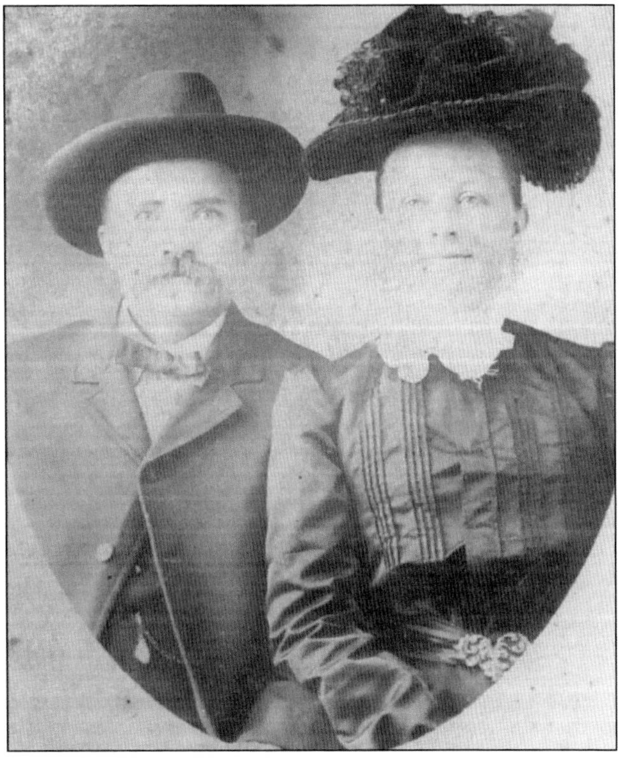

MR. AND MRS. J.R. GRICE.

O.O. SNELL AND ELLEN LAMB SNELL.

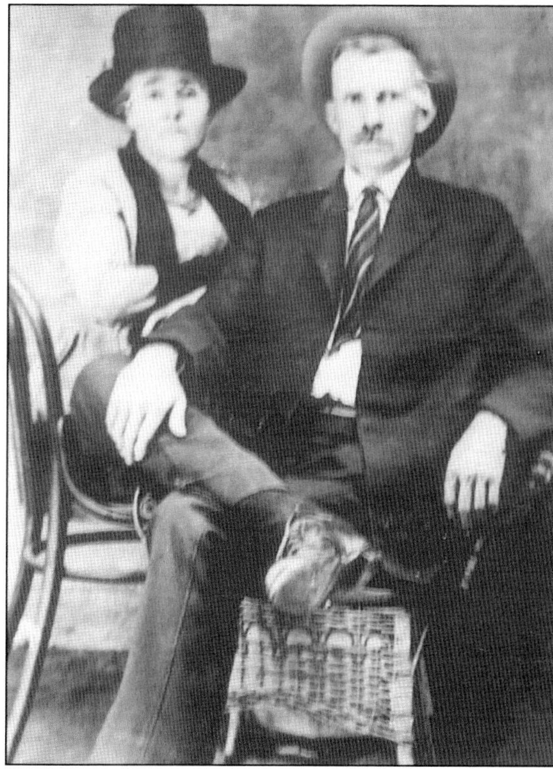

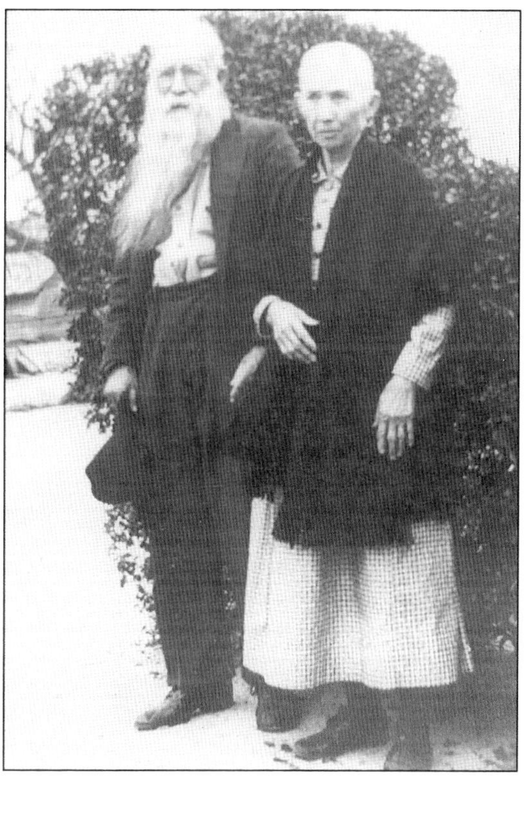

GID RAINES AND EMMA MIXON RAINES.

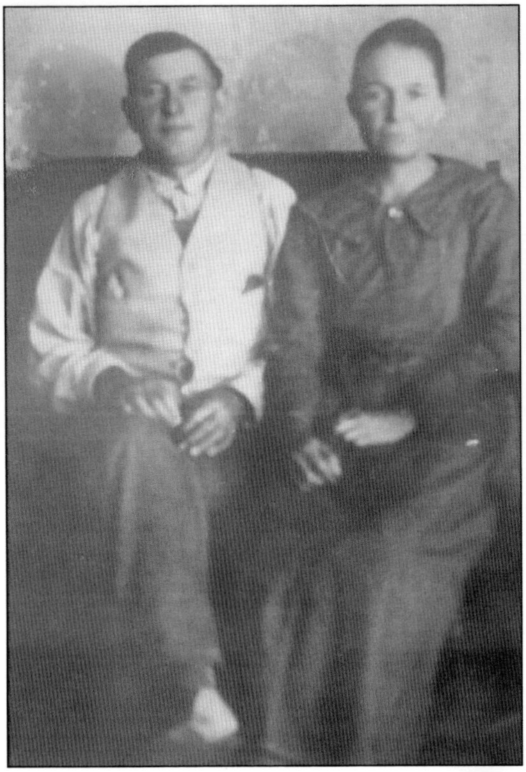

Morgan and Dessie Stapleton.

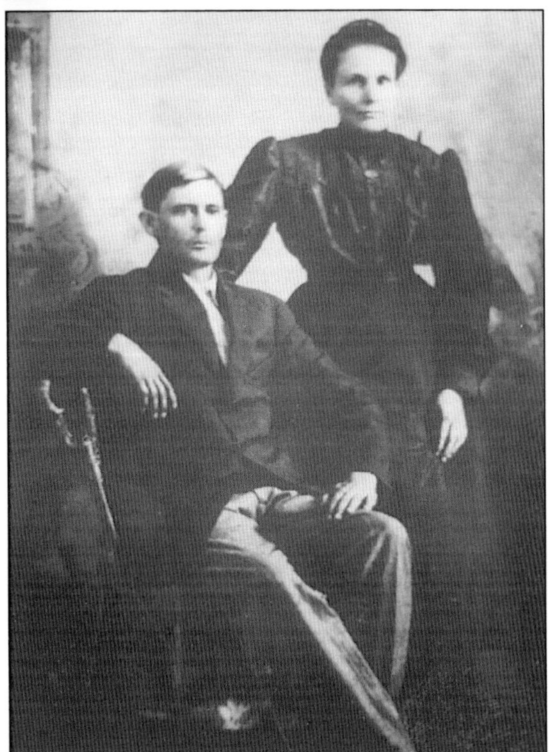

George Wesley Price and
Emma Elizabeth Williams Price.

BESSIE MAE MAYO LINDSEY AND J. THOMAS LINDSEY.

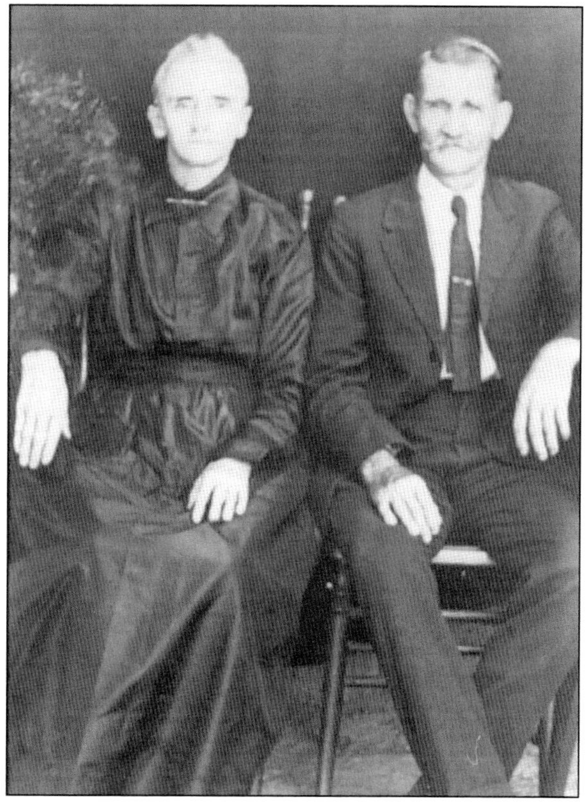

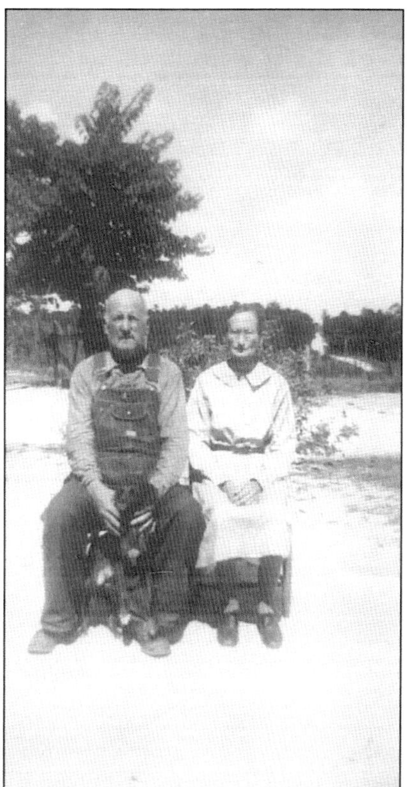

JOHN CLAXTON AND RILLA KIGHT CLAXTON.

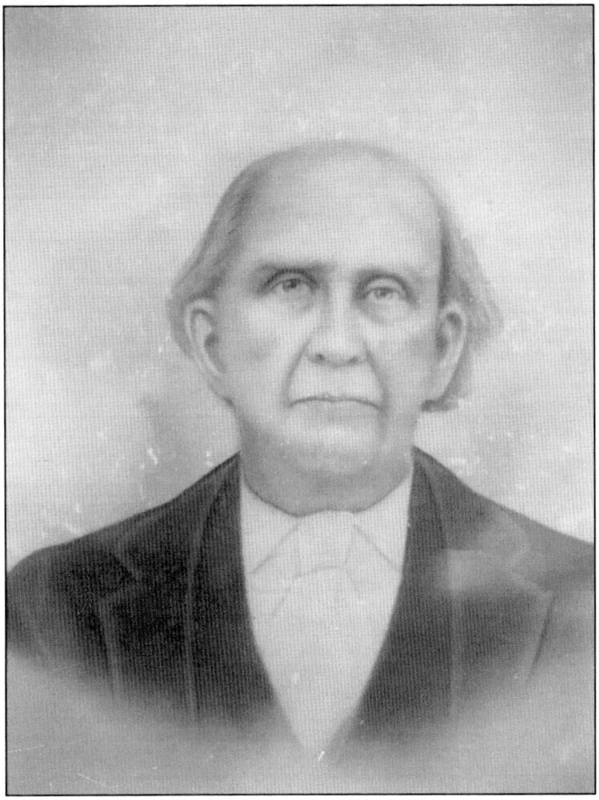

LOTT WALKER.

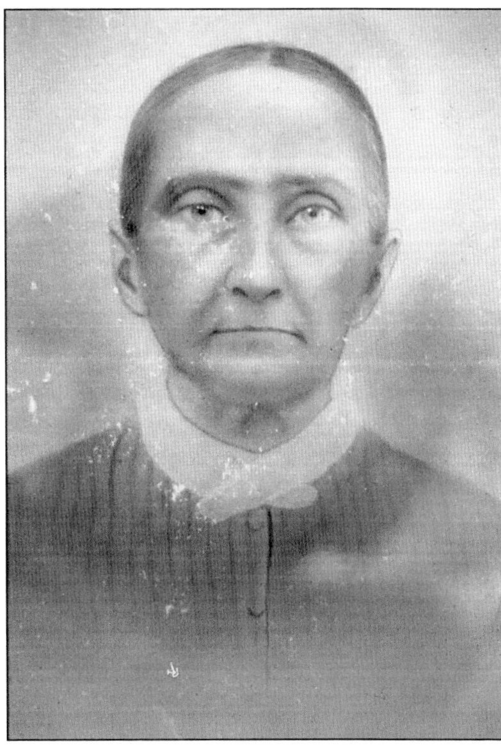

MARY WALKER.

THOMAS CARTER JR.

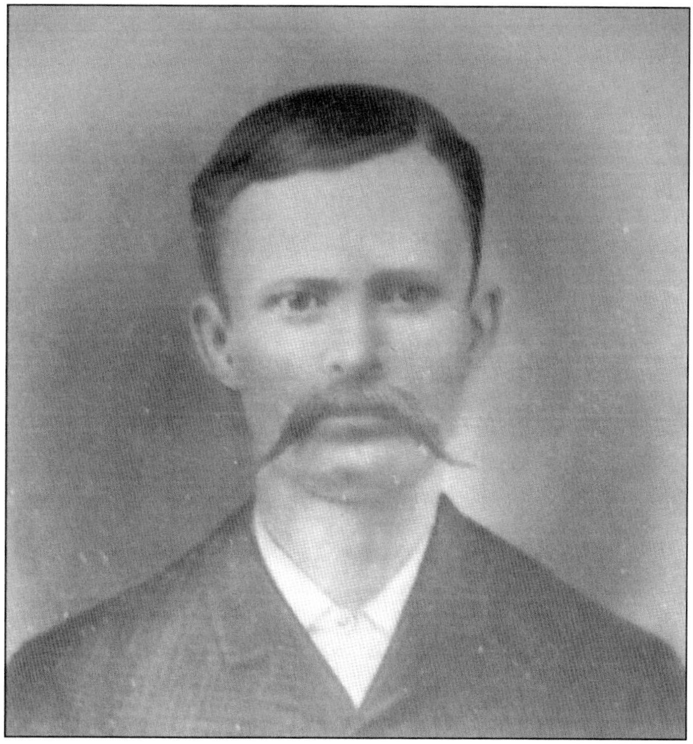

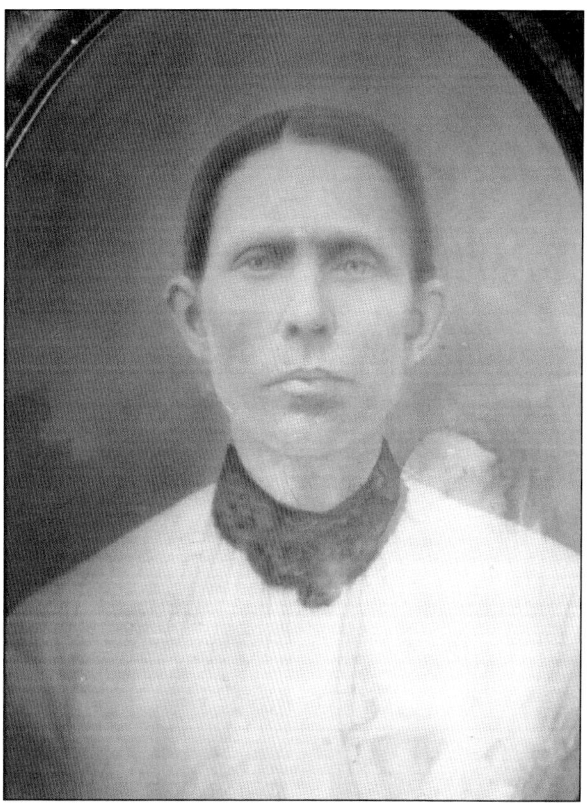

ISABELLA HALL CARTER.

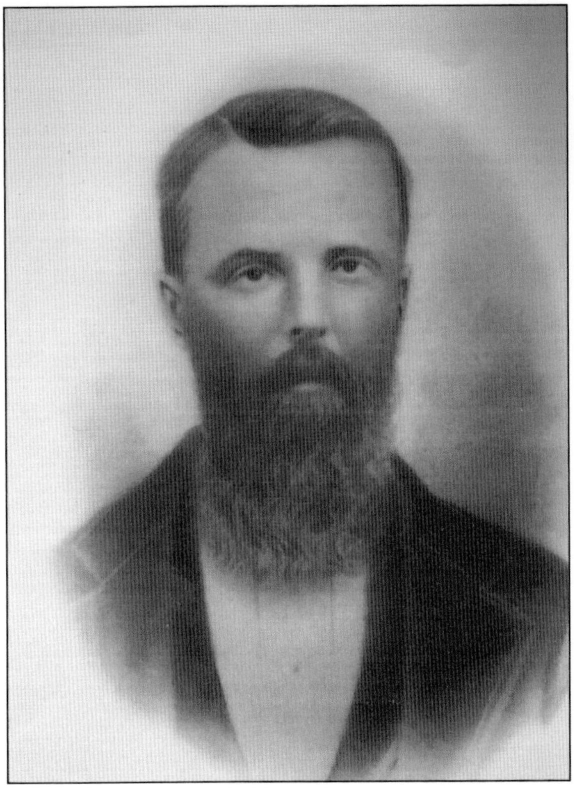

Samuel K. Smith.

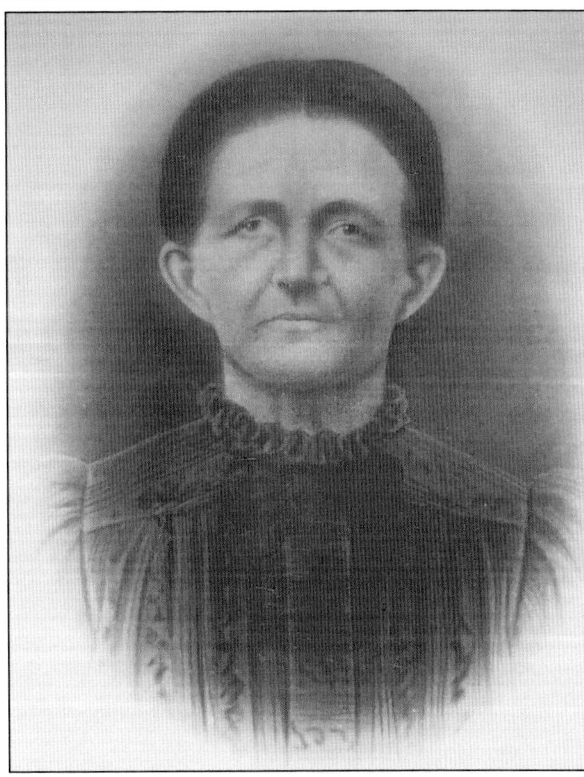

Mahala Brantley Smith.

Doctor Franklin Kemp.

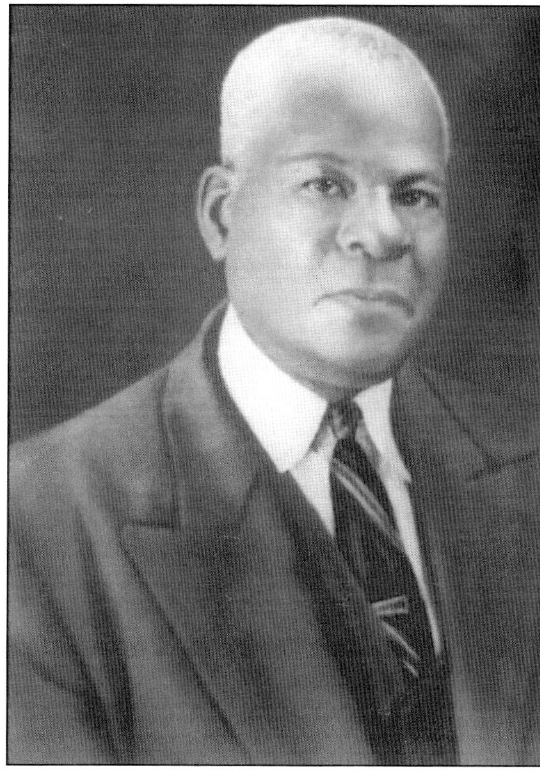

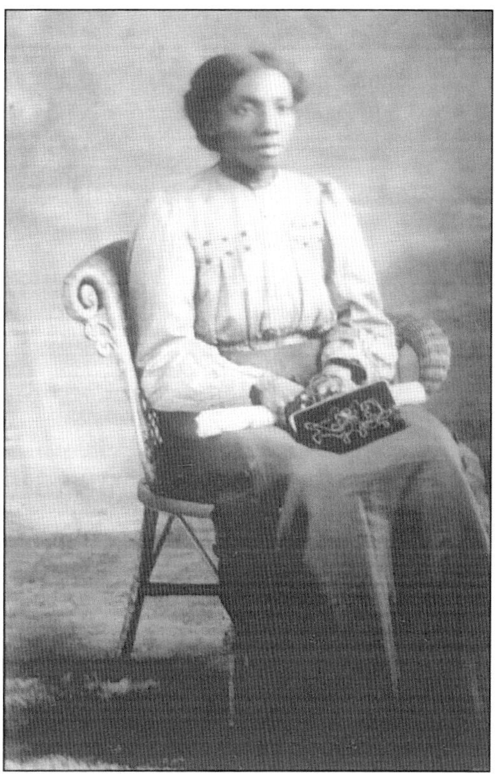

Elizabeth Moorman Kemp.

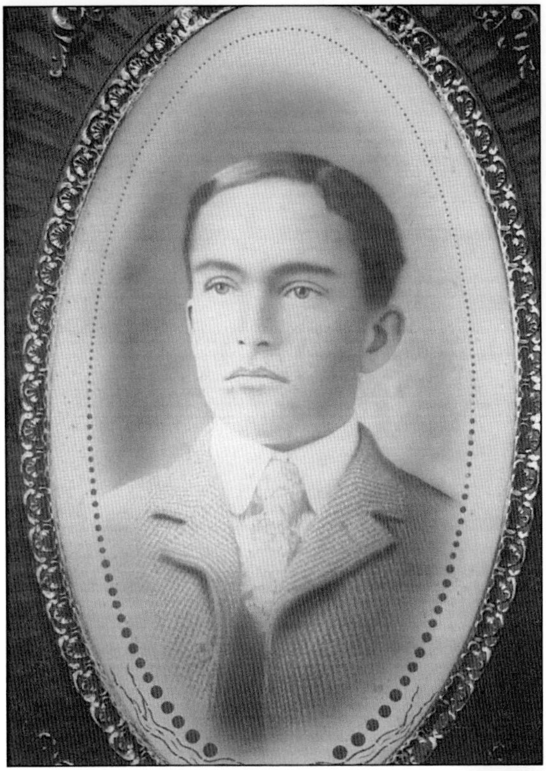

NORMAN GRICE.

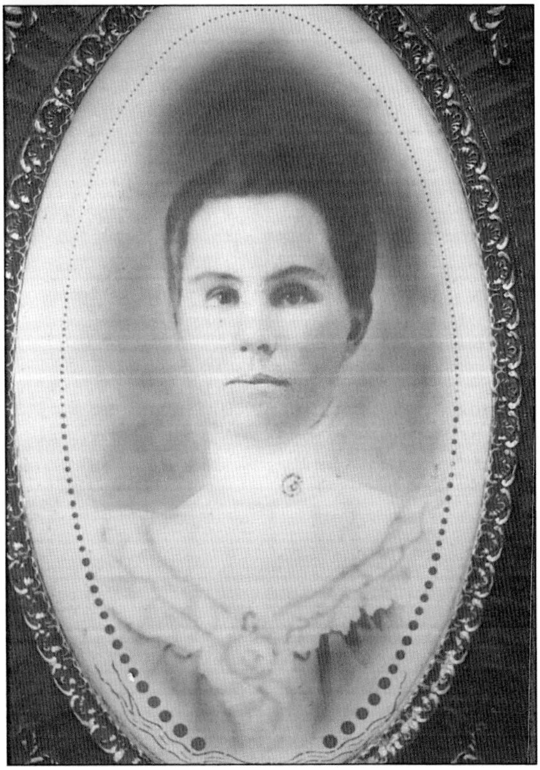

CARRIE JENKINS GRICE.

HENRY BRINSON CANEEGA.

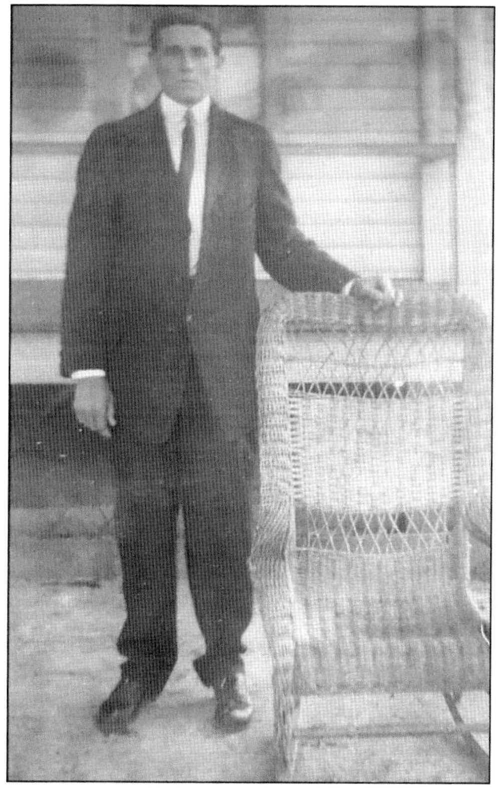

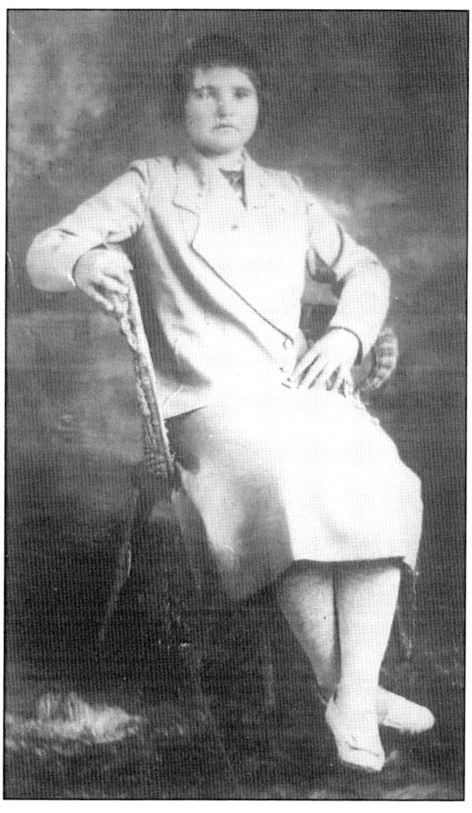

ADDIE CRAWFORD CANEEGA.

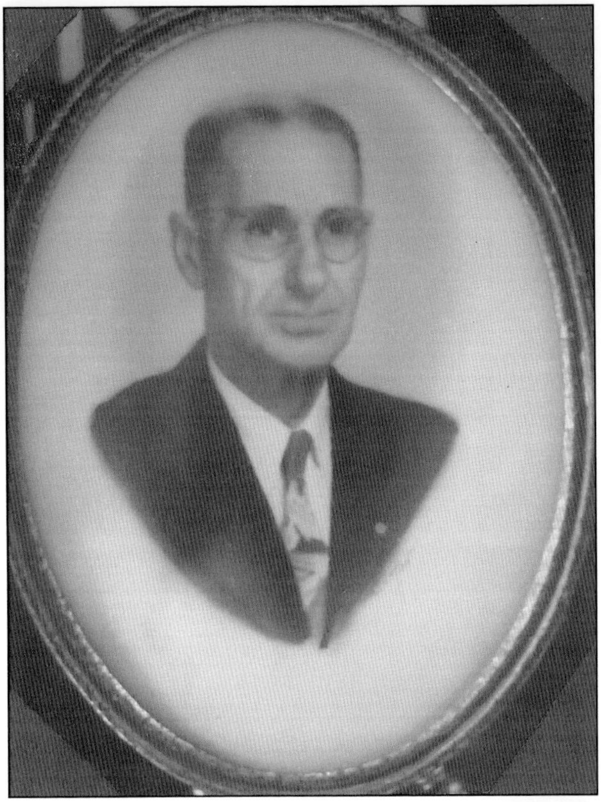

John Hall.

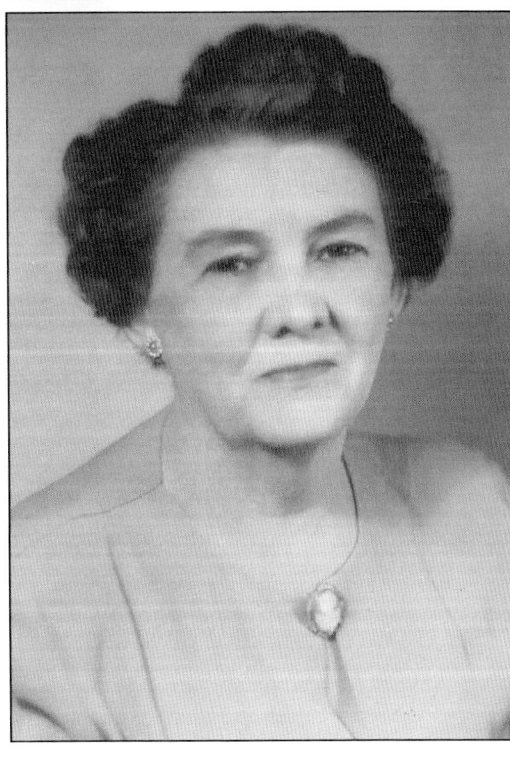

Johnnie Ennis Hall.

Christopher Columbus Colston.

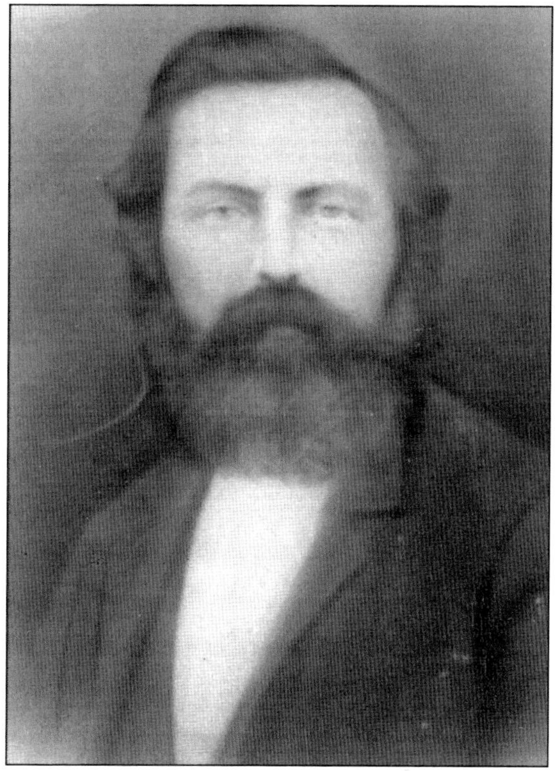

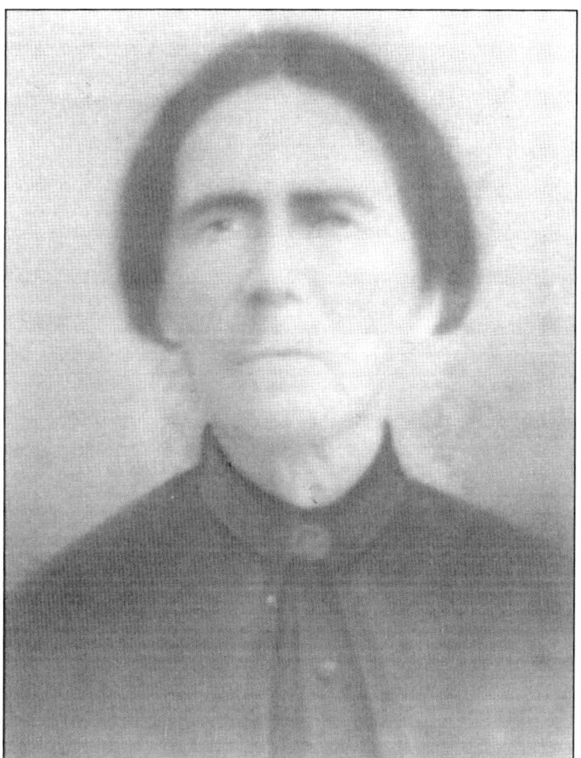

Virginia Colston.

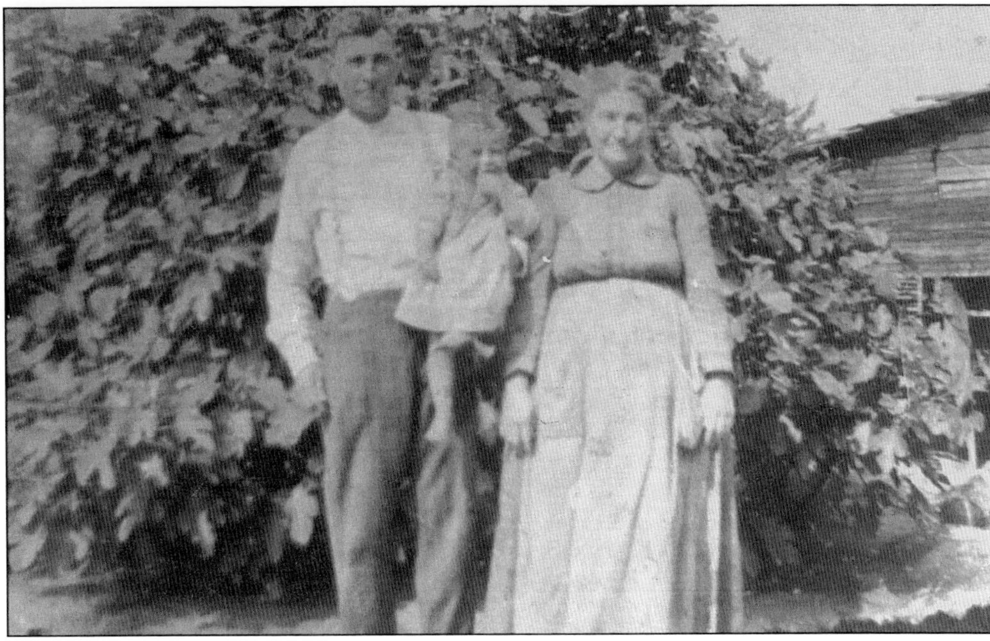

Bill and Carrie Oliver.

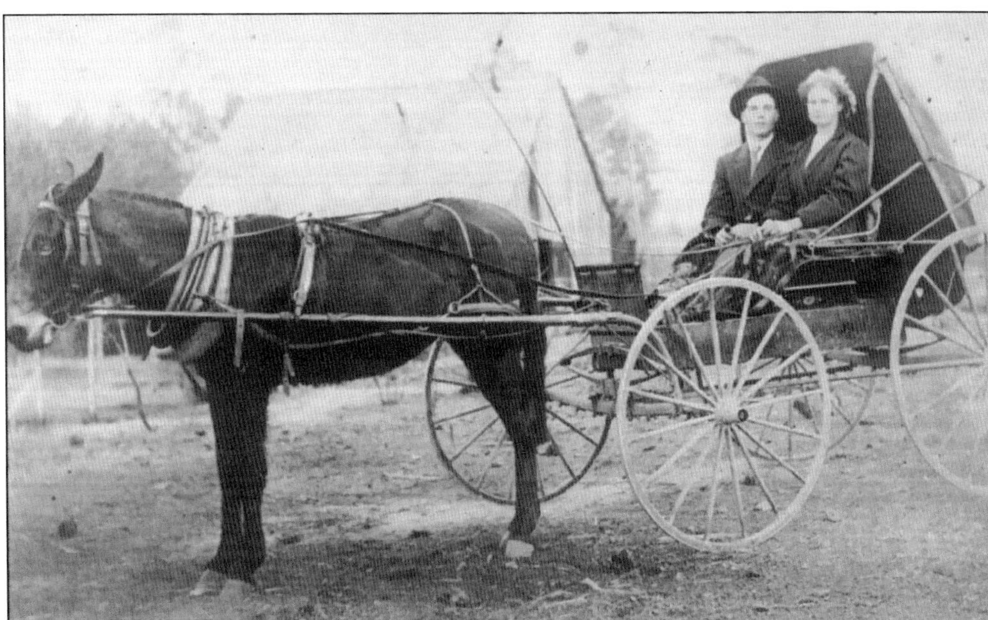

A Young Couple on Their Wedding Day.

Four

Styles and Fashions

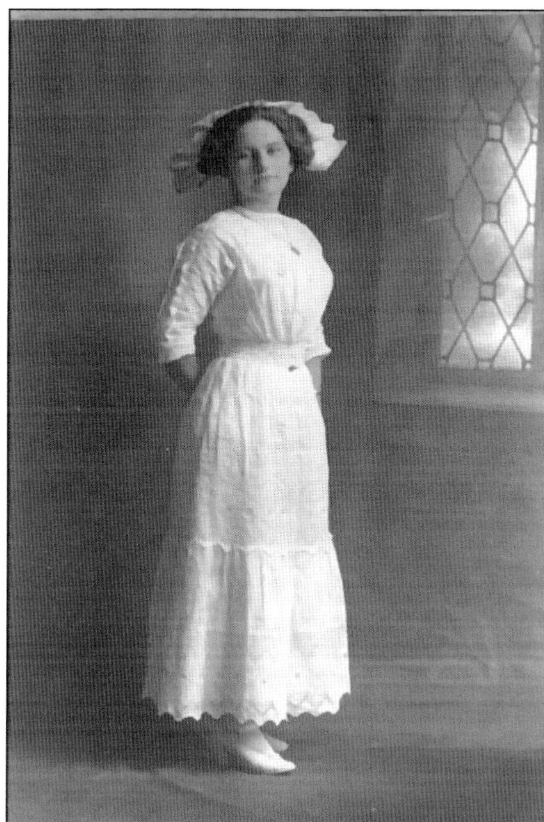

Geneva Bray, c. 1905. Geneva taught at Montee (c. 1918–1935) and Ball's Ferry (1935–late 1950s), where she was the only first-grade teacher. She retired from Wrightsville Elementary School.

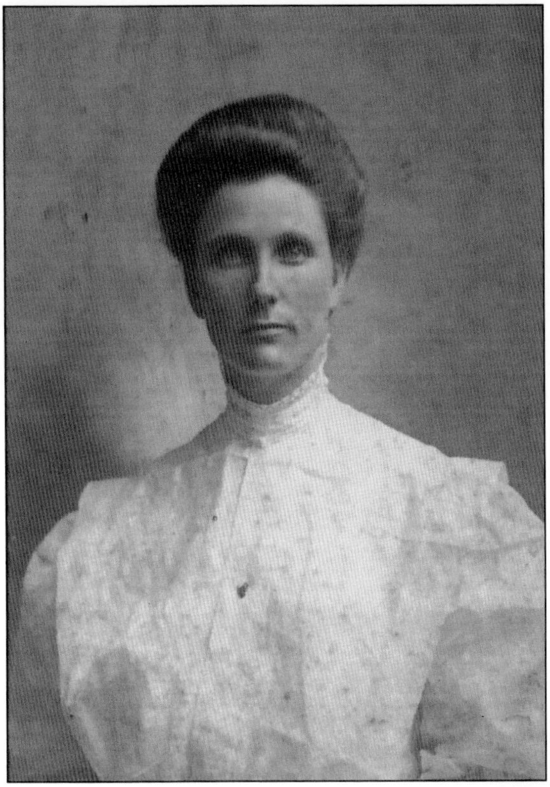

MRS. TRUDIE KIGHT GODFREY ROUSE. Here, Trudie shows off the style of the 1930s with her high-neckline blouse.

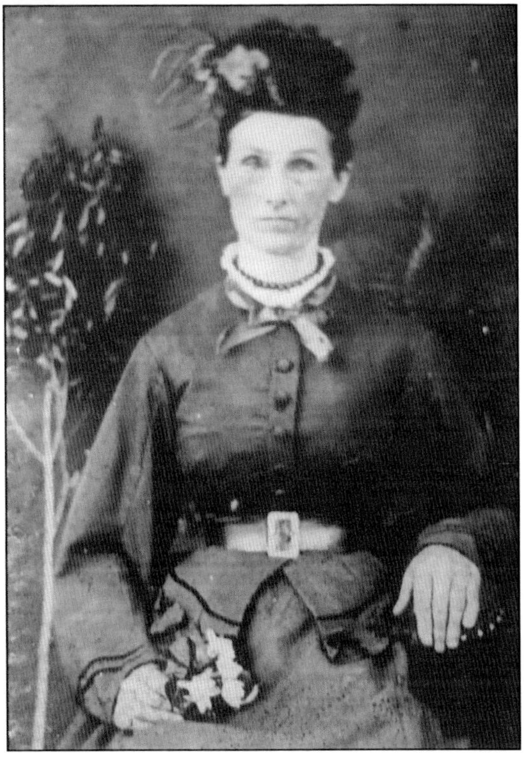

MRS. ELIZABETH SNELL RINER. Mrs. Riner is pictured in her "Sunday best." Notice the elegance of her hat and the style of her purse.

MR. LAFFEE HALL. Mr. Hall poses for the camera in his suit of the early 1900s.

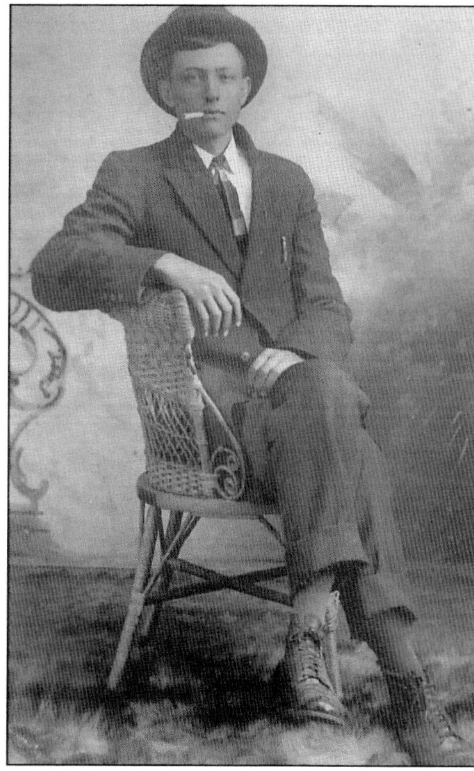

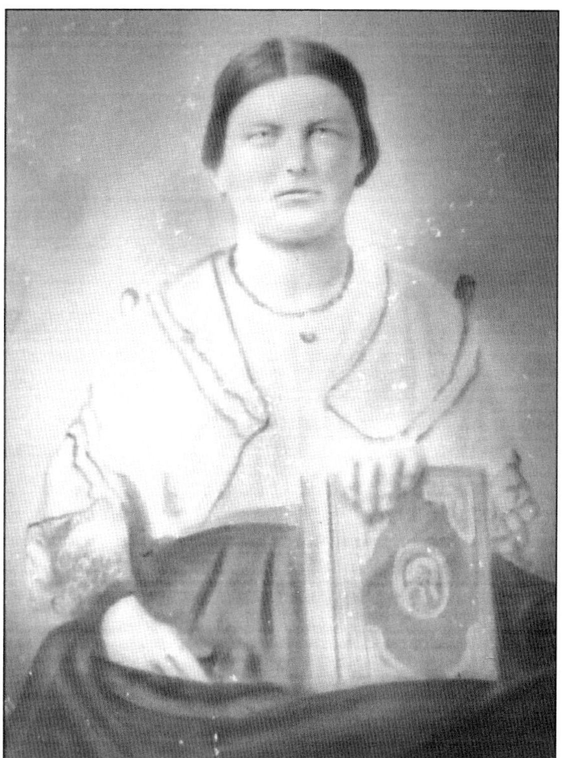

NANCY RAINES JOHNSON. This daughter of John Raines shows off the beautiful detail of her blouse.

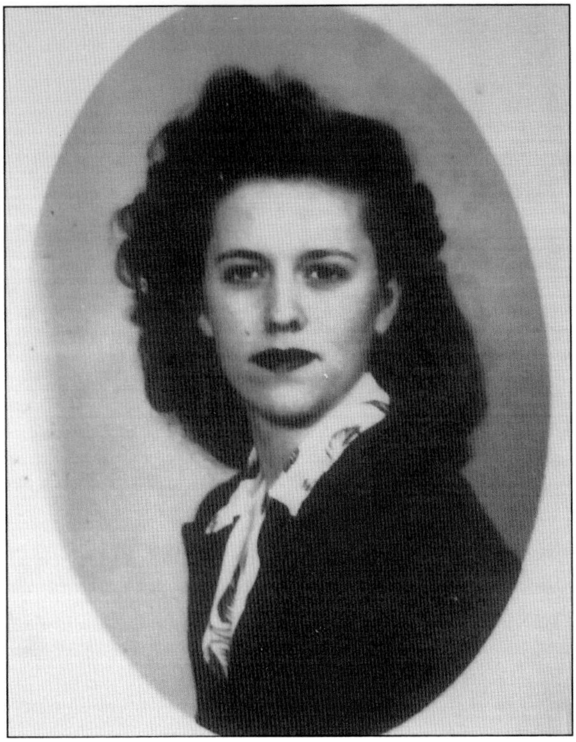

Mrs. Lucille Claxton Brantley. Mrs. Brantley, with her stylish hair, posed for this photograph to give to her sweetheart in the 1940s.

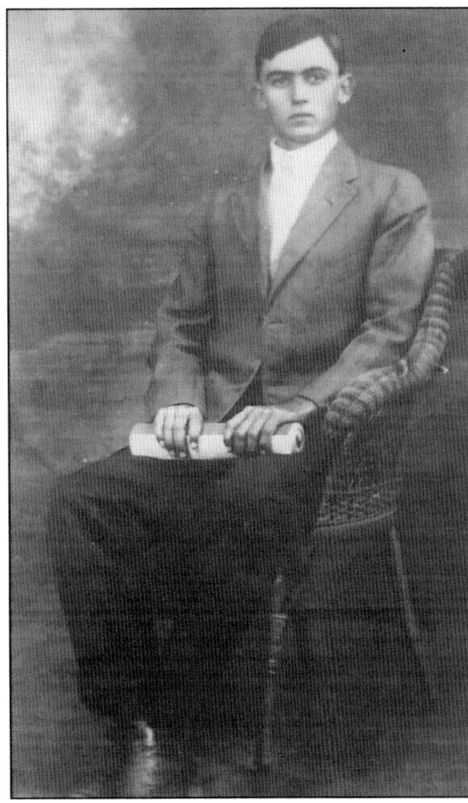

Harvell Mayo. Mayo sports a nice suit as he sits up tall for this photograph.

JOHN JOHNSON JR. Here, John shows off his pin-striped suit and his "Sunday" hat.

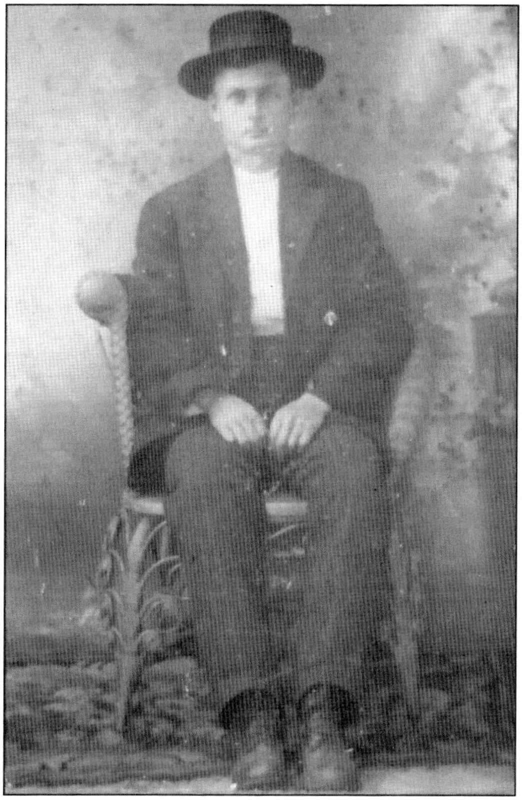

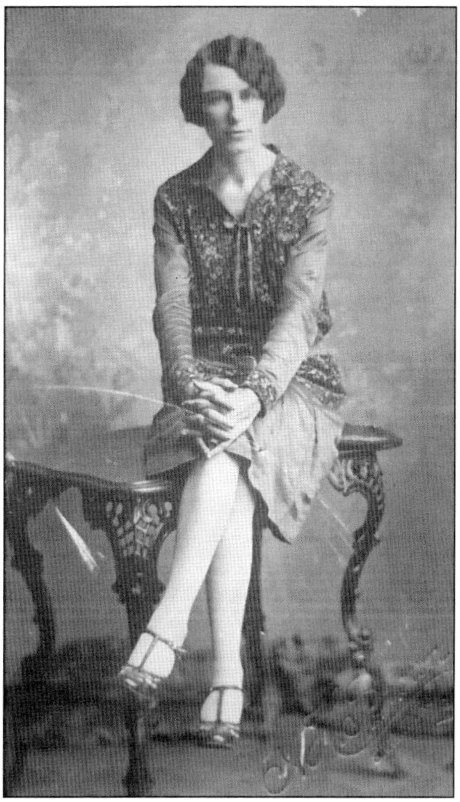

MRS. ANNIE BELLE CARAWAY SHEPARD JOHNSON. Mrs. Johnson is seen here in the new style of the late 1930s. Notice the neckline of her dress and the detail on her bodice and the hem of her sleeves.

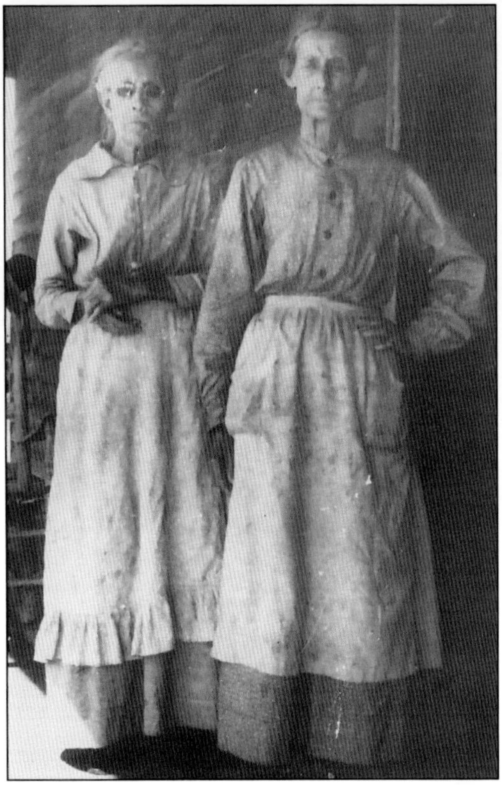

ISABELLE SWEET HALL (LEFT) AND HER SISTER EXEY HALL BROWN. These two women depict the style of dress suitable for life on the farm.

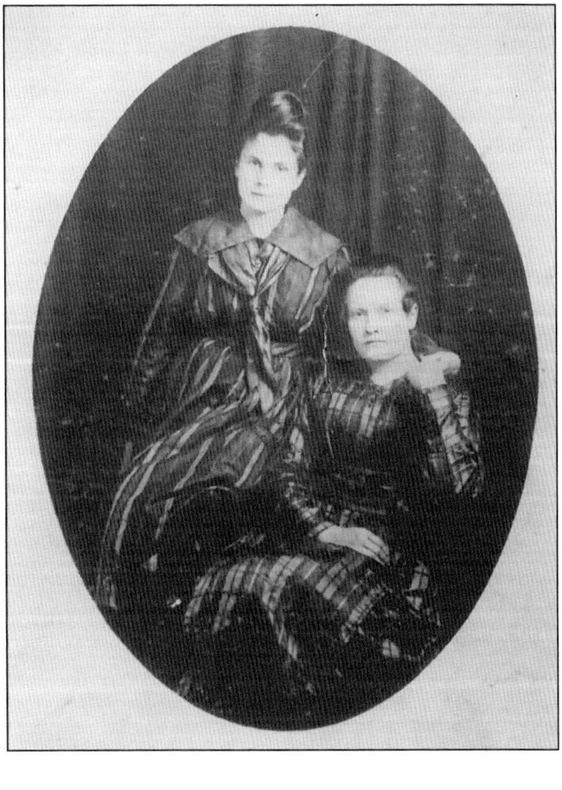

CALAR DELL PRICE (LEFT) AND VIOLA WILLIAMS, C. 1918. These ladies are pictured in the fashions of the day, including plaid dresses and pinned-up hair.

MATTIE SNELL HIGHTOWER.
Ms. Hightower shows off her good taste with this beautiful blouse.

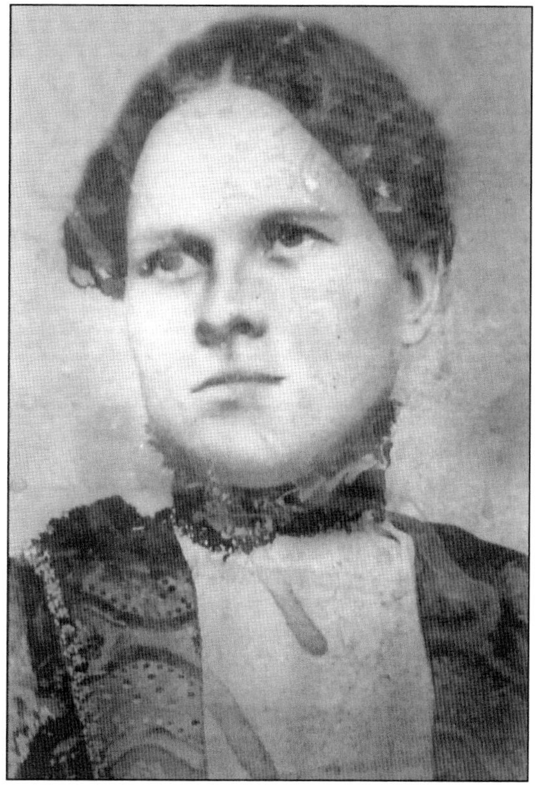

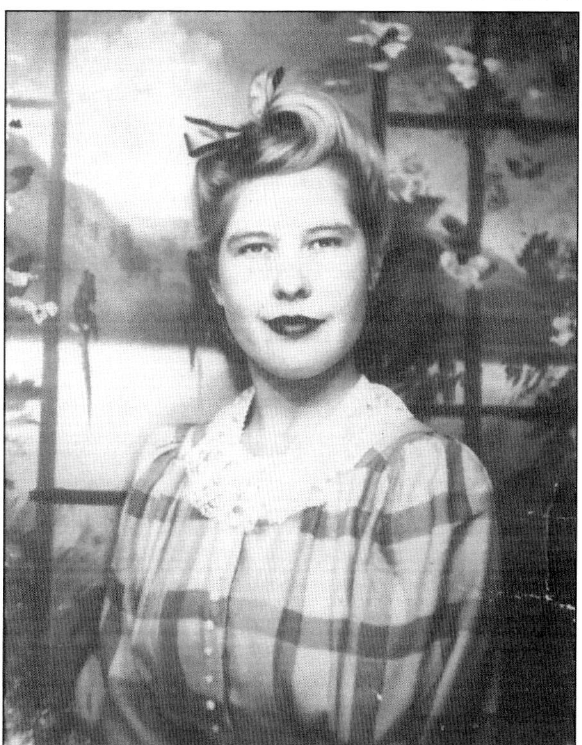

MRS. EDDIE MAE PRICE SHEPARD.
Mrs. Shepard poses here in a blouse designed and created by her mother, Mrs. Corean Price.

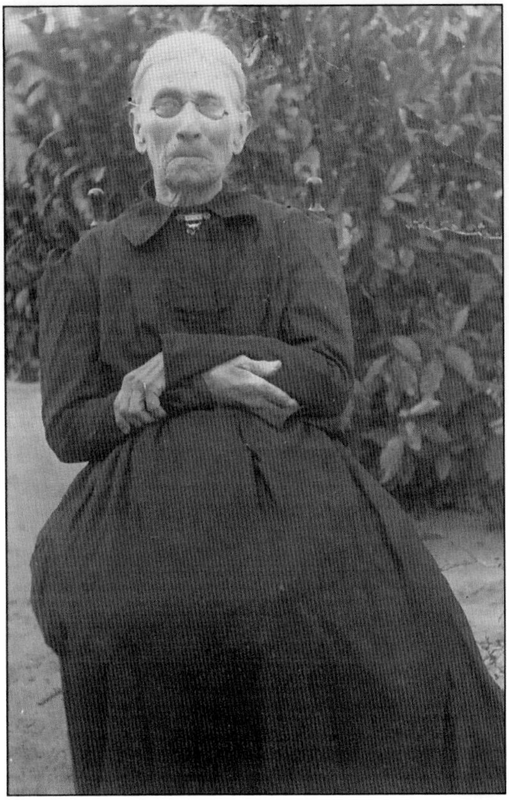

Mrs. Lenora Christian Hall Shivers. The daughter of William B. and Polly Ann Kight Hall, Mrs. Shivers shows off a style from the late 1930s. Notice the detail of the pleats on the bodice of her dress.

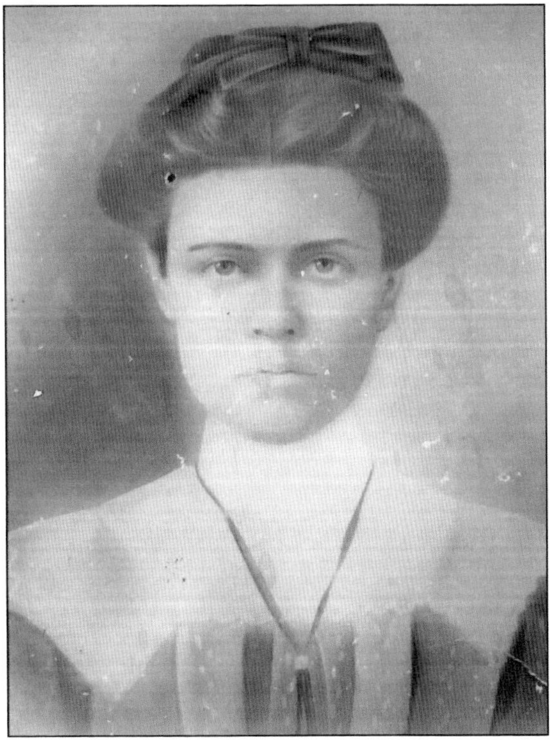

LaBelia Cordry. This lovely young lady poses for the camera in her best dress. Notice her beautiful hair and the border collar on her dress.

MR. VIRGIL SNELL. Virgil is pictured here in his suit in the late 1930s or early 1940s. Note the decorations on the chair used by the photographer during this time.

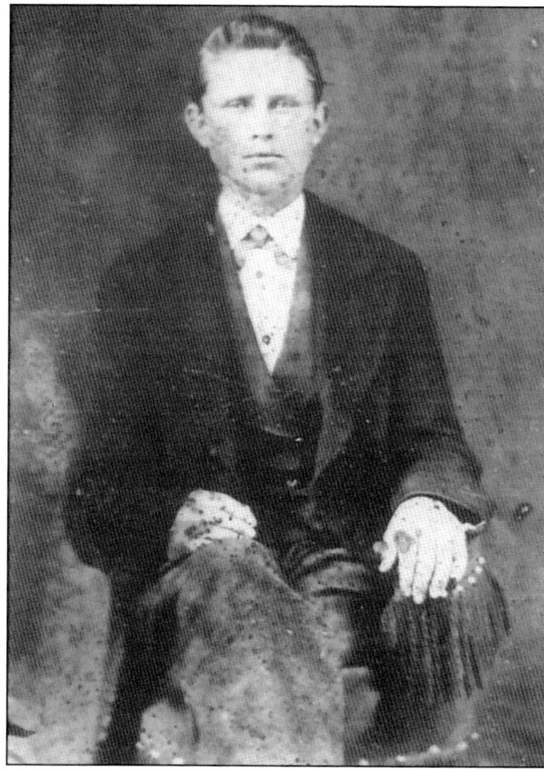

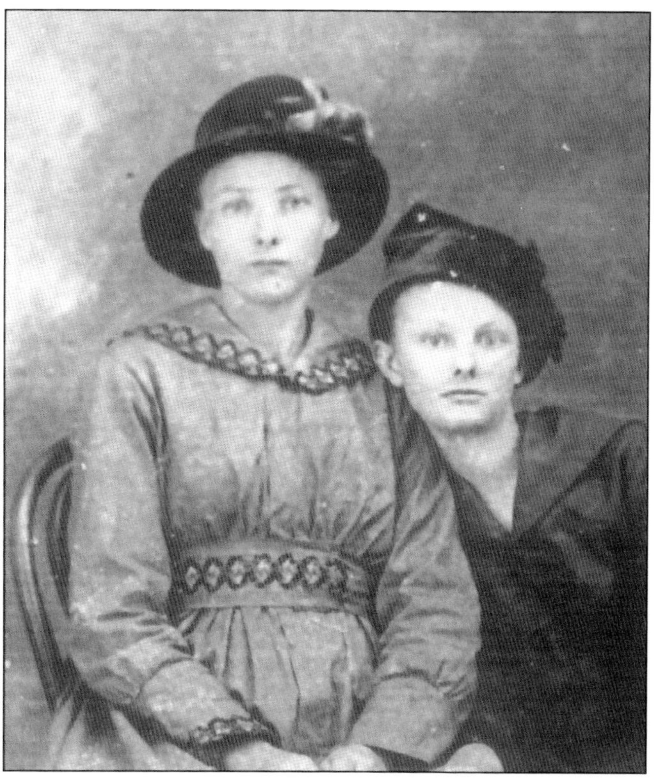

MISS OZELLA HALL (LEFT) AND HER SISTER NORA HALL. These two women are pictured in beautiful dresses and lovely hats.

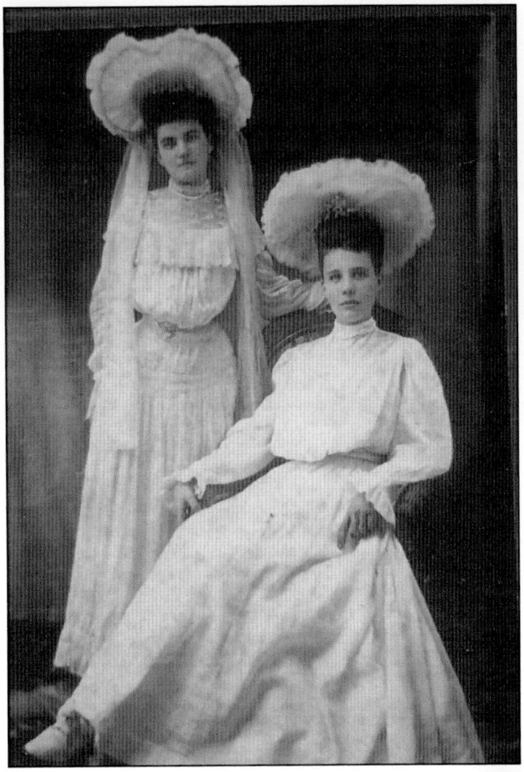

Nannie Martin Dunlap (Seated) With Her Maid of Honor, Tessie Duren. Notice the sophistication of their hats and the beauty of their gowns.

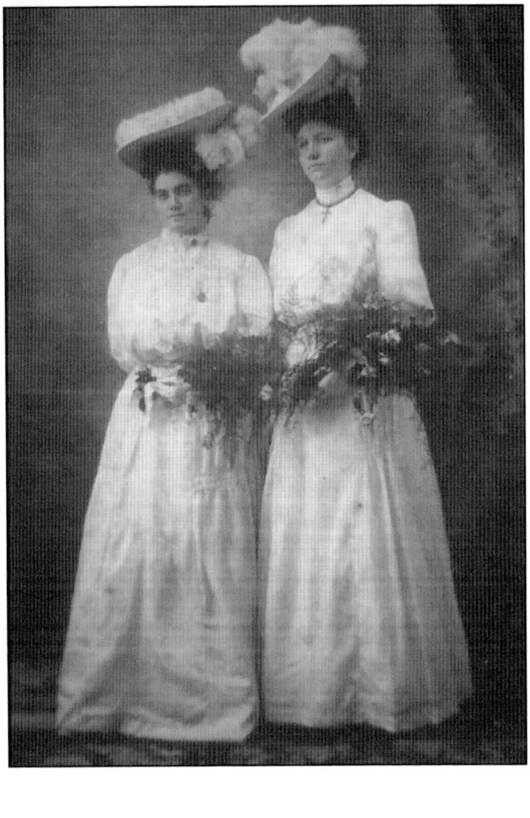

Nannie Martin Dunlap's Bridesmaids. These ladies wear hats similar to those worn by the bride and her maid of honor, pictured above.

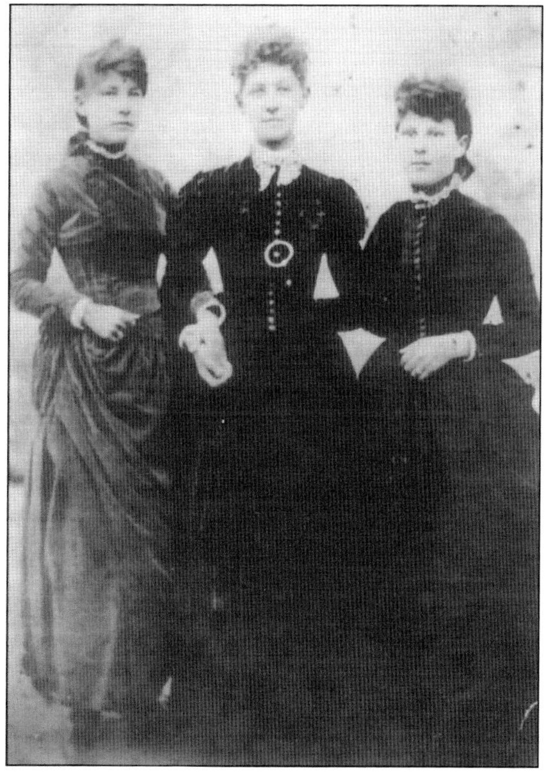

THE DAUGHTERS OF REVEREND F.W. FLANDERS, LATE 1890S. Pictured, from left to right, are unidentified, Ethel Flanders, and Sarah Salina Flanders. Note the detail of their button-up bodices and their high collars with lace.

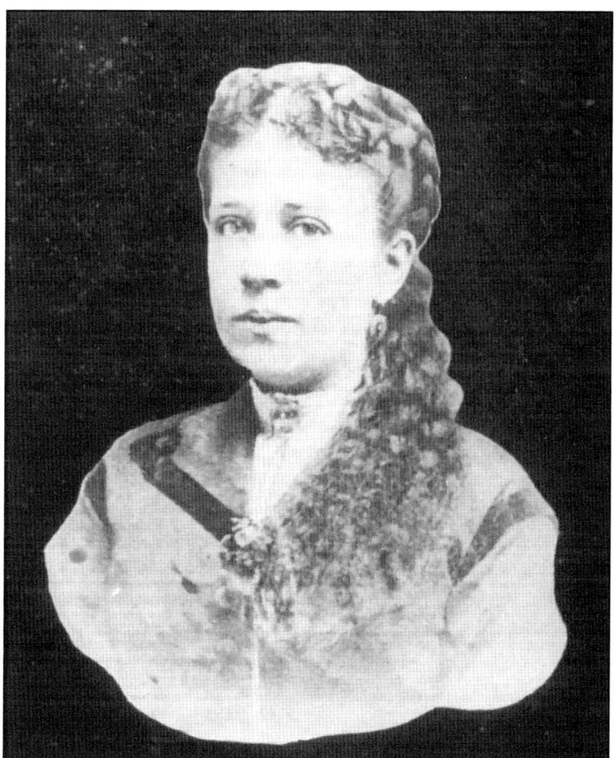

LIZZIE WRIGHT MARTIN. The daughter of J.B. and Mourning Wright, Lizzie was married to Captain John L. Martin. Note her beautiful hair.

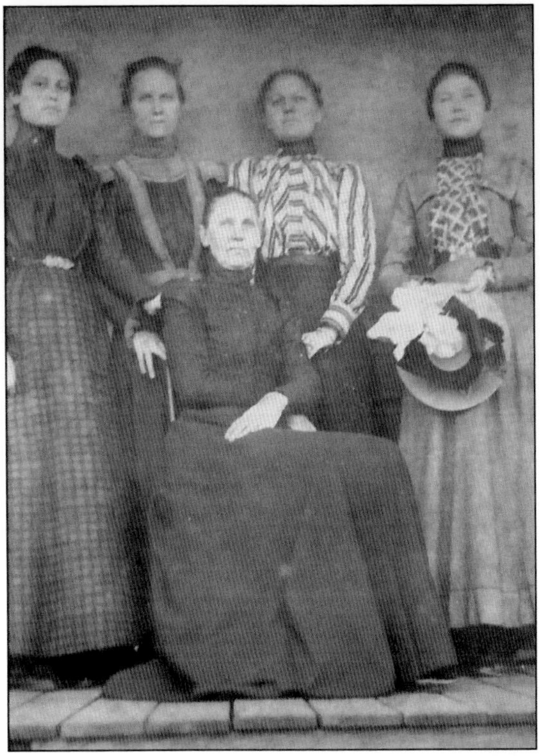

School Clothes. From left to right, Mady Griffin, Corine Q. Griffin, Ida Griffin, Essie Mae Griffin, and Pauline T. Attaway Griffin show off the styles that were appropriate for going to school. Notice the length of their dresses and the highness of their collars.

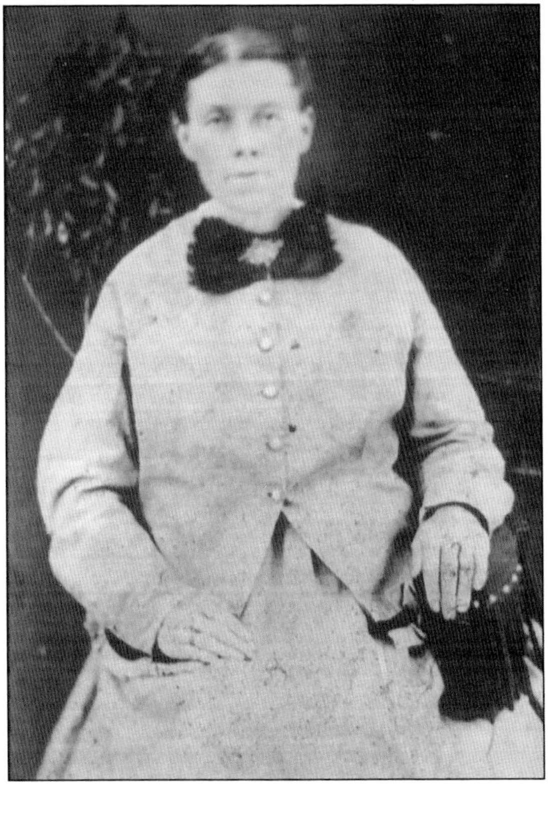

Margaret Tapley Snell. She poses for the camera in her button-up jacket and her long skirt. Notice the style of her purse and the bow on her jacket.

Five

People of the Past and Present

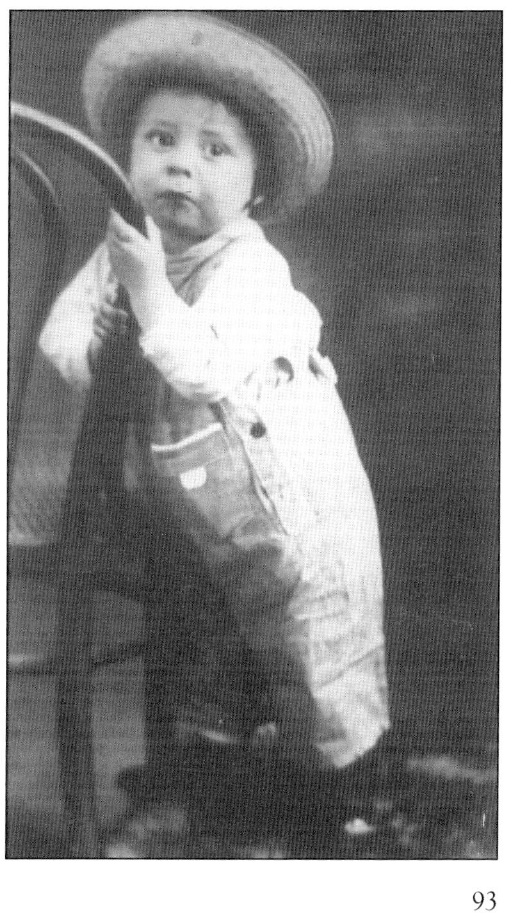

Little Johnny Grice. Dressed to go with his daddy to the fields, this boy has on overalls, popular attire for the time, and astraw hat that was sure to help shield him from the sun.

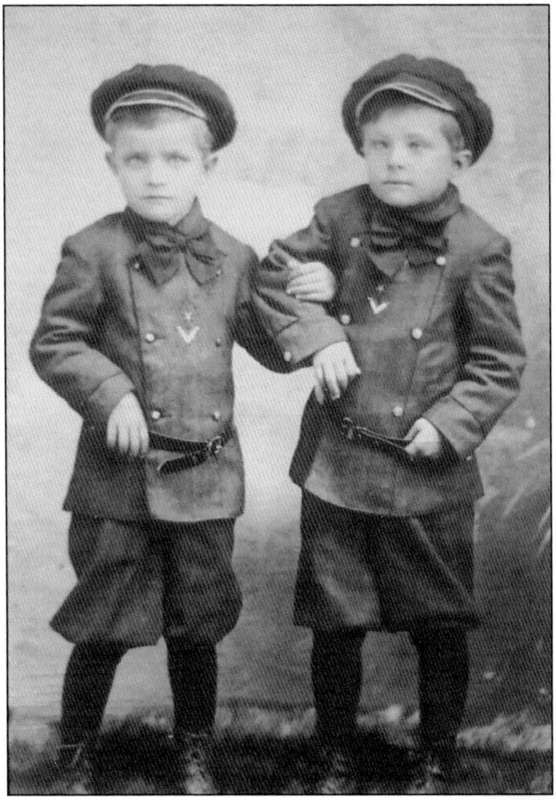

Cleo Dismuke (Left) and His Brother Clifford Dismuke. The sons of Tom and Amanda Carter Dismuke, these brothers lived in the Maple Springs area on Highway 15 South.

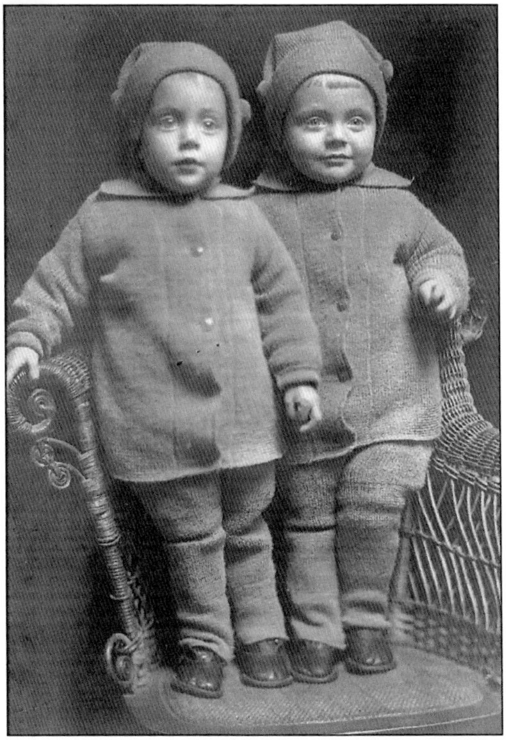

Margaret and Marion Brantley. The twins of Dr. Brantley are dressed for a cold winter day.

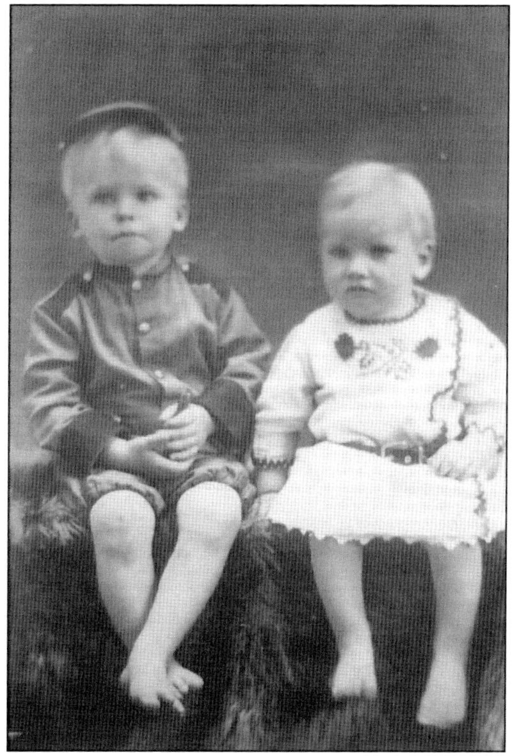

Robert and Julian Blizzard. Note the detail of the stitching in the dress and the trim work. Robert's outfit resembles that of a soldier's uniform with short pants.

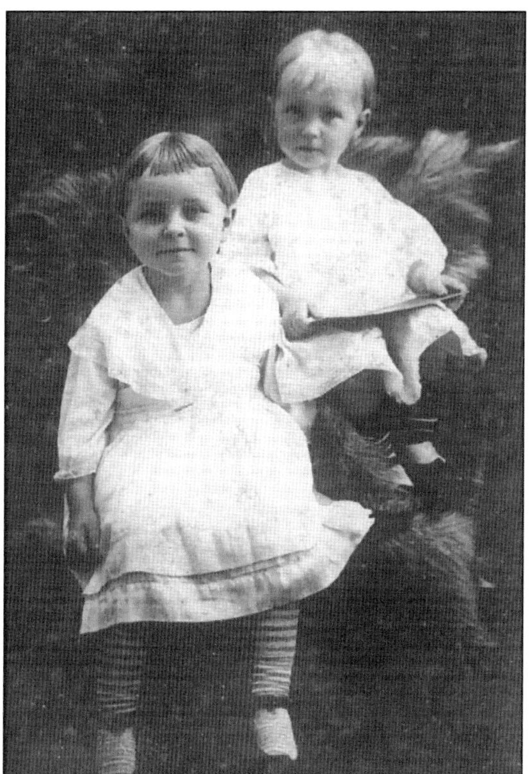

Louise (Left) and Dora Etta Vickers. The two are dressed in their Sunday best as they pose for the camera.

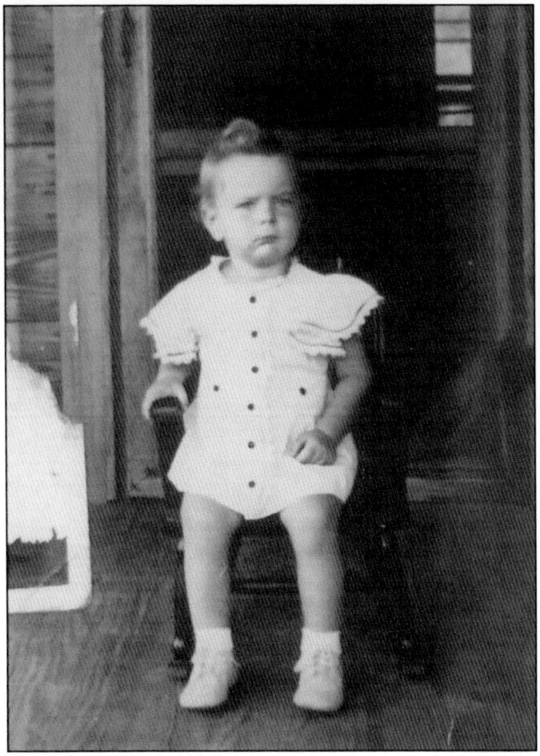

Virginia Copeland Josey. Notice the detail around the sleeves of Virginia's outfit and her flat-bottom, white hightop shoes.

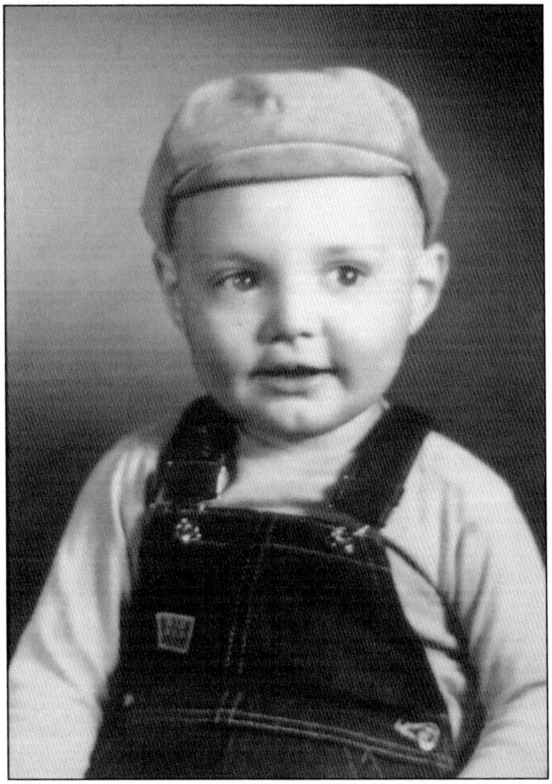

Jimmy Copeland. He is pictured here in overalls and a little hat.

NANNIE AND J.D. SMITH. These two children pose here for a postcard. Note the short pants with the high-top boots. The large bow Nannie wears was typical of the day and resembles a hat; it was used to complete an outfit.

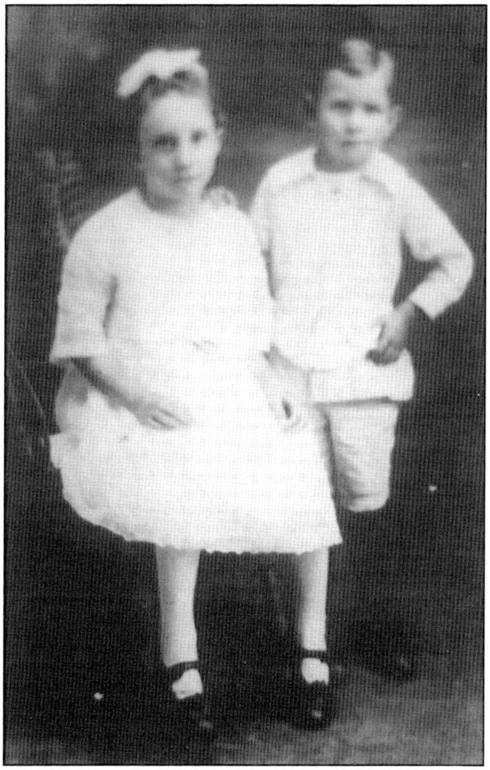

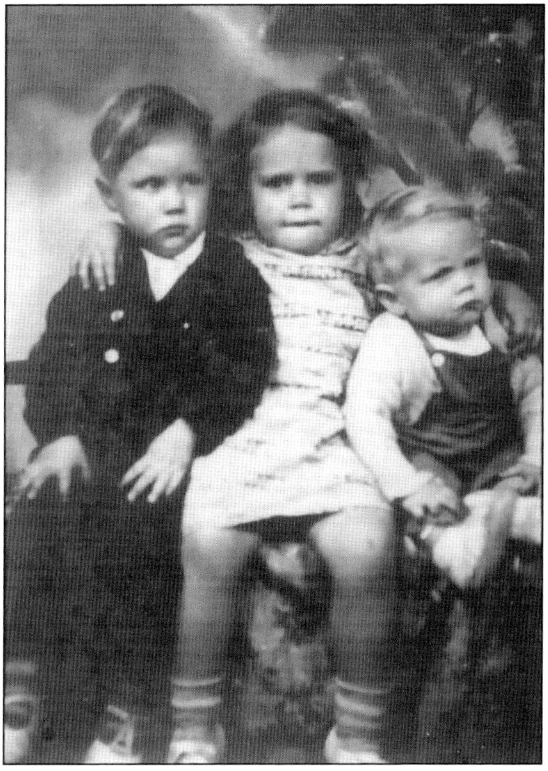

FAMILY PHOTO. From left to right, Elize Stapleton, Claudia Stapleton, and Ellie Stapleton pose for the camera in their Sunday best.

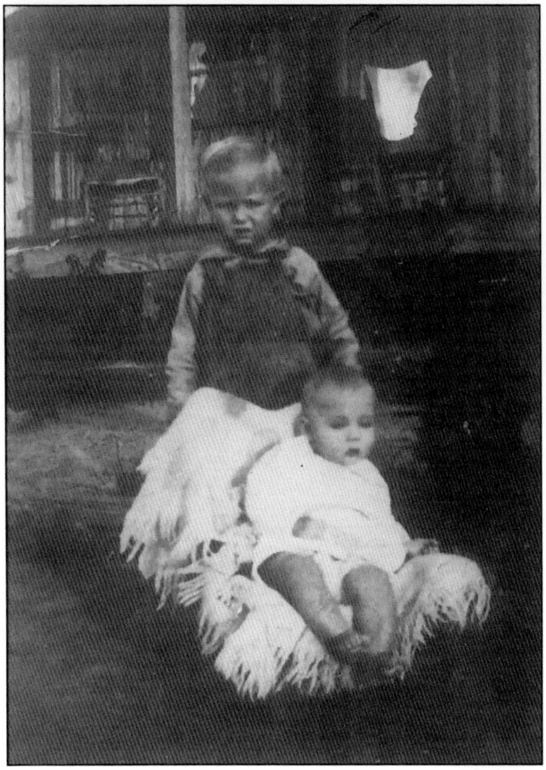

Claud Webb. Dressed in his overalls, Claud stops from his playing to pose for a picture with his younger brother Paul, *c.* 1934.

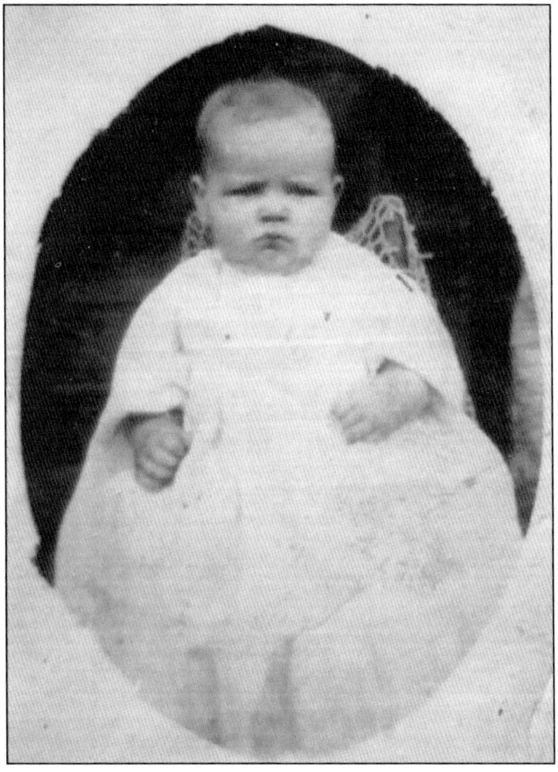

Harrison Copeland. Pictured here in his baby gown, Harrison is the son of James Paul Copeland and Maggie Wilkerson Copeland.

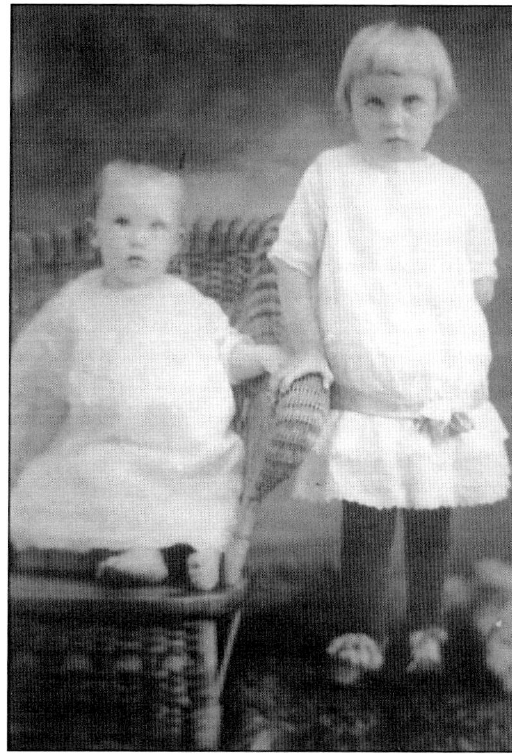

Buck Blizzard and Nannie Rea Blizzard. These two posed for this postcard photo, which was probably made to be sent to relatives. Note the long stockings and the ribbons on the dress.

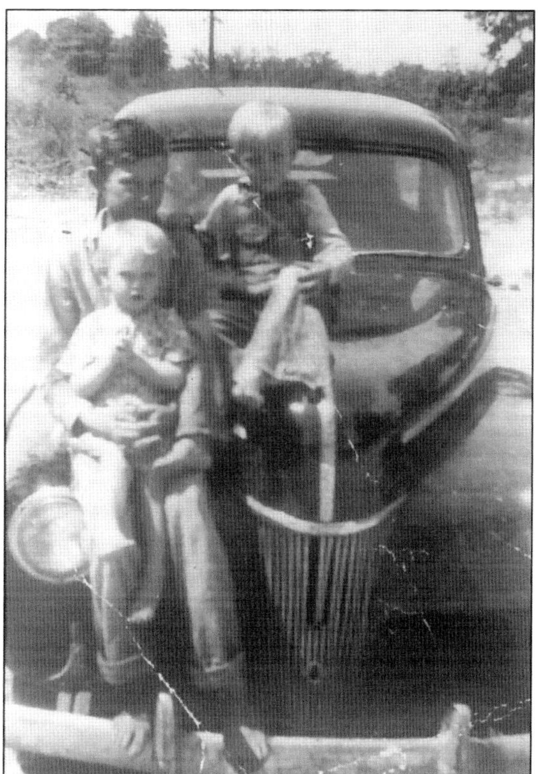

Posing on the Car. Pictured here are Perry Webb, Gwinette Webb on Perry's lap, and Marvin Webb. These siblings pose for this picture on top of their daddy's car and are dressed in everyday clothing typical of the late 1940s.

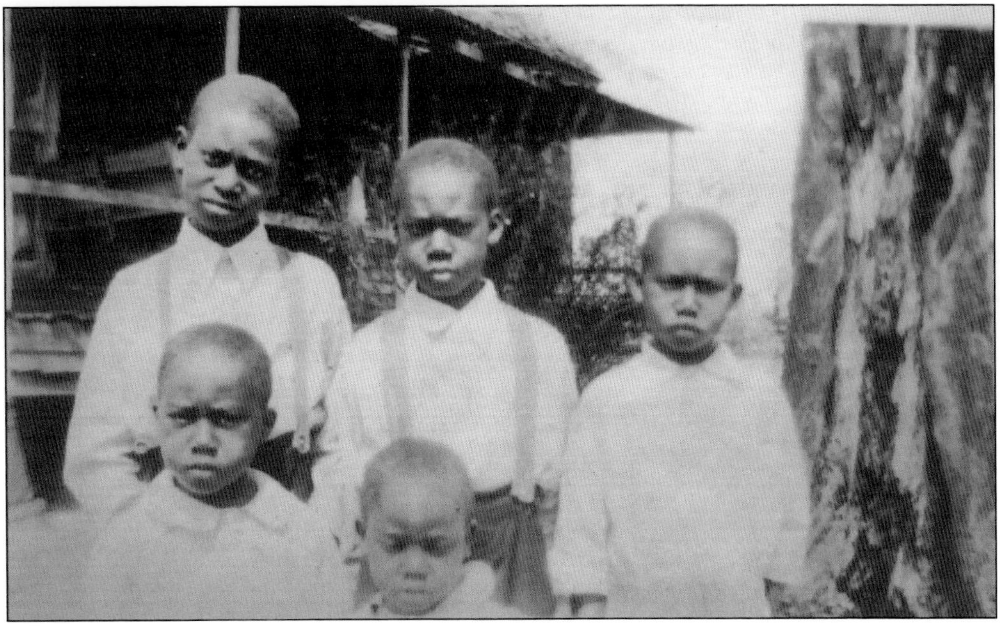

The Wesley Children. Pictured here, from left to right, are L.D., Clarence, P.W., James, and Willie Wesley.

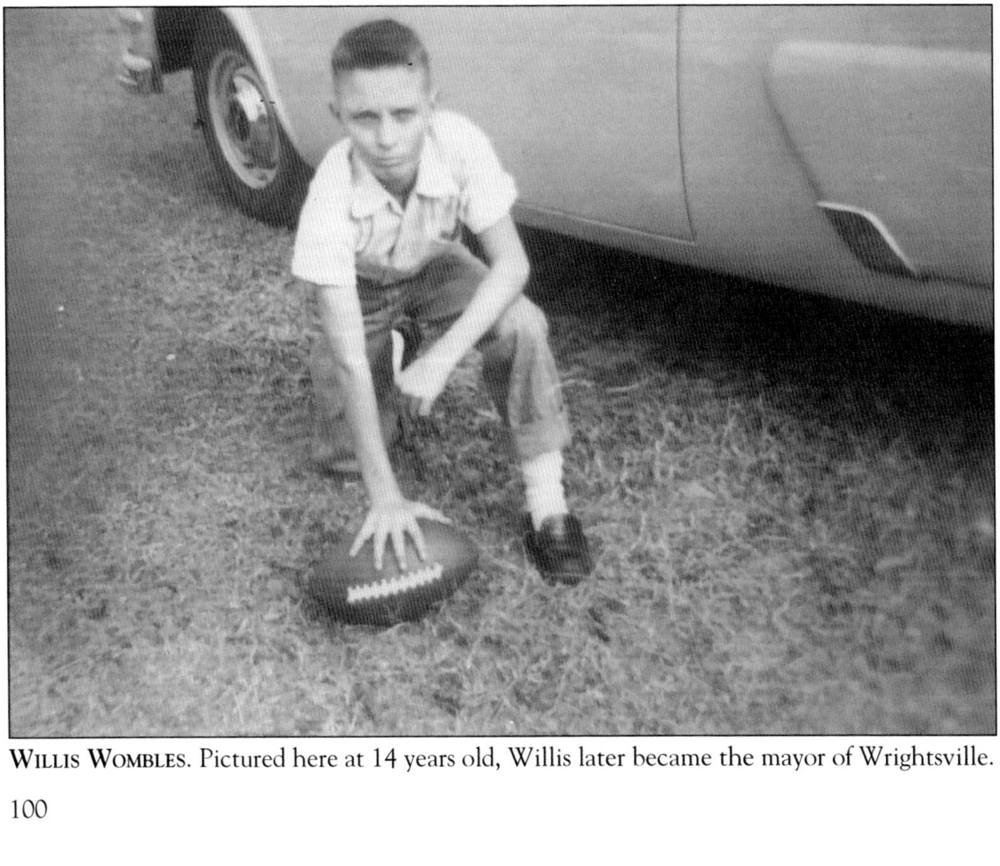

Willis Wombles. Pictured here at 14 years old, Willis later became the mayor of Wrightsville.

GORDON HOLMES BRANTLEY. He is seen here at age 12 months in 1918. He appears to be ready for a "cold" winter and some outside play.

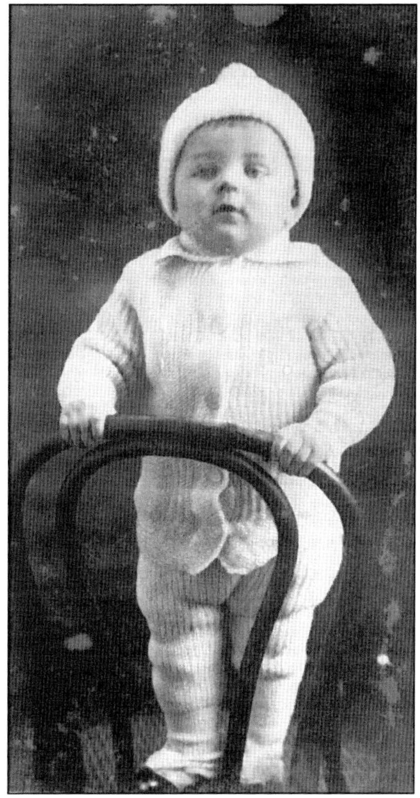

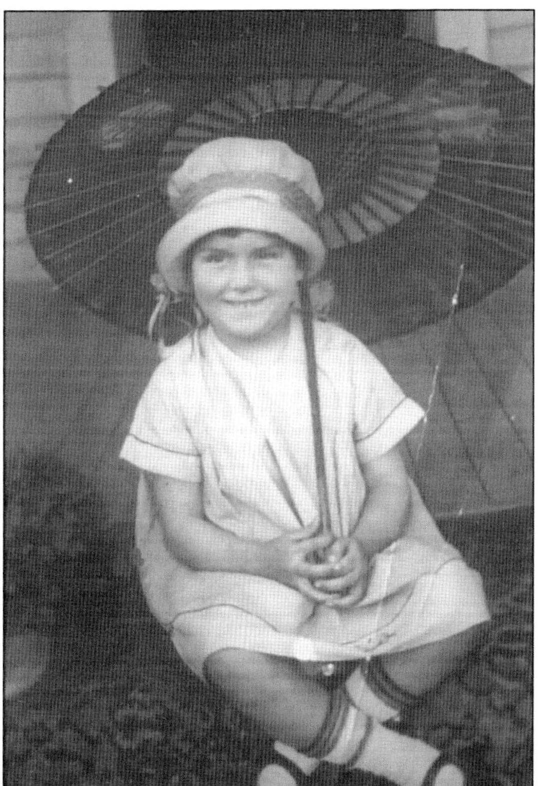

JOSEPHINE WILLIAMS. She shows off her beautiful hat with its embroidery and ribbons. Note the design on her socks and the little details of her dress.

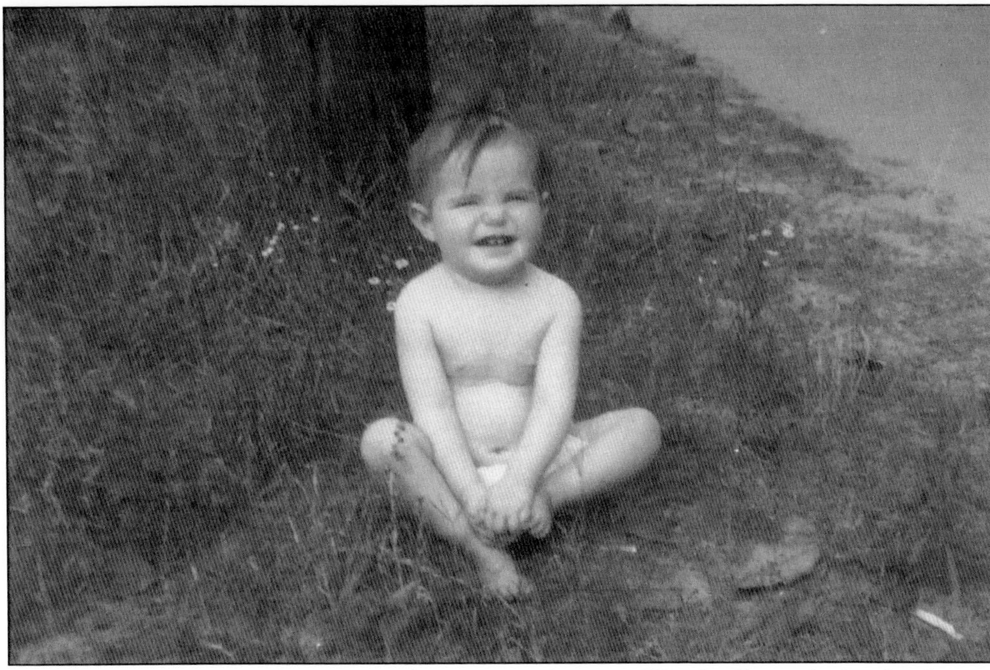

WANDA SHEPARD. On a hot, sunny day in Kite, Georgia, Wanda Shepard, the daughter of Randolph and Eddie Mae, tries to find a cool spot to rest for a while.

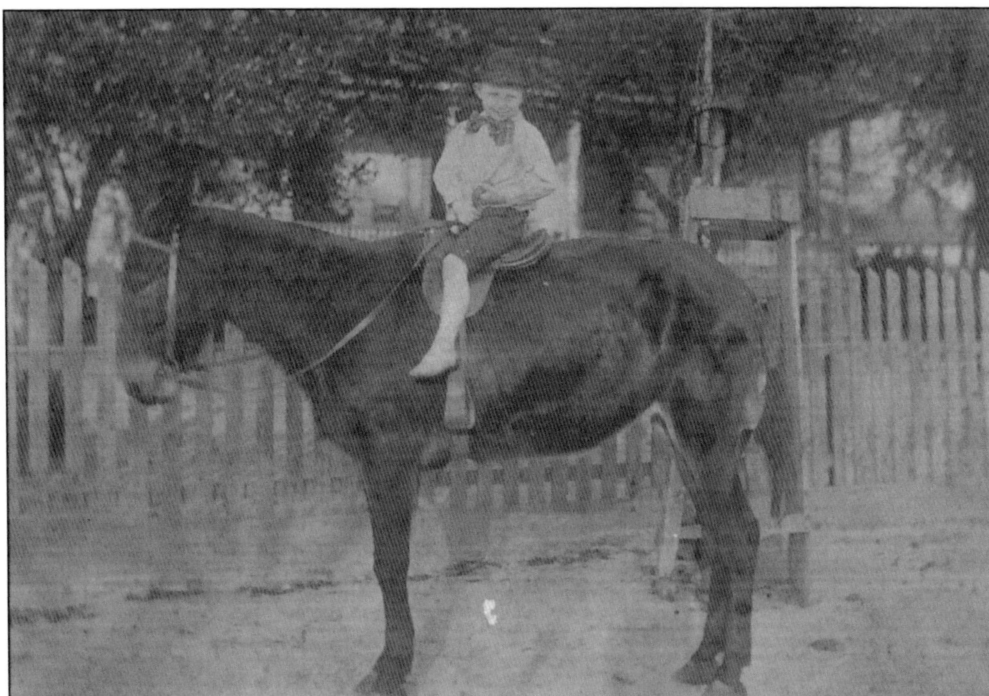

OSTELLE BRAY, C. 1910. The home of Tom Bray is pictured in the background. Even with a large bow tie and hat, Ostelle is still barefooted.

GEORGE THOMAS VICKERS. This little boy is pictured here as an adorable two-year-old child.

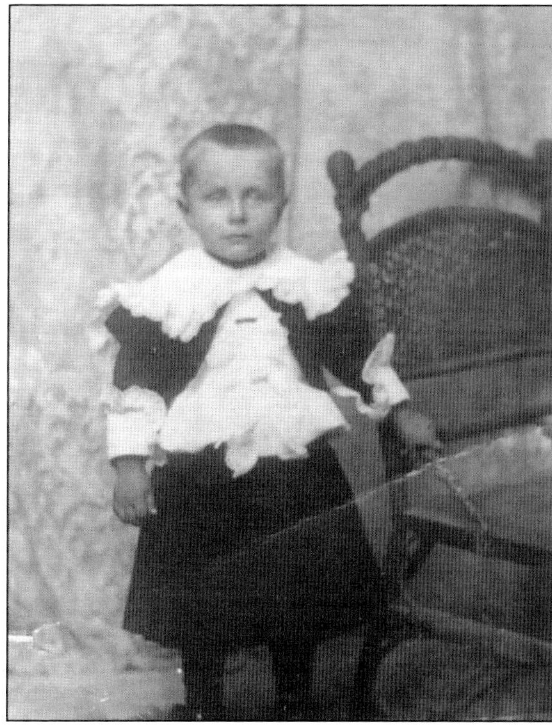

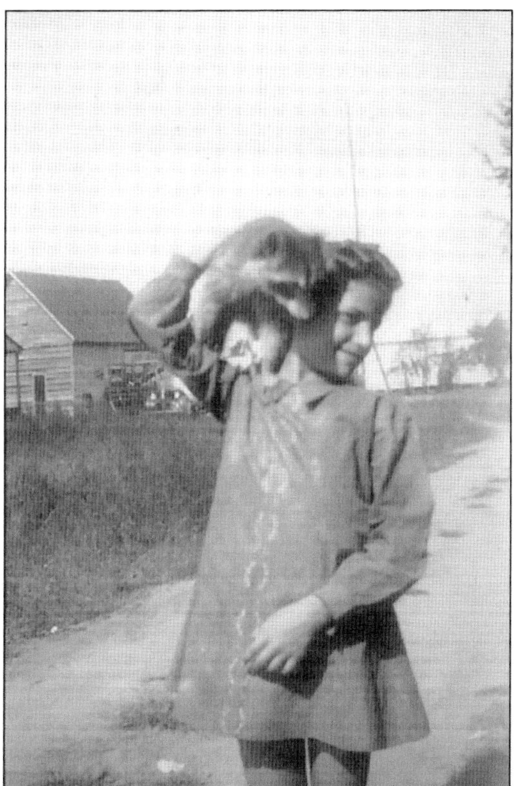

DORIS TOWNSEND AND HER PET RACCOON "BOZO." She is pictured in front of the Goob Lindsey Cafe in Kite, Georgia. Notice the length of the dress and the embroidery details down the front of it.

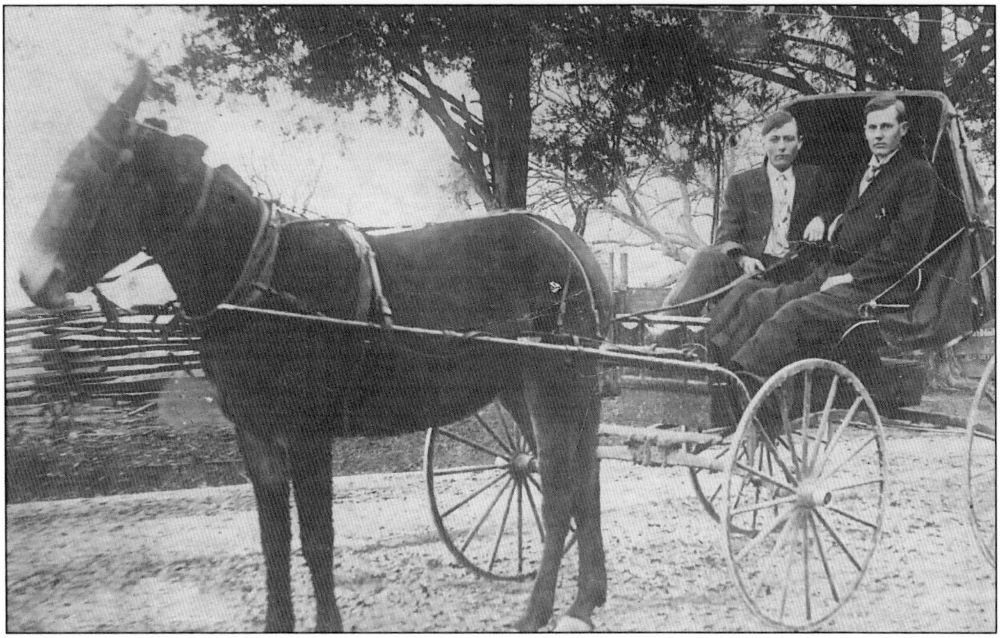

LAFFEE HALL (LEFT) AND LEO SCARBOROUGH. This pair stops on their ride into town to pose for the camera.

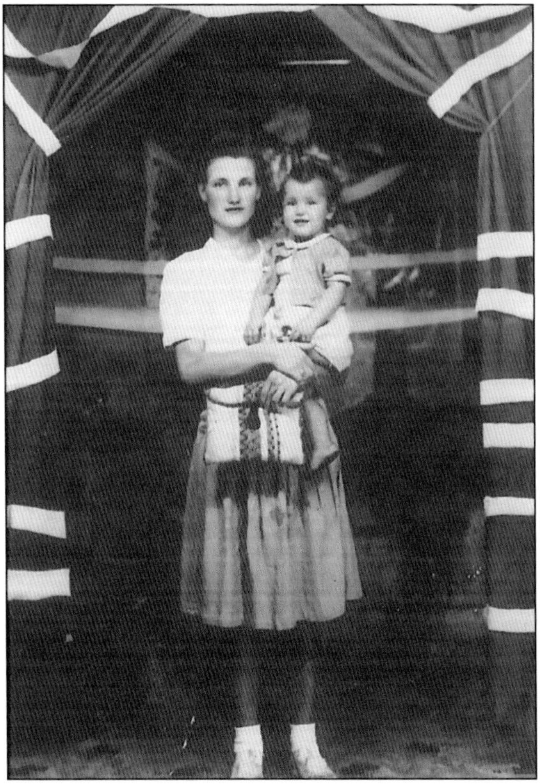

LAVANNAH POOL COPELAND (LEFT) AND DOMA COPELAND.

Charlie Hall and Two of His Daughters, Mary Lizzie (Left) and Menty Hall.

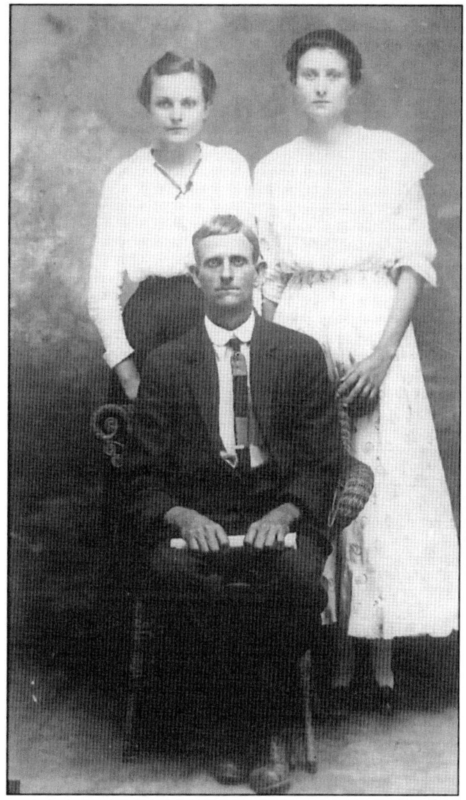

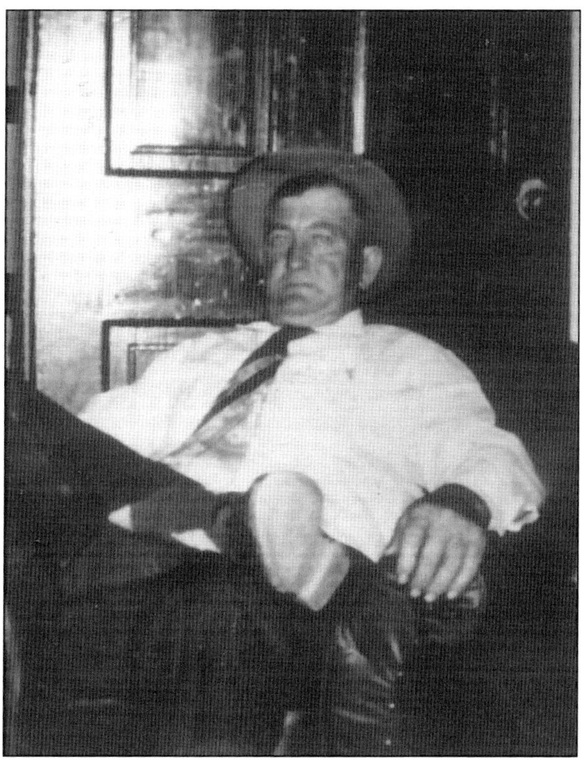

Teddie Manson Webb.

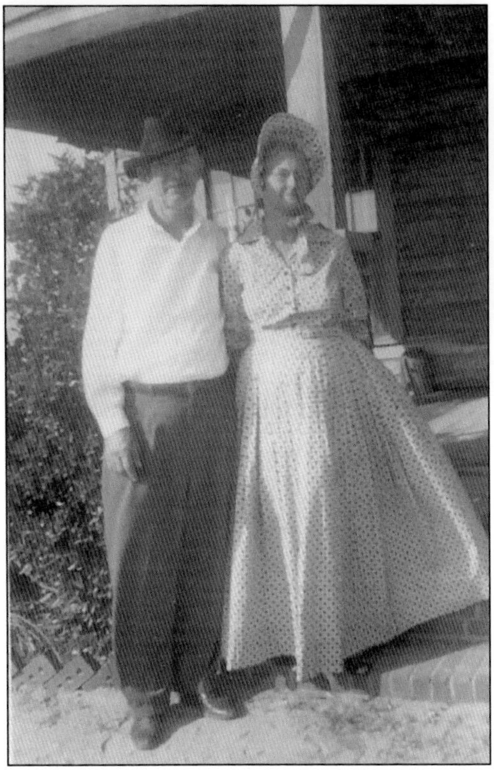

Ollie Raines and His Wife, Olga Dent Raines. The couple is dressed for Johnson County's 100-Year Celebration in 1958. They are the parents of Jewell Parker and Joy Hortman.

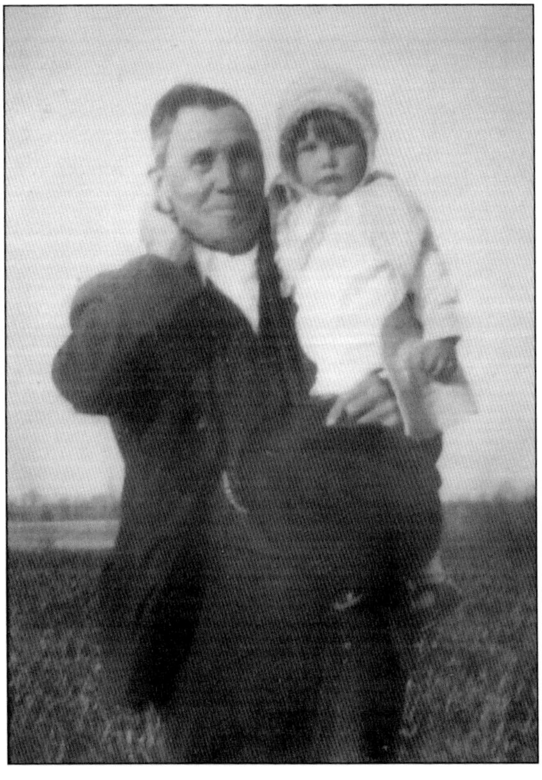

Bill Oliver. He proudly shows off his granddaughter Wanette Johnson.

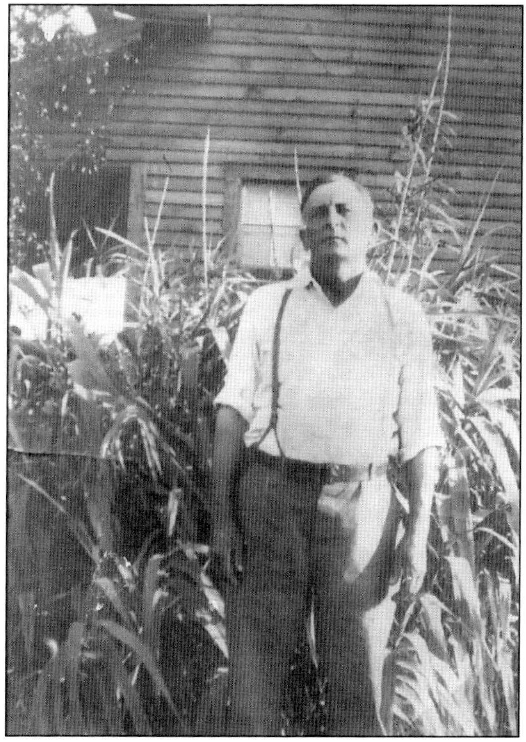

EVAN WILLIAMS. Mr. Williams poses for the camera next to his reed cane from which he made fishing poles.

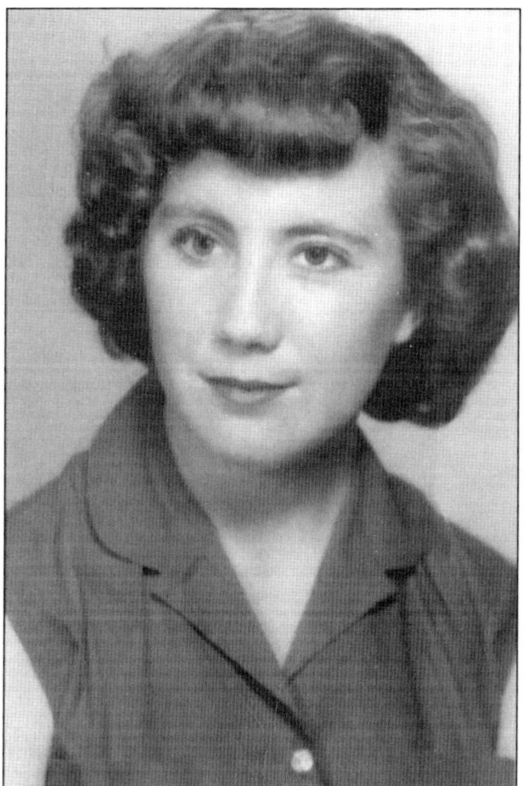

IONE MASON WEBB. Mrs. Webb is the daughter of John and Lorene Mason and the wife of Claud Webb.

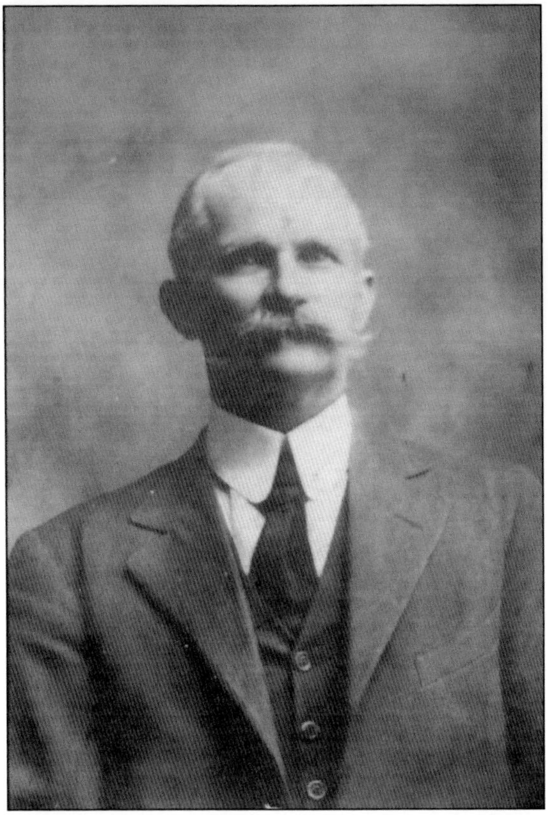

Mr. William N. Kight. He was the founder of the town of Kite and a former senator.

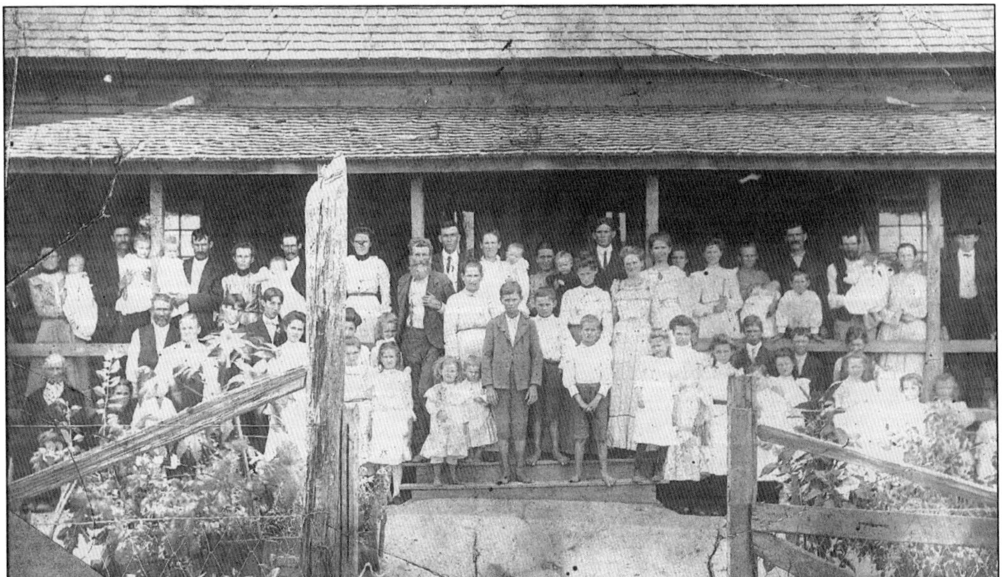

Pool Family Reunion, 1902. The family of William Bateman "W.B." Pool and Susan Walker Pool gathered at the home of their son William "Billy" Freeman Pool and his wife, Fernissia "Nissy" Pitman, near Donovan. Many of W.B. and Susan Pool's descendants live in Johnson County today.

ANNIE ELMORE TANTRY BLACK. Mrs. Black was the third wife of William Henry Black and is pictured with the children she helped raise, (clockwise from top) Leon Copeland, Arie Ethel Black, Tom Black, Luther Black, and Andrew Tant.

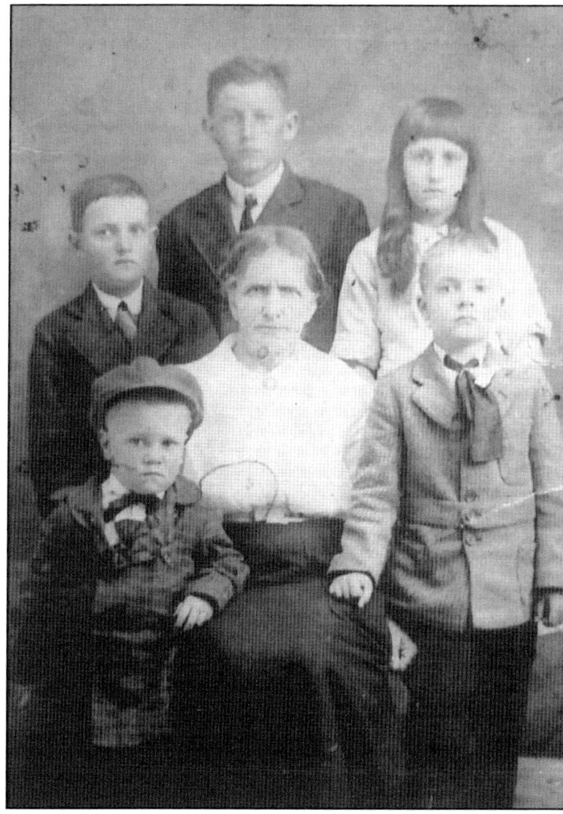

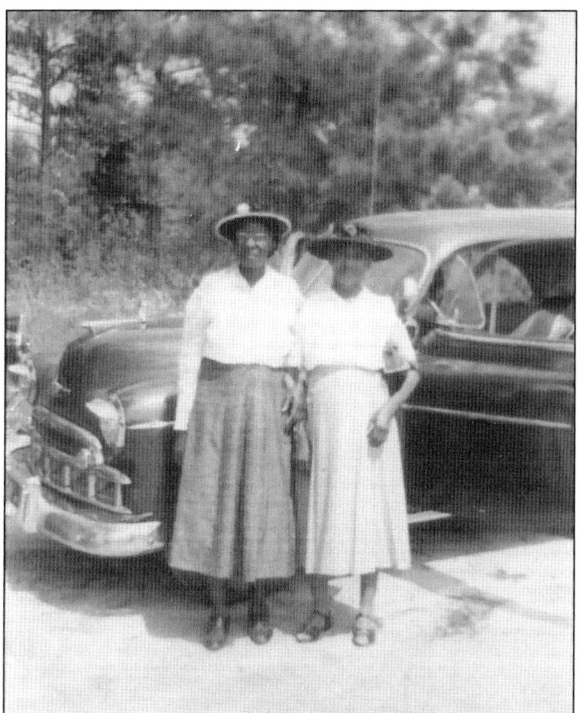

MARY B. KEMP WESLEY AND ELLA MOORMAN, 1952. These two are all decked out in their Sunday hats.

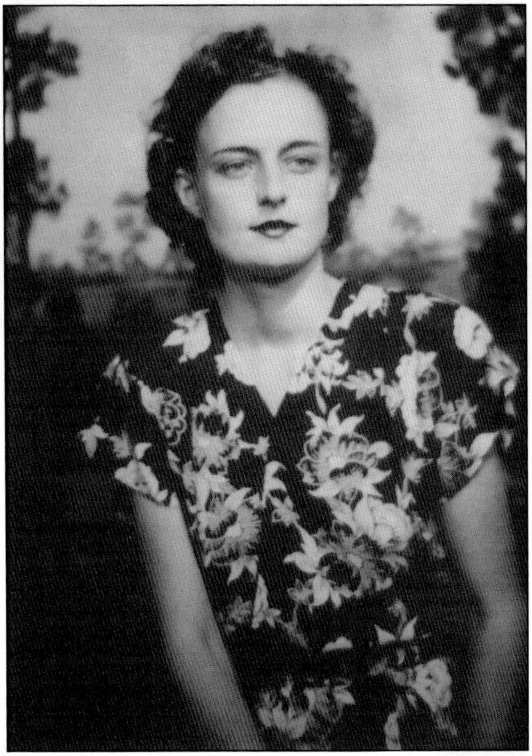

Ellies Copeland. The daughter of Freeman Sheppard and Missie Dixon Sheppard, Ellies was about 19 when this picture was taken.

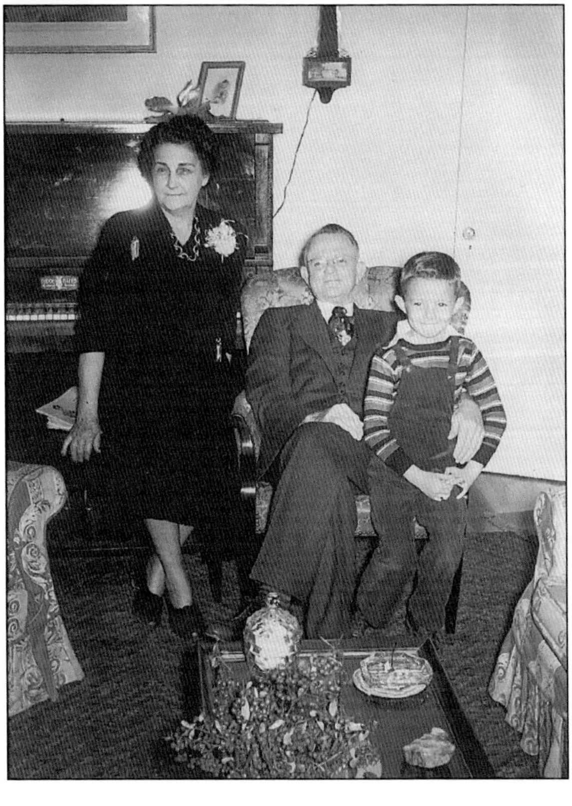

Dr. and Mrs. Brantley With One of Their Grandchildren, Jimmy Brantley.

Bertha Flanders Brantley (Left), Reverend Pompeii Flanders, and Minnie Flanders Wheeler (Right).

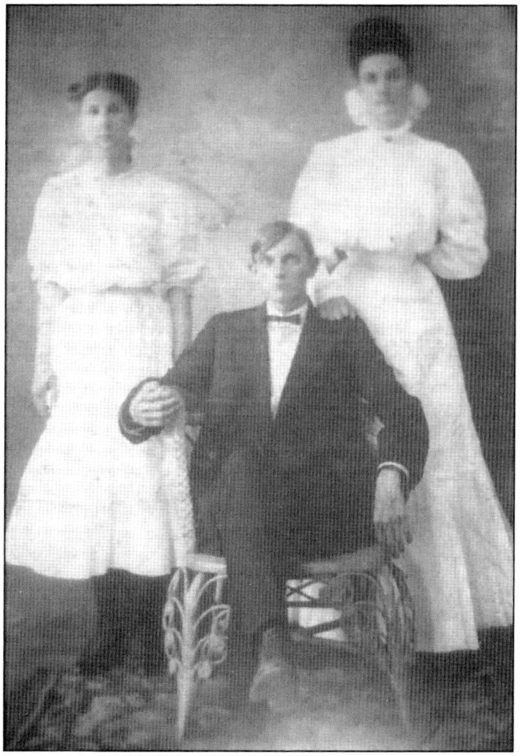

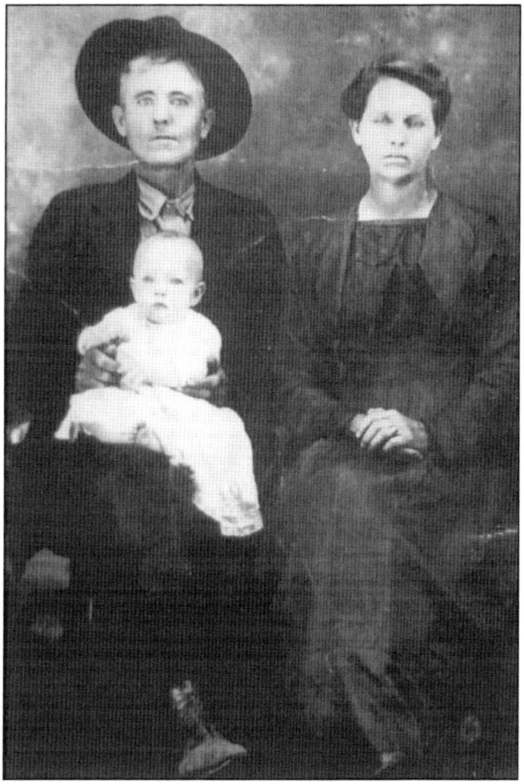

Robert F. Webb With His Wife, Minta Raines Webb, and Child.

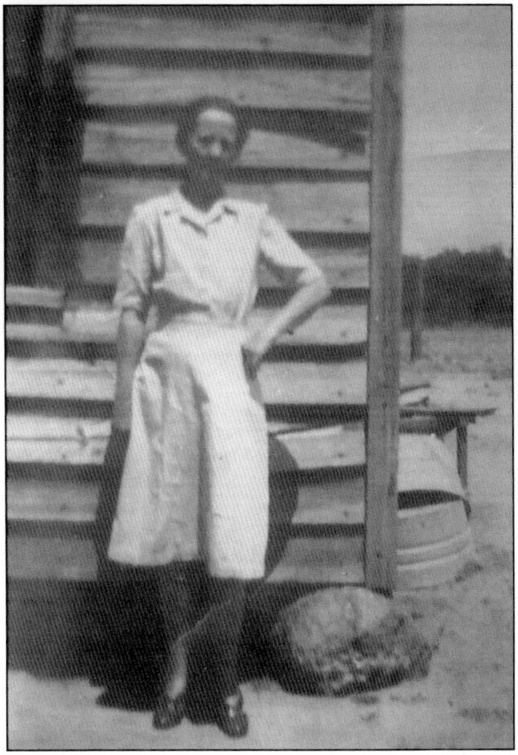

Corean Johnson Price. She was the wife of Clem Price and the mother of Eddie Mae Price.

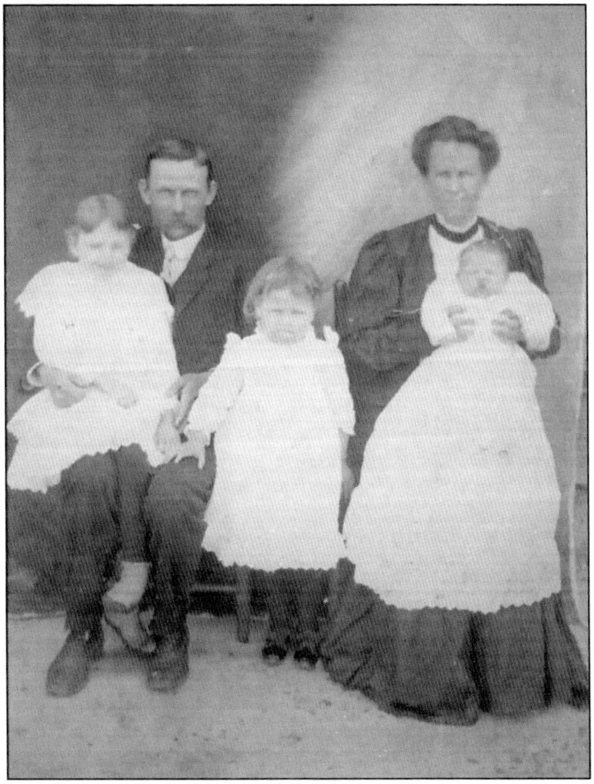

Morgan and Corine Snell. They were the proud parents of Pauline, Mildred, and Adeline, who are pictured here from left to right.

George and Lizzie Price. The Prices show off their two babies, Dawson and Hattie May, in 1900.

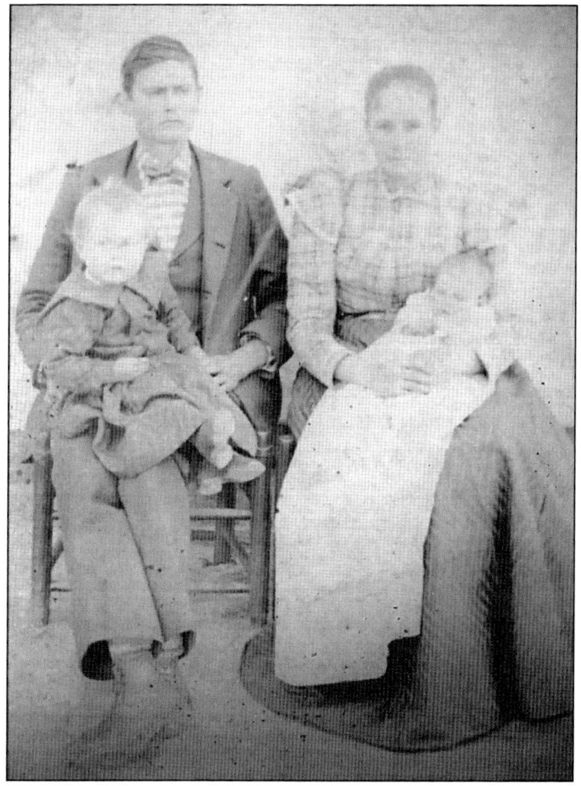

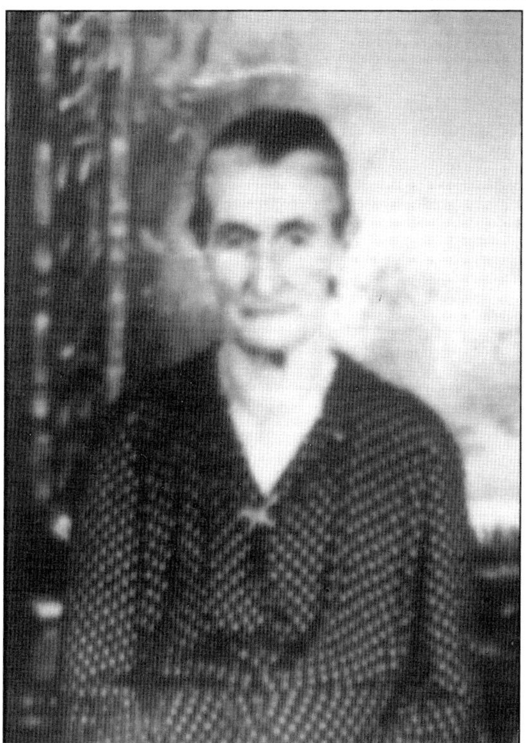

Sally Copeland Sheppard from Kite. Sally was the wife of Riley Sheppard.

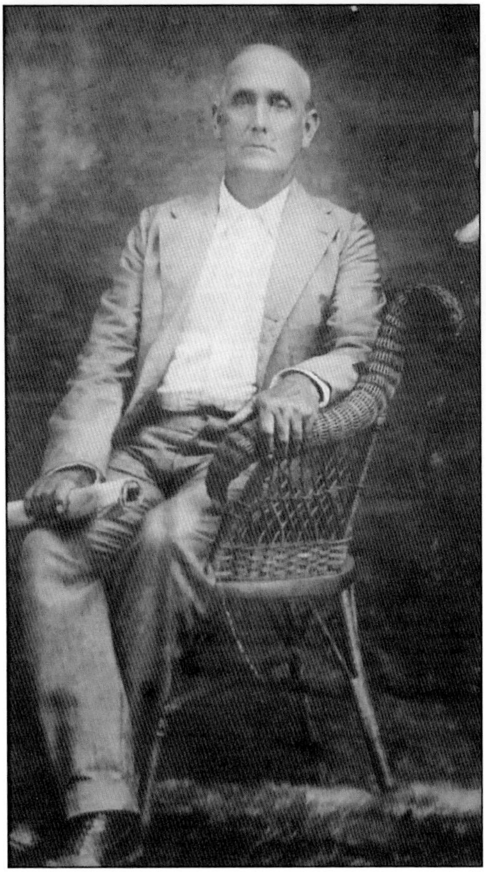

Henry Hightower Caneega. Born on August 5, 1859, Caneega died on June 22, 1936 and is buried at Westview.

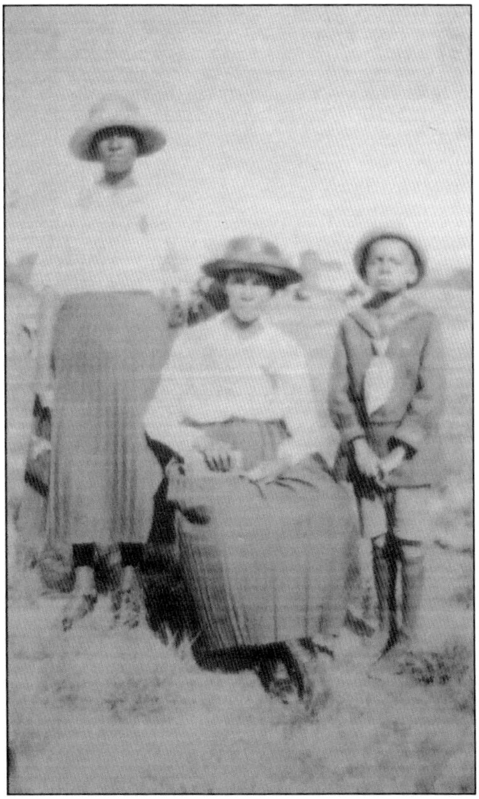

A 1925 Portrait. Pictured, from left to right, are Nannie Moorman Cordy, Ella Moorman, and Benny Moorman.

ANNIE DIXON AND HER MOTHER, MAZZIE BLACK DIXON. Annie is holding a doll and Mazzie has a doll pinned to her dress.

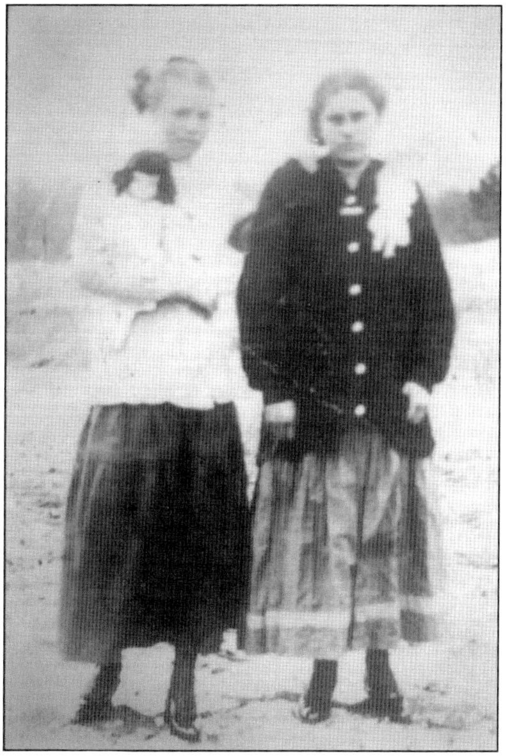

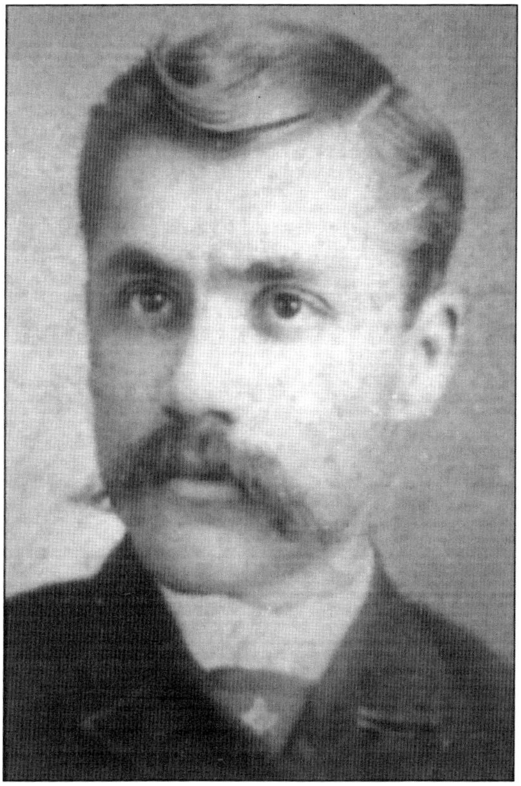

DR. JEFFERSON DAVIS TYSON. Tyson took a moment from his work to pose for the camera.

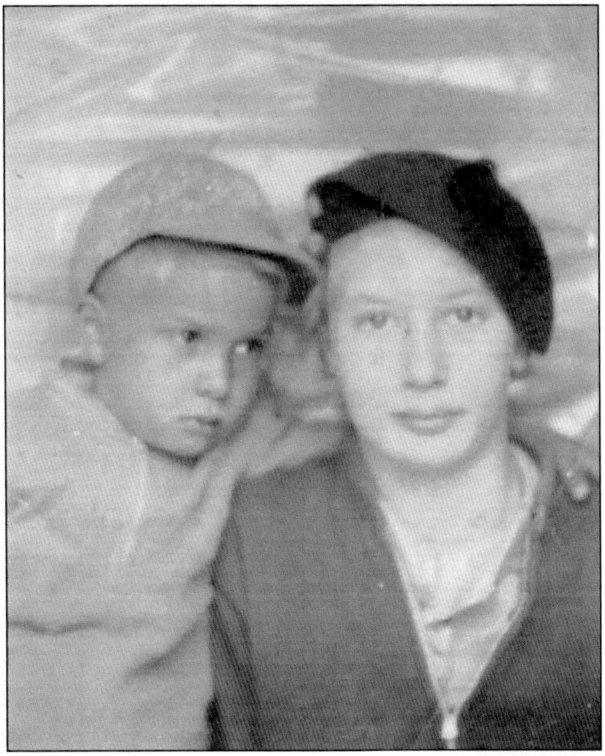

Carl W. Holt (Left) and Holt Peavy, c. 1933.

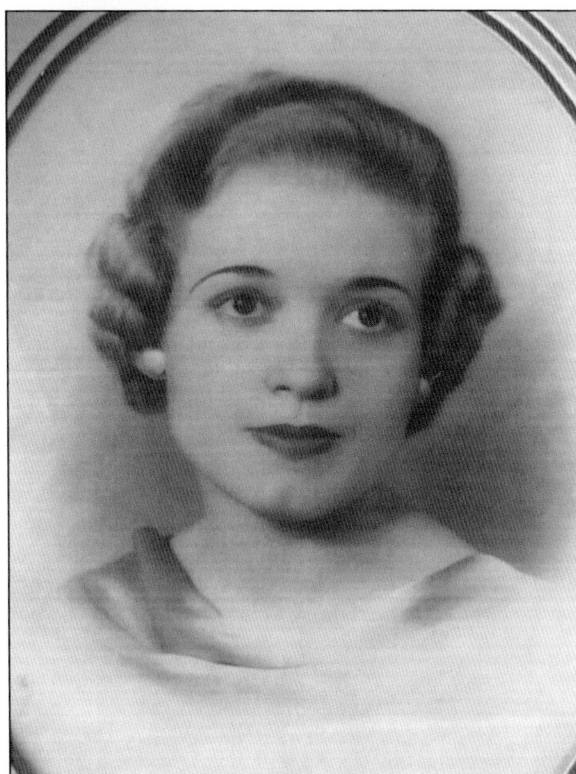

Mrs. Grace Outlaw, Wife of Hubert Outlaw.

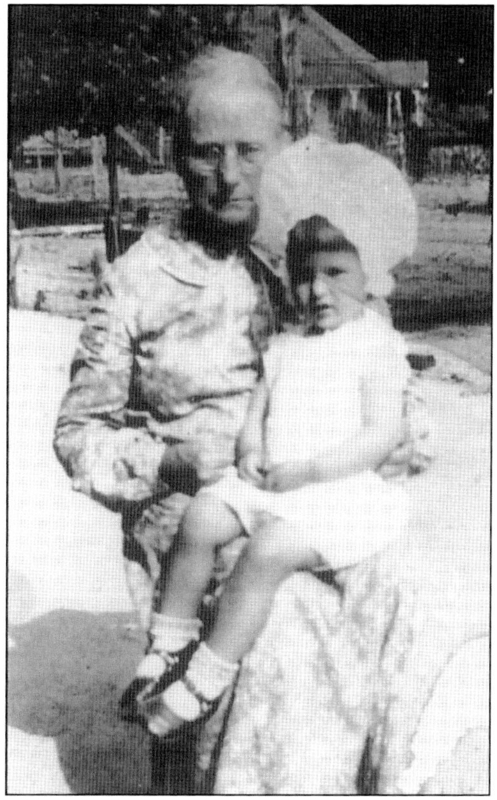

SUSAN SCHWALLS TOWNSEND AND HER GRANDDAUGHTER DORIS TOWNSEND CAMPBELL BATTS. This photo was taken in Kite, Georgia in 1933.

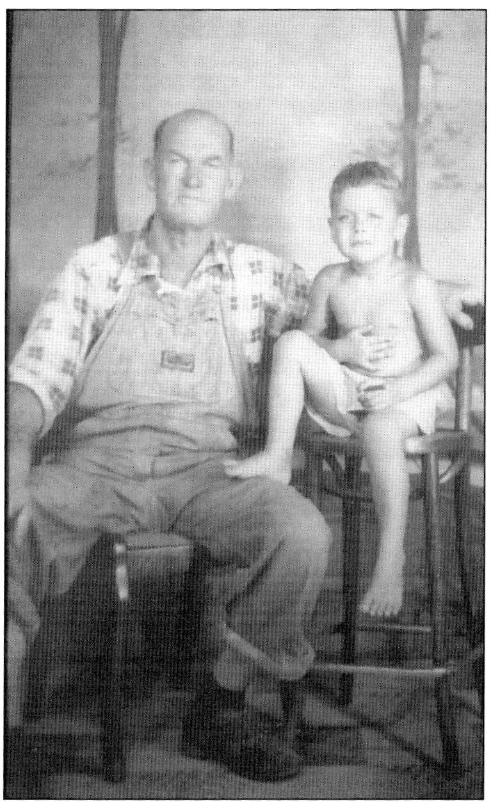

FREEMAN SHEPPARD AND ONE OF HIS GRANDSONS, RONNY COPELAND. Ronny was feeling a little sick from smoking the cigar shown in his left hand.

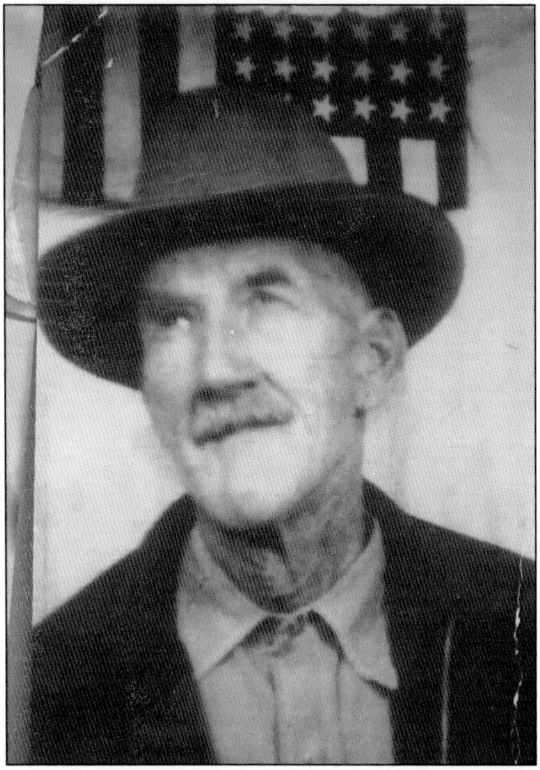

Tom Brantley, One of Johnson County's Farmers.

Willie J. Raines and His Sister Ellen Raines Maddox. Willie was the grandfather of Jewell Parker and Joy Hortman.

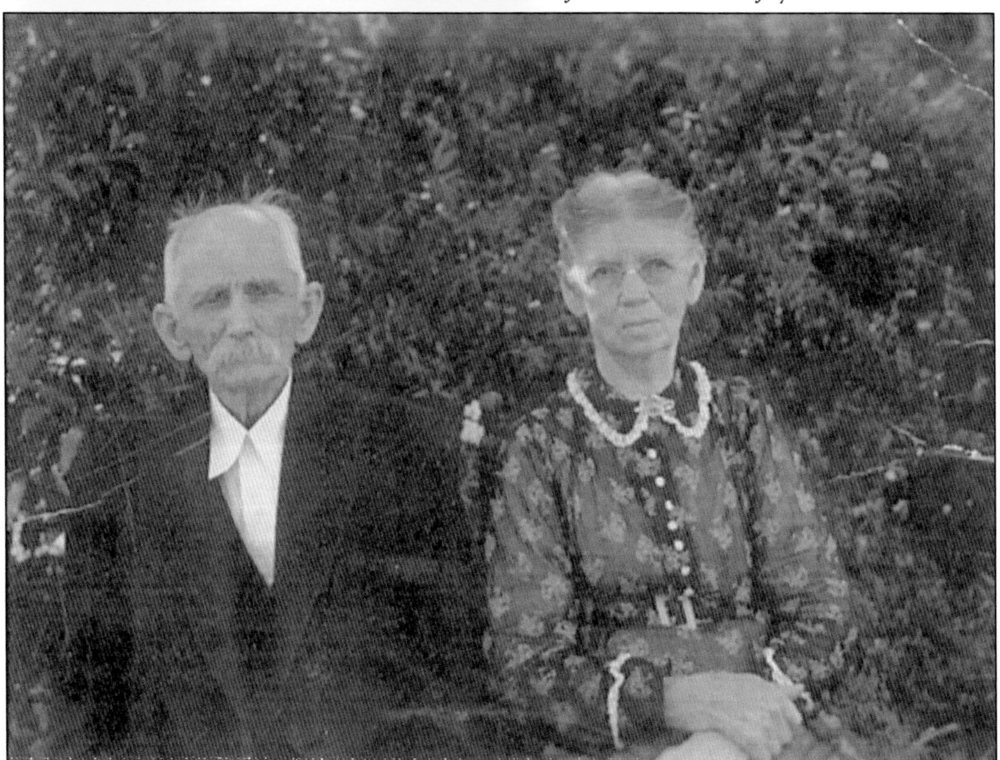

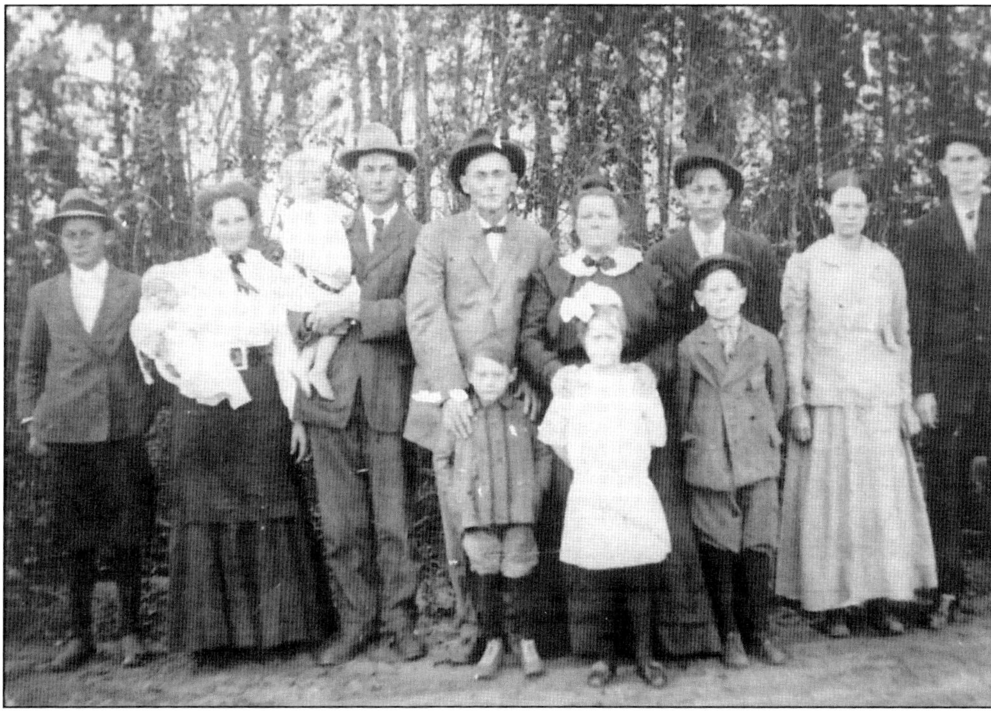

The Smith Family. Pictured here are, from left to right, (front row) J.W. Smith, Nannie Lou Smith, and Newman Smith; (back row) Eugene Smith, Lokella Smith holding Mary Lee Smith, Will Tom Smith holding G.T. Smith, William Riley Smith, Georgia Ann Hammock Smith, Lester Smith, Ada Smith Blount, and John Blount.

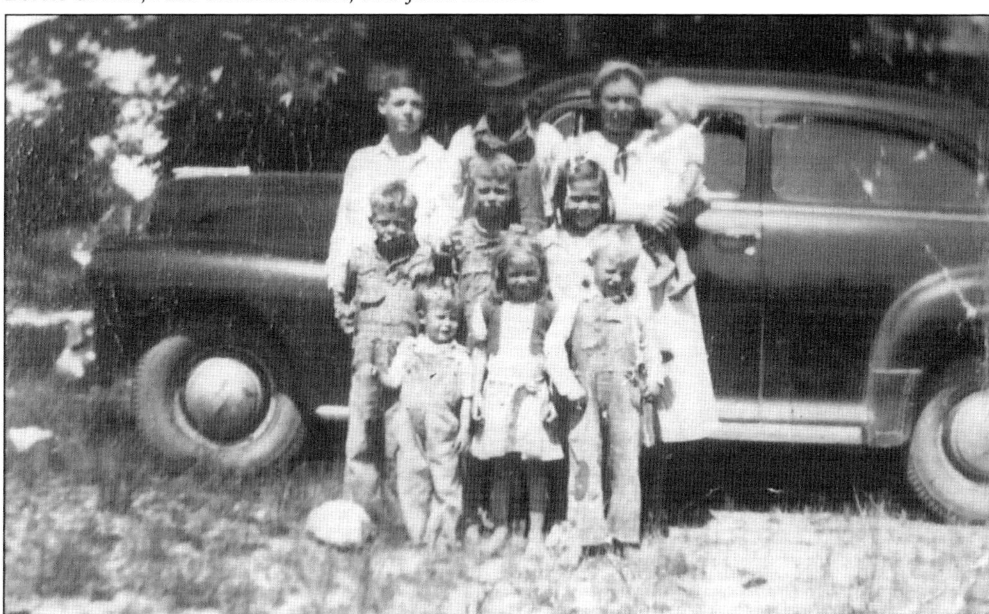

The Stapleton Family. Mr. Stapleton, his wife, and children take time out from farming to pose for this family photograph. From left to right are (front row) Jimmy Lee, Vadie Lee, and Ellis; (middle row) Ellie, Elize, and Claudia; (back row) W.H., Jim, Ethel holding Lynn.

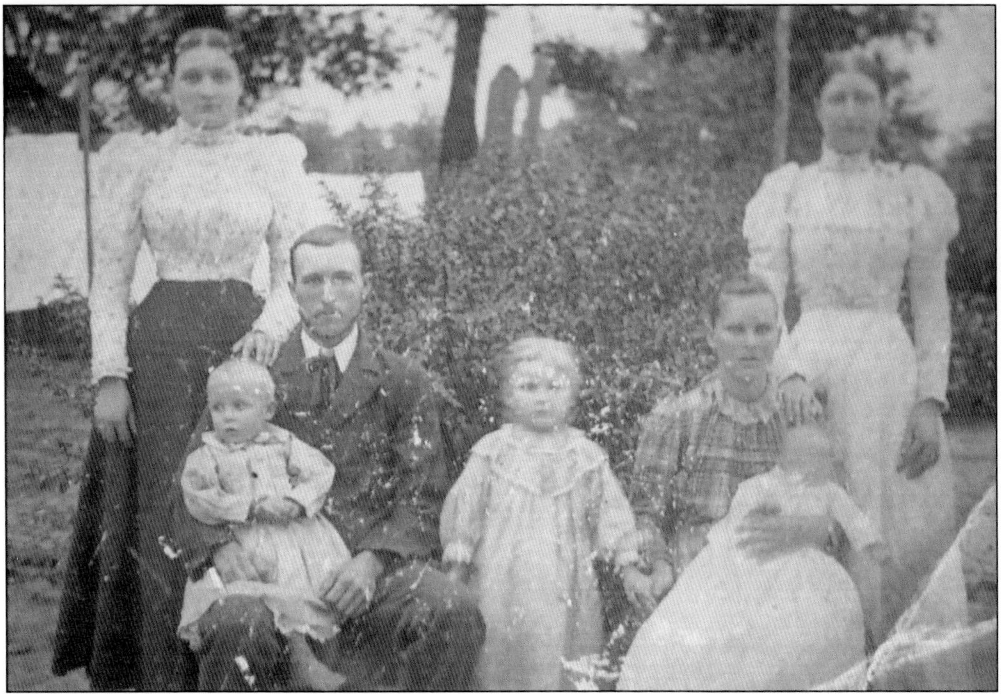

THE WEBB FAMILY. From left to right are Mollie, Loylar, Everett, Minnie Lee, Lou Ann, Charlie Raphael, and Sallie Webb.

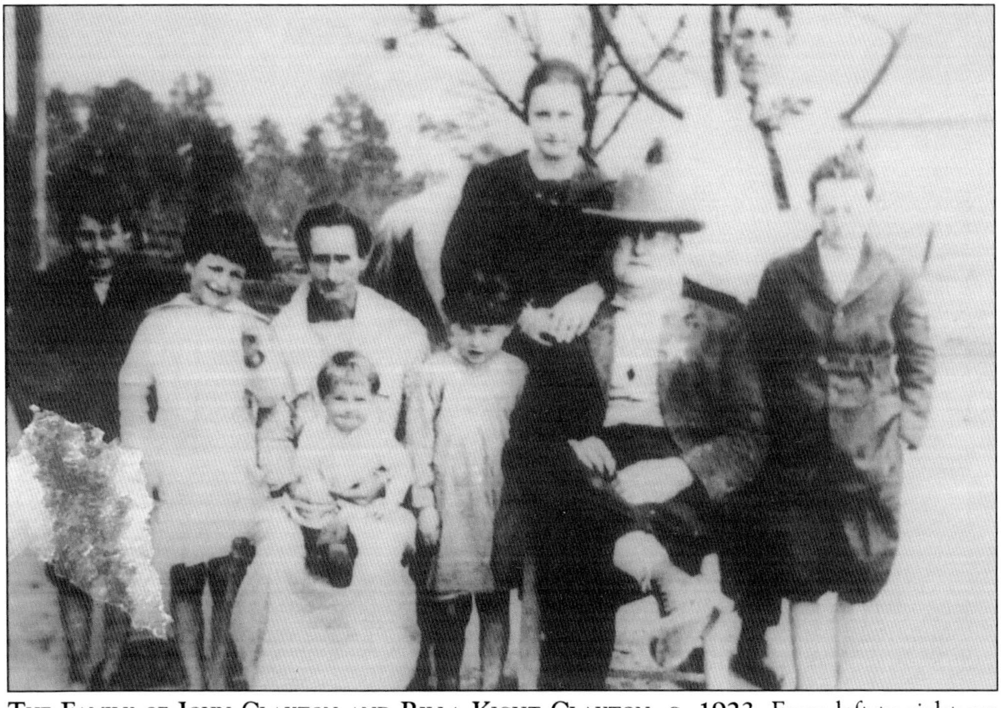

THE FAMILY OF JOHN CLAXTON AND RILLA KIGHT CLAXTON, C. 1923. From left to right are Albert, Pauline, Rilla holding Ruby, Maudie, Bessy, John, Eddie, and Clifford. John is wearing a star because he was a marshall in Kite.

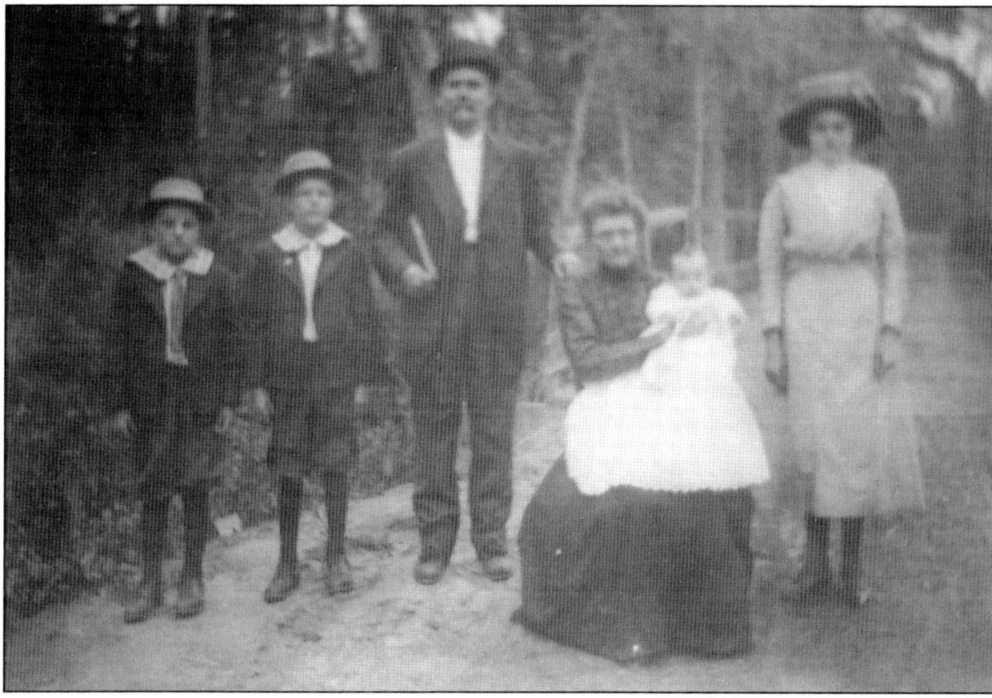

The Tom Dismuke Family. From left to right are Cleo, Clifford, Tom, Amanda holding Ethel Pearl Smith Logue, and Harriet Carter Smith. Amanda and Harriet were sisters. Harriet was the mother of Dicie Smith Wombles.

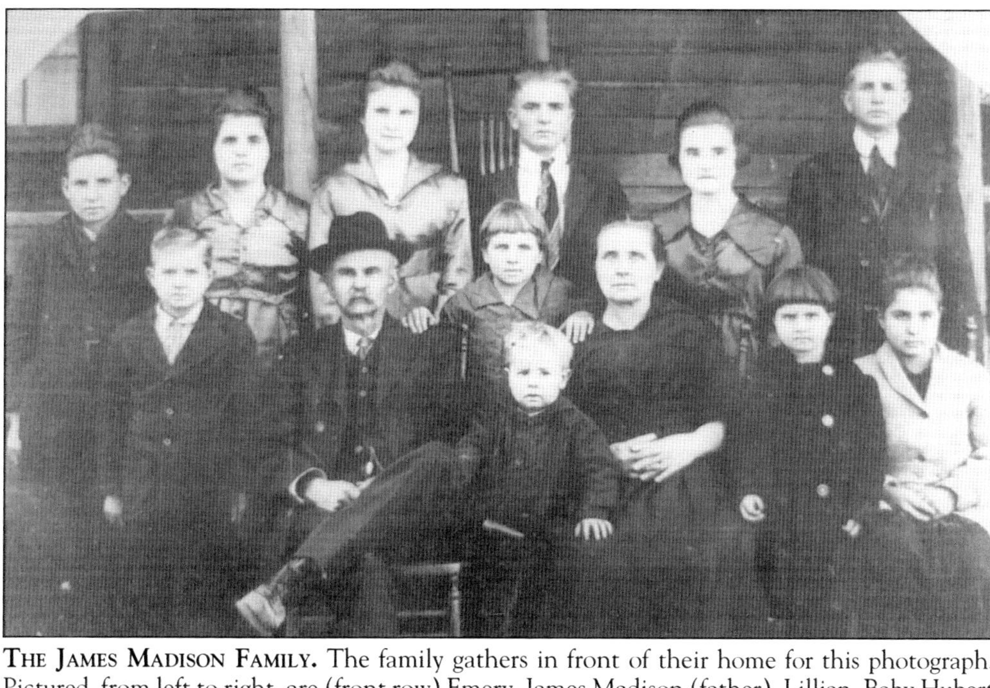

The James Madison Family. The family gathers in front of their home for this photograph. Pictured, from left to right, are (front row) Emery, James Madison (father), Lillian, Baby Hubert (in front), Nettie (mother), Ruby, and Grace; (back row) Lamar Crawford, Mattie Lou, Ida, Lonnie, Addie, and Loftin.

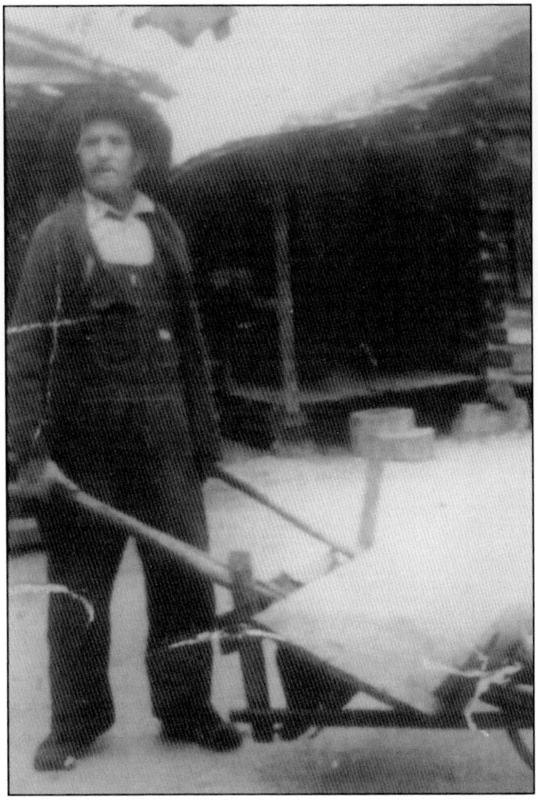

Wright Copeland Smith. Smith ran a grist mill at Archer's Pond on Highway 15 south of Wrightsville. Everybody who knew Wright said he never wore shoes, but this is the only picture of him and here he is wearing shoes.

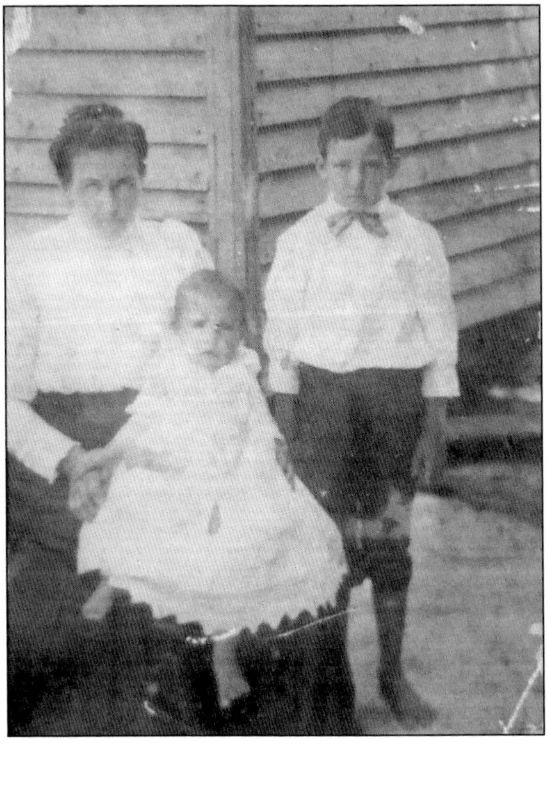

Nora Holton Parker With Baby Ben Parker Sr. and L.E. Parker Sr., 1901.

Bill Williams. He is pictured here in his pinstriped pants and Sunday coat.

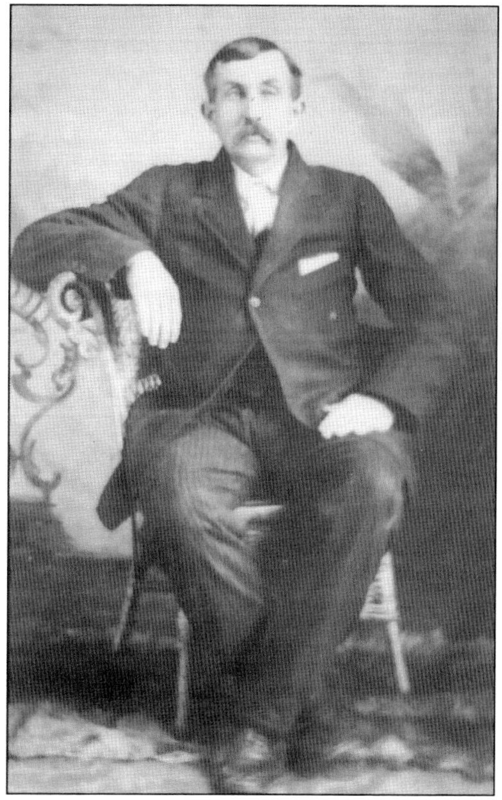

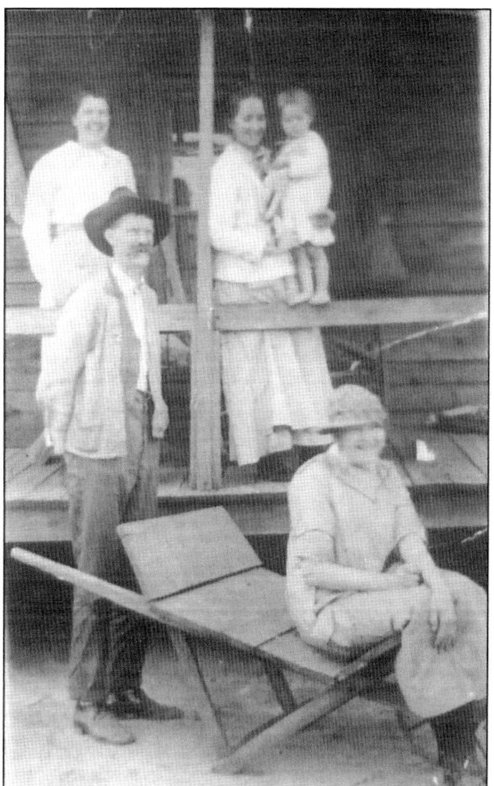

George and Martha Brantley. These two are seen playing around while Mazzie Brantley (left), Dallie Kight (center), and Georgia ? look on.

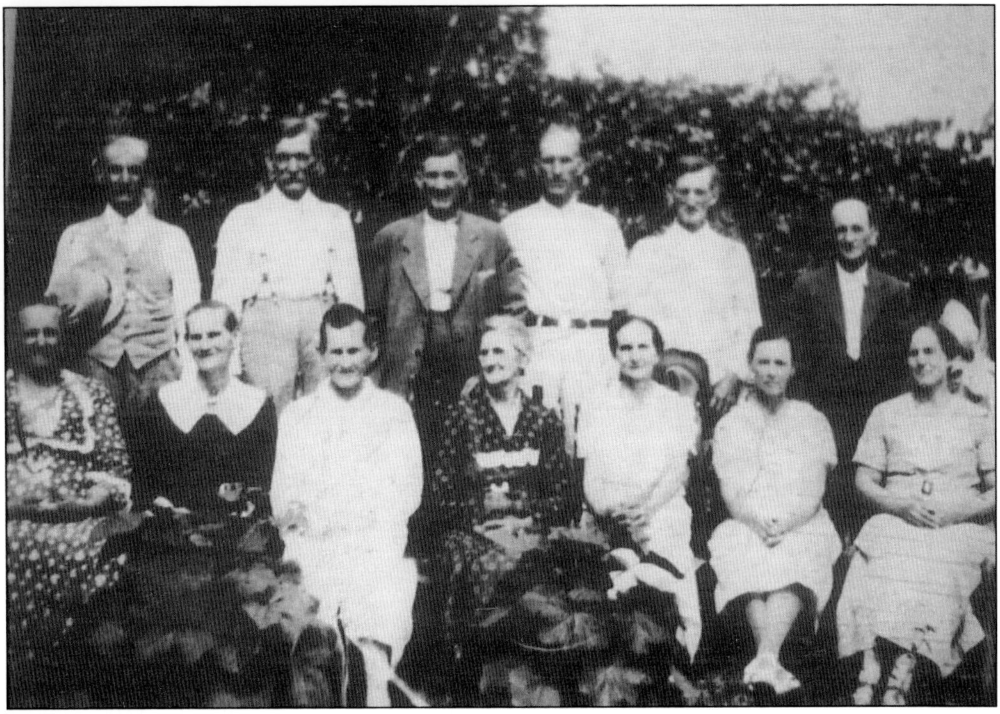

THE TOM "BOOKY" BRANTLEY FAMILY.

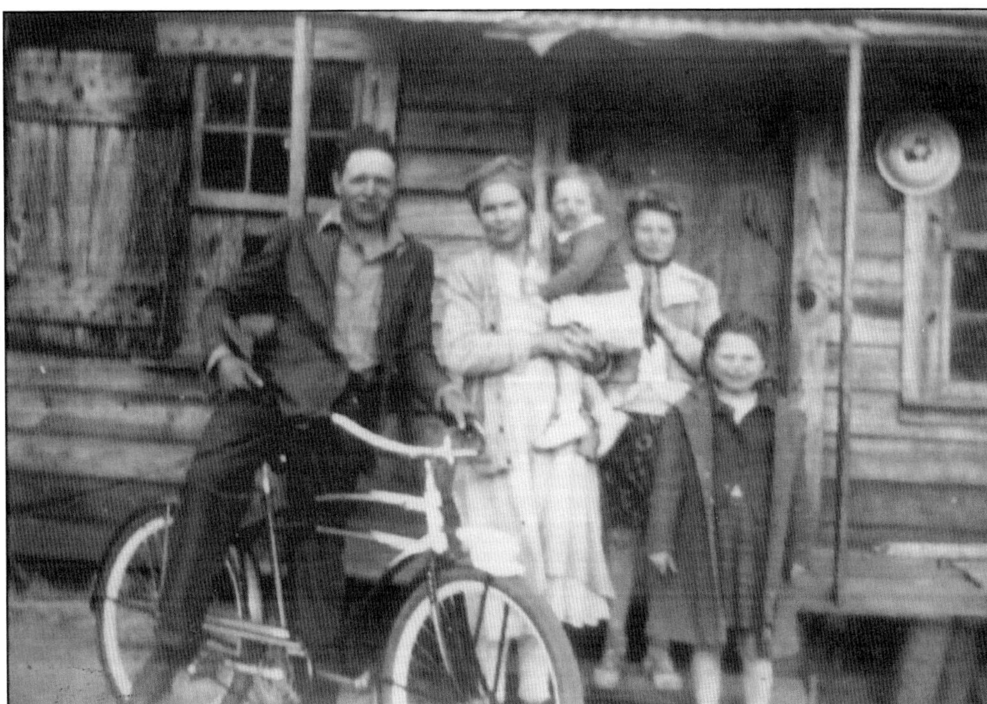

J.P. COPELAND AND HIS MOTHER, MAGGIE WILKERSON COPELAND. The children pictured are J.P.'s nieces, the children of Harrison Copeland: Maggie (left), Inell (center), and Jimmie.

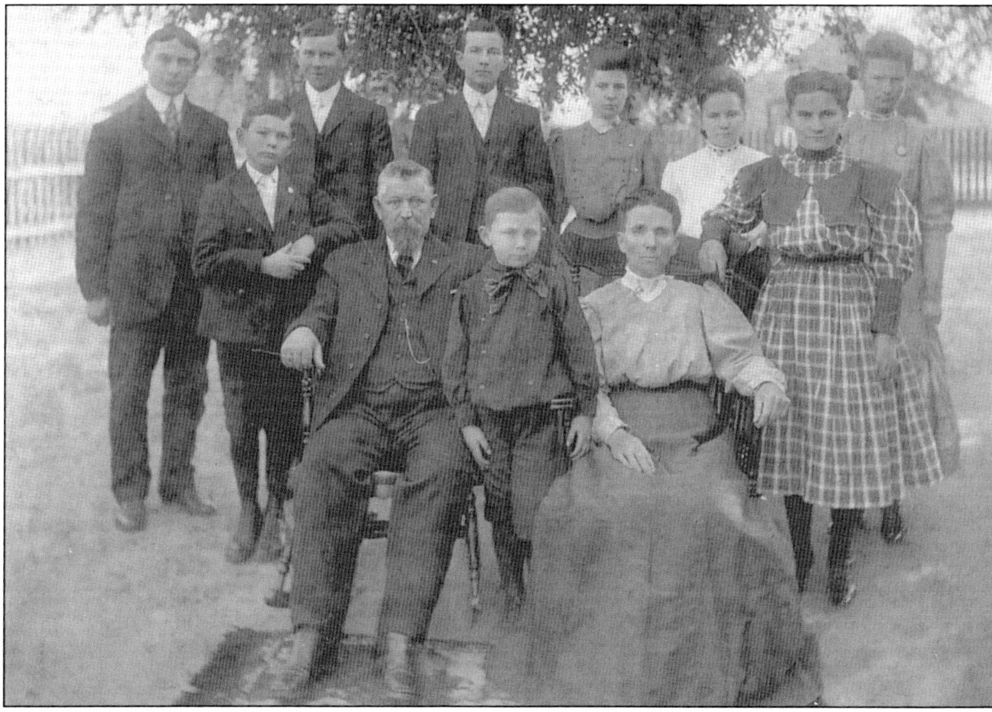

The Bray Family, 1908. Charles Thomas "Tom" Bray and his wife, Dealphia Stokes Bray, are pictured with their children. From left to right are (front row) Herschel B., Tom, Ostelle, Dealphia, and Geneva; (back row) John C., Charles "Charlie" T. Jr., Nathaniel "Nat" F., Bertha (Martin), Laurie (Hampton), and Clio (Hutcheson). The Brays living in Johnson County today are either descendants of Tom Bray or his brother Freeman Bray.

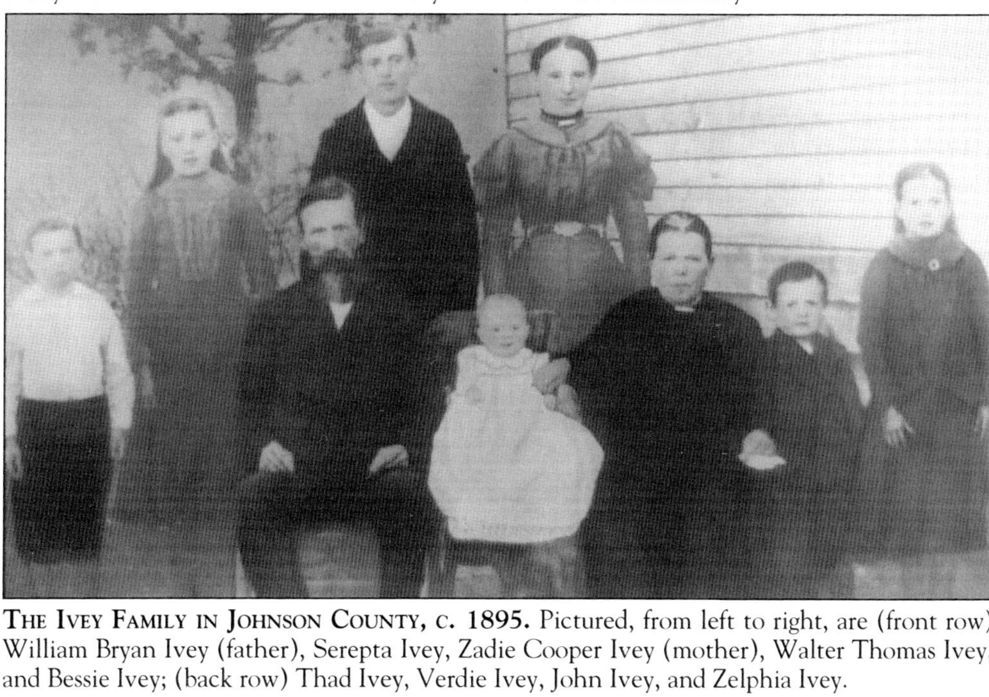

The Ivey Family in Johnson County, c. 1895. Pictured, from left to right, are (front row) William Bryan Ivey (father), Serepta Ivey, Zadie Cooper Ivey (mother), Walter Thomas Ivey, and Bessie Ivey; (back row) Thad Ivey, Verdie Ivey, John Ivey, and Zelphia Ivey.

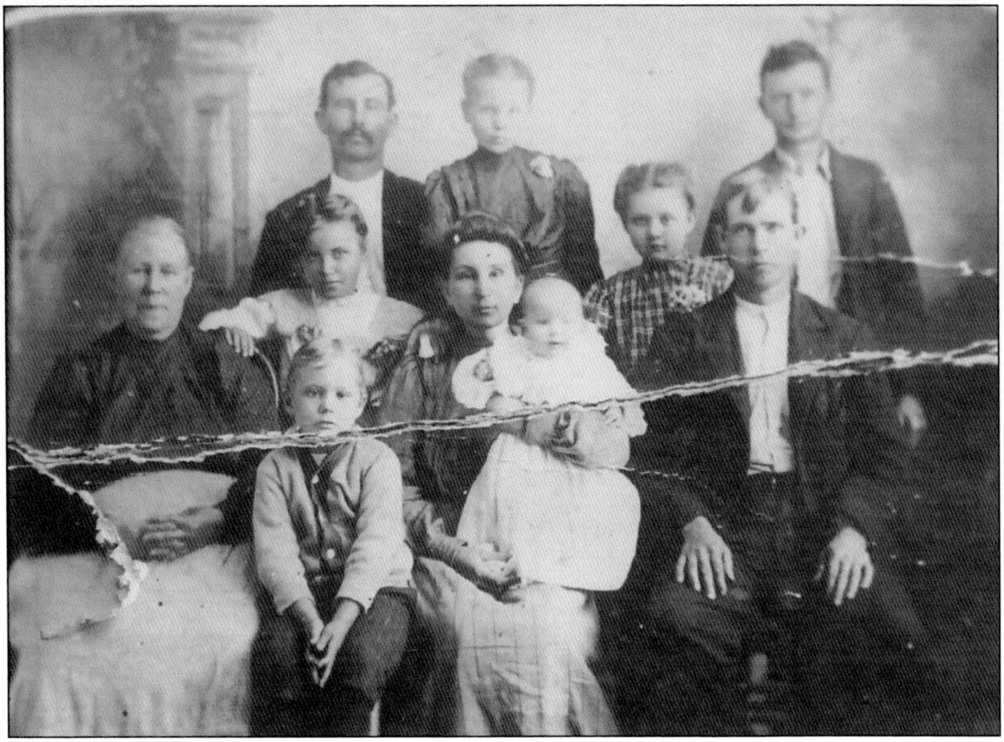

The Peavy Family. Pictured here, from left to right, are (front row) unidentified, Herschel Peavy, Emma Holton Peavy holding John Peavy, and Bose Peavy; (back row) Willie Robenson, William "Will" Holton, Videllea Peavy Brantley, Ann Lee Peavy, and Nelious "Pat" Johnson.

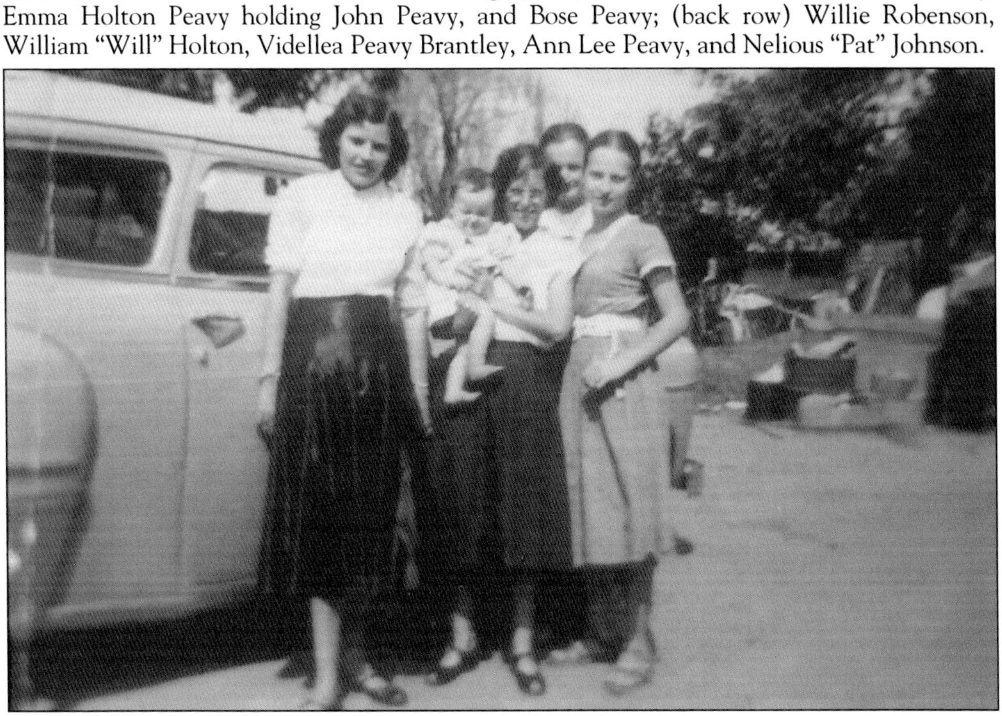

John Lois Smith Zellener, Dicie Smith Wombles, and Her Daughter Marie. Annie Laura Foster Snell appears behind Geraldine Snell Kitchens, far right.

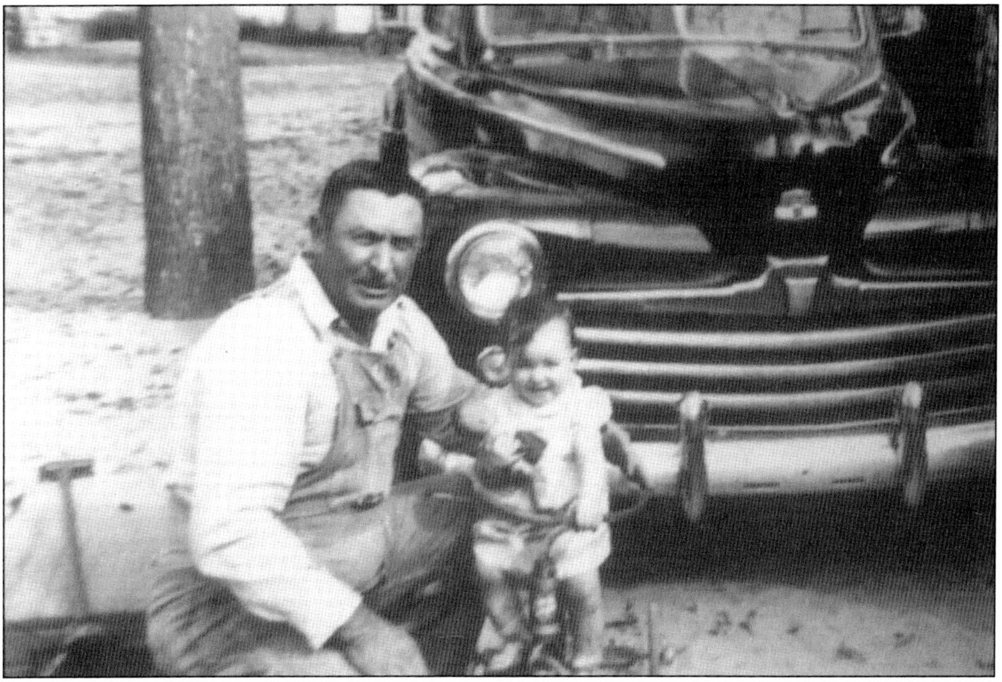

BURL WOMBLES WITH HIS DAUGHTER MARIE WOMBLES. Burl was born on February 2, 1915 and died on July 7, 1973.

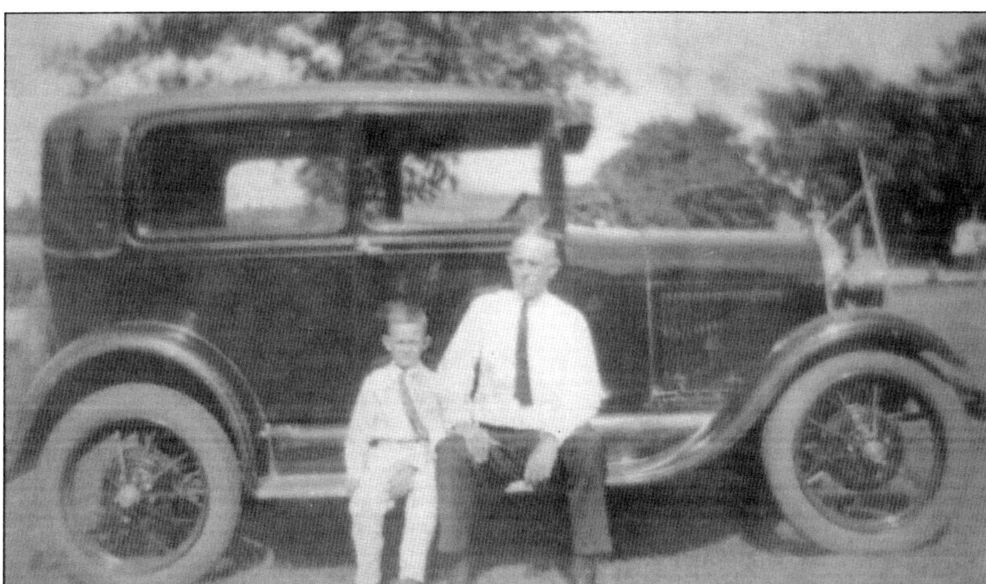

WILLIE KIGHT WITH HIS SON FRED AND THEIR CAR.

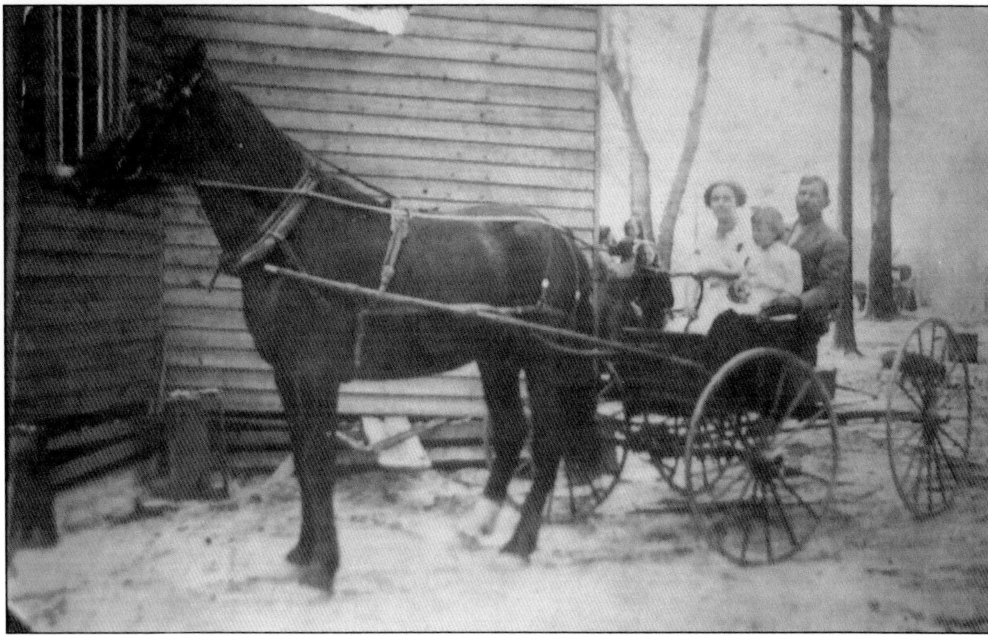

JIM SNELL. Snell gives Annie Bulyer(a schoolteacher) and Adeline Snell a ride to school.

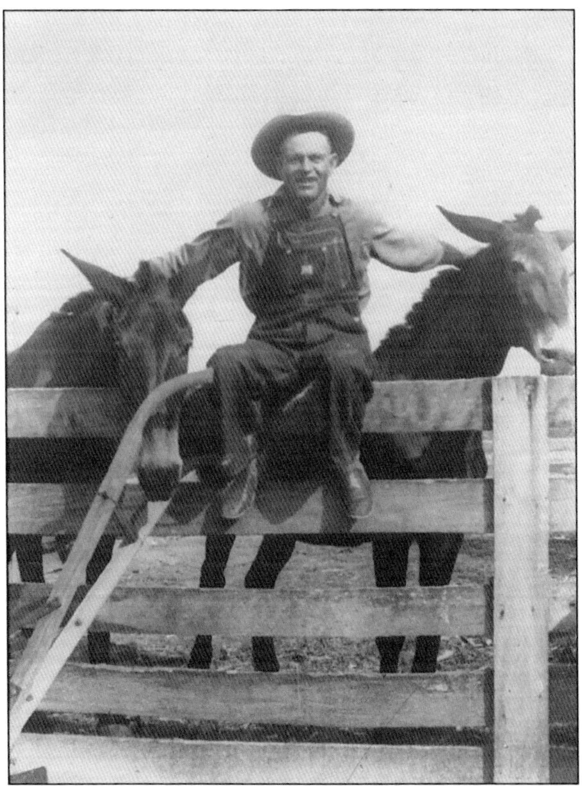

FOSTER GRAHAM, 1942.
Mr. Graham shows off his mules, Black Gal and Kate.